4/65
6/20

D0122178

COUNSELLING THE CATHOLIC

COUNSELLING THE CATHOLIC

*Modern Techniques
and Emotional Conflicts*

GEORGE HAGMAIER, C.S.P.
and ROBERT W. GLEASON, S.J.

Sheed & Ward - NEW YORK

© SHEED AND WARD, INC., 1959

LIBRARY OF CONGRESS CATALOG CARD NUMBER: 59–12094

IMPRIMI POTEST:
 THOMAS E. HENNEBERRY, S.J.
  PRAEP. PROV. NEO EBORACENSIS

NIHIL OBSTAT:
 JOHN R. READY
  CENSOR LIBRORUM
 AUGUST 28, 1959

IMPRIMATUR:
 † ROBERT F. JOYCE
  BISHOP OF BURLINGTON
 AUGUST 29, 1959

FIFTH PRINTING, AUGUST, 1961

MANUFACTURED IN THE UNITED STATES OF AMERICA

ACKNOWLEDGMENTS

Father Hagmaier wishes to acknowledge permission granted him to include in this book the following previously published material:

"The Priest and Mental Health," *The Homiletic and Pastoral* Review, LV, No. 9 (1955).

"The Catholic Counsellor's Two Hats," *Contemporary Psychology*, II, No. 11 (1957). (Portions of the chapter "The Priest as a Listener.")

"The Pastoral Counselling of the Homosexual," *The Proceedings of the Second Institute for the Clergy on Problems of Pastoral Psychology* (New York: Fordham University Press, 1958).

Father Gleason's chapter 11 of this book, "Moral Aspects of the Problem of Homosexuality," was originally read as a paper at the Second Institute for the Clergy on Problems of Pastoral Psychology and appears in the published *Proceedings* (New York: Fordham University Press, 1958). It was also published in *The Homiletic and Pastoral Review* in December, 1957. He wishes to thank both sources for permitting him to reprint it in this book.

Both authors wish also to express their thanks for permission to reprint the passages from various books and periodicals to which references are made in the notes sections of this book.

CONTENTS

INTRODUCTION: WHY THIS BOOK?   ix

Part One: Psychological Perspectives on Counselling

1. EMOTIONS AND BEHAVIOR   5
2. THE PRIEST AS A LISTENER   31
3. THE PSYCHOLOGY OF HUMAN WEAKNESS   51
4. MASTURBATION   73
5. HOMOSEXUALITY   94
6. ALCOHOLISM   113
7. SCRUPULOSITY   145
8. MENTAL ILLNESS AND MENTAL HEALTH   174
9. USING COMMUNITY RESOURCES   200

Part Two: Moral Perspectives on Counselling

10. MORAL ASPECTS OF MASTURBATION   215
11. MORAL ASPECTS OF THE PROBLEM OF HOMOSEXUALITY   228
12. ALCOHOLISM AND MORAL GUILT   239
13. CATHOLICISM AND PSYCHIATRY   247

APPENDIX I: THE CHIEF MENTAL ILLNESSES   271
APPENDIX II: REFERRAL FACILITIES   283
BIBLIOGRAPHY   295

INTRODUCTION:
WHY THIS BOOK?

"Quite often, the psychopathologist is given a well-deserved reproach for forgetting, under the spell of his professional bias, that at least some human acts are emanating from clearly conscious judgment and free determination. On the other hand, we must humbly recognize that, as human beings, theologians are no more exempt than others from the temptation of neglecting the facts which do not immediately fit into the sphere of their current personal thinking. Totally absorbed in building up the well-integrated structure of moral virtues, destined to become the flexible and efficient instrument of Divine Grace, we often show some reluctance at giving due consideration to serious obstacles encountered in the acquisition of fully rational functioning which supplies the normal basis for the higher achievements of supernatural life. No wonder, then, that we can do so little for those who require our help in all confidence and with the best intentions, while they feel desperately hampered in their spiritual development by uncontrollable vicious habits, degrading addictions, and neurotic impulses or inhibitions."

Father Noël Mailloux, O.P.*, who wrote the above, pleads that we improve the art of spiritual direction by seeking to give it the "necessary empirical basis it is still awaiting." This book is one small effort toward that goal. The Church, in her efforts to lead

* Chairman of the Department of Psychology, University of Montreal. Quoted from *The Proceedings of the Institute for the Clergy on Problems in Pastoral Psychology* (New York: Fordham University Press, 1956).

her children to salvation, has always earnestly applied herself to anything and everything which touches man significantly. She has, from the first days of her foundation, acknowledged the place and importance of the body and the emotions, as well as the soul, in the definition and destiny of human nature. Consequently the Church has always promoted Christian social and humanitarian objectives, for she acknowledges that man's eternal and spiritual happiness must be worked out in the midst of temporal and mundane concerns.

Modern psychology is a new science which has contributed much to our deeper understanding of why man thinks, feels, and acts as he does. This book examines some of these concepts. Today's more exact behavioral studies merely confirm many of the psychological observations and principles intuitively sensed in centuries past by saints and spiritual writers. Our readers will undoubtedly want to weigh and even challenge other findings of modern psychology. But most students will agree that this newly developed science has at least demonstrated beyond a question of a doubt that man's emotional life is highly complex, and that man's personal problems are therefore not always open to easy and quick solutions. There are many more "grays" than there are "blacks" and "whites."

Every priest, sooner or later, finds himself in the role of a counsellor. He hopes, by exercising his prerogatives as an instructor and as a channel of grace, to build confidence and strengthen the spiritual commitment of his people so that they can face and solve their personal problems with the insight and courage of true faith. Today's priest, however, has found that faith means most and works best when it functions in a mature, well-adjusted, emotionally healthy individual. Often the priest counsellor discovers that he must first help his parishioner to understand and even rebuild his emotional life before the supernatural life can really take hold with full effectiveness.

This book, then, is largely dedicated to an exposition of the *emotional stratum* of man's functioning and of its influence upon his behavior. Many splendid treatises which deal with the development of rational and supernatural virtue are available to the reader.

The book which describes in any complete way the technique by which the counsellor blends the timeless tenets of supernatural growth with the modern psychological principles presented in this volume has, as Father Mailloux indicates, still to be written.

This book, as far as we know, is a first and therefore a primitive attempt to perform an admittedly difficult, perhaps impossible, task. We propose in these pages to present a simple outline of fundamental counselling concepts and techniques which will serve as a text book for seminarians and a reference volume for priests who face the day-to-day appeals for help from parishioners with personal problems. Present "pastoral" courses taught in Catholic seminaries define quite adequately practical aspects of the administration of the Sacraments, the canon law of marriage and, occasionally, the management of church finances. Most of these courses, however, deal insufficiently or not at all with the fundamental precepts of contemporary counselling theory. In the light of the urgent counselling demands made upon today's priests, the authors feel that a basic course in guidance principles, pastoral counselling, practical psychology—call it what you will—should be as important a part of seminary study as the fundamental courses in theology, philosophy, canon law and scripture. We hope this book will encourage this curriculum change.

The chapters which follow do not attempt, in any sense, a detailed or exhaustive treatment of the subjects outlined. Nor should this book be seen as a training manual for counsellors. The priest who wishes to specialize as a counsellor will find this material insufficient, and must pursue further and more intensive study elsewhere. Our aim has been to write a compendium of practical psychology which contains a certain *minimum* of information to which we feel *every priest* should be introduced.

We trust, therefore, that our readers will be charitable and perceptive enough to accept this volume for what it is—an introductory, overview text of pastoral counselling. It will surely disappoint those who expect a catch-all, "do-it-yourself" handbook which will provide simple, clear-cut, ready-made answers to typical human problems. Indeed, our chief goal has been not so much to answer questions or solve difficulties as to build *attitudes* about the problem-solving process itself. The content of the various chapters is intended to have a cumulative effect, and we hope the reader will reserve judgment about the adequacy of our presentation until he has read the entire volume. If, at that time, the reader finds that there has been a significant change in his views of human problems and the theory and technique of solving them, we will feel that our labors have been more than justified.

A deeper insight into the unconscious motivations behind much of human behavior; a conviction that most human conflicts are far more complex than they appear; a recognition that the same problem in two people can have wholly dissimilar causes, and therefore quite different solutions; a reluctance to jump quickly to "diagnostic" conclusions about the reasons and remedies for behavior difficulties; a readiness to listen more and say less in counselling relationships; the clear recognition that many specific human problems require specific information and training to be solved; an informed readiness to refer professional problems to professional experts; a deeper grasp of the relationships and distinctions between emotional and religious, psychological and supernatural influences, and the ways by which both the priest counsellor and his parishioner can take them into account—these are some of the longitudinal objectives the authors see as important in the training of today's young priests.

Since our objective, therefore, is to build a counselling philosophy rather than to solve many individual problems in a few words, we have decided not to include an *index* in this book. It is fatal for the would-be counsellor to look up "stealing" or "envy" in an index, read a few pages of text, and then feel himself qualified to hand out a solution to some troubled inquirer.

Because this book is intended as an overview or a primer of pastoral counselling, the authors have tried to avoid the use of complicated, technical concepts and professional jargon. Where specific psychological vocabulary was unavoidable, we have tried to give a simple explanation on the spot. Whether we have succeeded or not is for our readers to decide. On certain subjects we have quoted extensively from other authors. We feel their clear and simple explanations say exactly what we are trying to convey. We could not find words of our own to say it better. Finally, the reader should be reminded that many of the subjects discussed are by no means as simple or obvious as they might appear. This is, of course, the inevitable handicap of communication inherent in any highly specialized and complex science.

Part I, the treatment of counselling theory and technique, is the work of Father Hagmaier. In Part II, Father Gleason discusses in more technical fashion those aspects of specific counselling challenges which touch the province of the moral theologian. However, both authors have carefully reviewed each other's material, have refined, qualified, and expanded each section in such a committed and complementary fashion that, despite some disparity of style, a complete unity of viewpoint has emerged.

It is hoped that a considerable portion of the subject matter will be self-explanatory to those who use this book as a reference work. Ideally speaking, however, this volume is intended as a supplemental text to an introductory counselling course, taught by a trained instructor to seminarians or young priests who have had little or no formal training in these areas. The basic material written up in these chapters was, in fact, the subject matter of such a course taught by Father Hagmaier to newly ordained priests at the Paulist Information Center in Boston, Massachusetts. The course, half lecture and half group discussion, made it possible for the author to add considerable pertinent material to the original text and revise the treatment of other sections at the suggestion of the student priests.

Incidentally, classroom use of this book reinforced our assertion that this book alone will not train a priest to be a counsellor. Young priests must have the opportunity, in supervised group discussions, to analyze and compare some of their practical apostolic experiences. They can learn much from each other. Most important, the trainee must be helped to recognize *within himself* the emotional influences described in these pages. He must come to see how his own emotional life developed and how his feelings affect many of his own attitudes and much of his behavior. Only then, as a counsellor, will he be truly capable of understanding these forces at work in others, thereby achieving that necessary degree of empathy which is the essence of compassionate counselling.

While this book is intended chiefly for Catholic seminarians and priests, it is the authors' hope that *lay Catholics*—parents, teachers, sisters, guidance counsellors, youth workers, psychologists, psychiatrists, etc., may also find a considerable portion of this material useful. This book may also help the *non-Catholic* specialist to understand some of the specific religious, moral and psychological difficulties of his Catholic clients, and may aid him to determine appropriate, acceptable and effective methods of guidance. Many non-Catholic counsellors will, we believe, be surprised and pleased to find that the counselling of the committed Catholic can involve the same sort of proven psychological techniques which are used by the good therapist or guidance person who works with any sincere client.

This book is only a beginning. It is, in every sense of the word, an experiment in communication. The authors most earnestly entreat the reader to offer, by correspondence, any comments, opinions, or criticisms pertinent to the objectives heretofore described. Favorable and unfavorable communiqués alike will please us, and our correspondents can be sure that their observations will help to clarify and refine at least a portion of the present needs and future practice of that vital and fast-developing talent: the science and art of pastoral counselling.

ROBERT GLEASON, S.J.
DEPARTMENT OF THEOLOGY
FORDHAM UNIVERSITY
NEW YORK 58, N.Y.

GEORGE HAGMAIER, C.S.P.
INSTITUTE FOR
RELIGIOUS RESEARCH
C/O 608 ISHAM ST.
NEW YORK 34, N.Y.

COUNSELLING THE CATHOLIC

PART ONE

PSYCHOLOGICAL PERSPECTIVES
ON COUNSELLING

1

EMOTIONS AND BEHAVIOR

Most religious books on counselling theory and technique stress character formation and the development of self-control. The essential philosophy behind this approach lies in the valid conviction that man's higher faculties, mainly his intellect and will, can be employed to order and subdue man's physical drives and emotional vagaries. Occasionally, however, the pre-eminence of man's rational and volitional faculties in regulating the emotional sphere is somewhat overstated. Often quite the reverse is true. In one very real sense, man's emotional life has a prior influence on his behavior. When St. Thomas Aquinas observed that nothing enters the intellect except through the senses, he might have included the emotions as a part of that gateway. It is difficult, indeed, to imagine a human activity which is purely rational in character; a thinking man is always a feeling man too. There are many instances of behavior which indicate that man's feelings and passions are directing the kind of thinking and choosing that he does. In other words, the intellect and will can only control and co-ordinate those emotions which are healthy, properly developed, and reasonably undisturbed by psychological handicaps of various kinds.

Unlike many Catholic counselling books, this volume will have very little to say about theology, philosophy, will power and grace in the development of desirable human behavior. Rather than duplicate the many excellent contributions already made in these areas, the authors hope in these pages to highlight the roles which feelings and emotions play in the development of sound or weak human personalities.

To illustrate this concept let us cite several examples. The homosexual, who seeks physical gratification through relationships with his own sex, has more than a "will-power" problem. His difficulty is essentially an emotional one. Somewhere deep in the past his ability to relate warmly and affectionately to members of the opposite sex was stifled and thwarted, whether by parents, society, or subtle force of circumstances. In any case, his is an emotional block, so powerful in some cases that it may influence his thinking to the extent that he is intellectually convinced that God intends him to be this way, and that he need make no effort to control his desires or to seek help.

Again, the individual who suffers from sudden, irrational bursts of temper cannot solve his problem through "positive thinking." His is essentially an emotional difficulty; he will have to find out why he *feels* the way he does, before he is able to *think* sensibly about his problem. In a very real sense then, emotions are often the rock foundation upon which other and higher human faculties build.

"Grace builds on nature" can have two emphases. This dictum can mean that grace ennobles, supernaturalizes, and illuminates those qualities in man which are singularly human. It can also mean that grace can do all these things most effectively only if "nature" is whole and healthy and capable of ennoblement. The priest does not casually give absolution or Holy Communion to the psychotic, whose human nature may be so twisted and blocked that grace cannot take hold and fructify what is there. To a lesser degree, the emotional life of most of us is in some way stunted, perverted, or otherwise undeveloped so that grace is not always able to work as fruitfully and perfectly as it might.

Most of the saints have been extraordinarily well adjusted individuals. There are some, however, who seem to have become saints in spite of emotional handicaps. It could very well be that the source of merit for them was the triumph of will and grace *despite* the neurotic handicaps which blocked the possibility of totally free and tranquil living. And yet, no one would defend such a *status quo* if these crippling neurotic elements could have been removed. We should be as interested in developing wholesome emotional qualities in a human being as we are in making sure he is free from physical deformities of any kind. "Mens sana in corpore sano" is surely a motto of the Catholic humanitarian as well as the stoic.

IMPORTANCE OF EMOTIONS IN CHILDHOOD

Why are emotions so important in the development of human personality? Hitler, Freud, and the Jesuits have been variously quoted as paraphrasing the truism "give me the child until he is seven, and then do with him what you will." There is a world of wisdom in this tribute to the significant role emotions play as major factors in the development of character and personality. While it is true that the use-of-reason develops gradually during these early years of life, the chief motive for most of infant behavior is *feeling*. It is the "education of emotion" during these first six or seven years which influences much of the later intellectual and volitional life of the individual.

Personality-wise, the newborn infant is little more than a bundle of feelings. Food and warmth are his only needs. Irritation and frustration when he is cold or hungry, satisfaction when he is fed and cuddled are the only significant experiences of his life. As the child grows, his purely physical needs and satisfactions emerge slowly into more complicated psychological awarenesses. He gradually learns that there are others in his world beside himself; that he is not as "omnipotent" as it first appeared. He comes to know the meaning of affection, of being loved and cuddled and wanted. He notices, too, that there are compromises to be made; affection can sometimes wear thin in the face of importunate demands for immediate food or attention. The young infant learns, gradually, to defer the personal need of the moment for the sake of gratifying love and acceptance in the long run. Gradually, too, the child learns the meaning of fear and insecurity. New experiences are often threatening, and the sudden and unexplained withdrawal of loved ones can be a frightening symbol of abandonment.

Note that all these experiences, which form the very core of early living, are almost entirely emotional in nature. Just as the infant's body grows upon the milk and cereal it feeds upon, so the embryonic personality of the individual is developing through the emotional experiences it encounters in infancy.

The young child learns many things about himself in his early years. Even more important, he develops many significant attitudes about his emotions and those of people around him—attitudes which will form an indelible part of his personality and influence a good part of his adult behavior. A great many of these attitudes are absorbed automatically by the child from the kinds of emotional behavior he observes in his parents and others close to him.

It is in these early years, for example, that the child begins to develop his own opinion of himself. By listening to an evaluation of himself by those near and dear around him, the young human being begins to see himself as endowed with certain desirable—or undesirable—qualities. His parents may speak of him constantly as "the problem child," or "the one with the temper tantrums," or "the poor eater," or "the stubborn member of the family." If a negative characteristic is often and strongly suggested, a child will usually come to think of himself in similar negative and pessimistic terms. If, on the other hand, parents obviously enjoy him, want him, make allowances for the shortcomings of youth, and speak of him in positive terms, he is much more likely to consider himself a wholesome, competent, promising, lovable young person.

During these early years the child learns to respond in a healthy or unhealthy fashion to a succession of primitive emotions essentially irrational in nature. The way in which the child learns to manage his basic emotions depends on how his parents manage theirs, and how the youngster is helped by them to manage his own. If a parent is constantly losing his temper, exploding in a haphazard or illogical fashion, the child is liable to have difficulty in managing his own temper and will develop a pattern of volatile feelings which will make it difficult for him to live with himself and others.

Other parents may stifle *any* show of emotion in their children.

They will not "tolerate" the kinds of rebellion and occasional hostility which are part of every child's normal behavior pattern. Such children, persistently blocked in their early efforts to give expression to their inherent emotional drives, often become tense, silent, cynical, timid, and even withdrawn. They are unreasonably afraid to "let go" with an expression of feeling, a necessary function of man's psychological life. Parents who ruthlessly discourage or forbid all manifestation of these "less lovely" traits of human personality—in themselves or their children—do not understand that such frustration often leads to even greater difficulties. The first step in learning control over our more primitive emotions is to understand them, accept them, respect them without fear. Only then can they be safely channeled into healthy and acceptable outlets.

Let us consider, in this connection, the relation of sex to self-acceptance.

IMPORTANCE OF SEX EDUCATION

A very important aspect of self-acceptance involves the kind of sex education, or lack of it, which the growing child is given. Sex education means not only a progressing familiarity with the processes of reproduction; it includes the concepts a child has of masculinity or femininity, his growing capacity to give and to receive affection, and the kind of relationship he has to his own father and mother. There is perhaps no single area of human development in which adult behavior is more significantly influenced by attitudes developed in early childhood. Pope Pius XII made it very plain that it is a grave duty of parents to instruct their children by revealing gradually, simply, and truthfully each fact and detail which the child has the capacity to assimilate.

A good sex education involves much more than the mere imparting of information. Far more important is the communication of healthy attitudes toward sex. A child's attitude toward sex is built up from his earliest years. Such an attitude depends on how his parents think and feel about sex, how they talk about it, laugh about it, or perhaps ignore it completely.

Although many of our young parents are quite comfortable when they speak of sex to their children, the majority of today's mothers and fathers are still affected by the Victorian, Puritan, or Jansenist tradition of their elders in this regard. Parents display their inhibitions and uneasiness with this subject in three possibly damaging ways. Some parents acknowledge sex, but in a threatening, fearful, or ashamed tone of voice. Questioning children are told "Don't ask about such nasty things"; "Don't let me hear you use that word again"; "Nice people don't talk about things like this." Children of such parents come to regard sex with uneasiness and misgivings, and are soon afraid to ask further about it.

Another type of parent does his best to communicate necessary facts to the child, but is so emotionally distraught and uneasy that the "feeling tone" speaks louder than the facts he is relating. All the good will in the world will not hide the fact that even a willing parent is personally embarrassed, disturbed, and ill-at-ease with this subject. The child will often be more impressed and disturbed by the *manner* in which the parent communicates than with the facts that are communicated. Such parents will often answer a child's question with fables and deceptions about the birth process and other facts of reproduction. Such untruths will all have to be undone later on.

Finally, there is the parent who remains completely silent about the entire matter. This is equally puzzling and disturbing to the young child. The curiosity of a youngster is universal and insatiable. He must begin to wonder why in one particular area of life he is kept in ignorance. Often the child who "never asks questions" knows beforehand that the parent does not wish to hear such questions, much less talk about them.

The emotional relationship between parent and child makes it especially desirable that the parent impart significant sex instruction to the child. At this particular time in our culture, however, it is still the small minority of children who receive adequate sex instruction at home. In practice, therefore, it is the responsibility of the clergy, and, in certain instances, of the school, to supply wholesome and accurate information when it is impossible for the parents to do so. Wherever possible, of course, the chief role of the clergy should be to educate the parents. By means of PTA meetings, Cana groups, and study clubs a certain number of parents in the parish can be reached. In many other instances, the priest must work directly with the children. Various moral and educative principles relating to these procedures have been outlined by Fathers Fleege, Haley, Juergens, and Duhamel.[1]

In any of these procedures, the following points seem important to remember:

Sex education is not only a matter of imparting information, but of communicating attitudes and values. Consequently it is of great importance that the adult who imparts such information learns to be comfortable with the subject, positive and open in his approach, and completely free of the embarrassed and evasive tone which proclaims his confusion to the young listener.

Sex education is a long-range project. The parent who plans to reveal all the facts of life at one sitting and have done with it has a completely false idea of the philosophy and technique of good instruction. Young children become gradually aware of the facts and fantasies of sex. They will, for example, be asking certain questions almost as soon as they are able to talk. Gradually their capacity to absorb more and more detail demands that the parent transmit more precise information.

Adults should constantly remind themselves that sexual information does not have the same emotional overtones for children as for grownups. Children do not read into their questions, and the resulting answers, all the highly charged, inhibitive, or stimulating implications which are present for the adult. This is one reason why it is important that young children absorb as many facts and attitudes as possible in the prepuberty years. The preschool and grammar school child can absorb the facts of human sex life a good deal more objectively and placidly than can the adolescent whose curiosity has been continually stifled and who is overwhelmed with sudden insight at a time when his own emotions are undergoing new and violent upheavals.

Young children are interested in sex just as they are interested in any other subject. They will want to hear the same details explained over and over again. "What are firemen?" "Where do babies come from?" "Why does the lake freeze up?" Such questions have equal interest value and are liable to be asked again and again. It is always important for the parent, priest, or teacher to make sure *what* the child is asking before giving him an answer. "Where did I come from?" could be a query about the city or country of one's origin, and have nothing to do with sex information at the moment. Often children will be satisfied with the most simple sort of answer. The very young child, for example, is quite content to be told, "You grew in a warm place inside your mother's body, and when you were ready to be born you came out through a special opening." Only as much information as the child is ready for need be given.

The single most important ingredient for sex education is *the truth*. Every lie or distortion told to the child will some day have to be corrected. Not only does every child resent deception from his parents in any form, but he will wonder why *in this particular matter* it was so important for the parent to tell a lie.

Sooner or later a Catholic child must, of course, have his sex information integrated with his religious and moral convictions. However, parents and educators are sometimes too anxious about linking the two at every turn. In the early stages of sex education, God and religion should not play a more significant role than in any other sphere of the child's interest. This is especially true of that kind of sex education which equates shameful and sinful possibilities with the exercise of sexual faculties. When the child is old enough and informed enough, the realities of sexual morality can be explained without the damaging effects of their negative implications coming too soon.

Overemphasizing the religious aspect of sex can also be misleading to the young child. A seven- or eight-year-old will be as dissatisfied with the answer "God brought you" as with the answer "The stork brought you." When an older child asks "I understand how the baby gets *out,* but how does he get *in?*" it does not help him to say "God makes the egg inside the mother begin to grow." Of course God does, but Daddy helps a little too! It is probably the latter information he is after, and he has a right to it.

Important aspects of sex education are the attitudes of the parents to such things as modesty, eliminative processes, and the sexual organs themselves. Households where the human form is so covered up that the very young child never has a chance to observe masculine and feminine sex characteristics for himself often create inordinate and anxious kinds of curiosity. If mother and father speak of the eliminative processes as "dirty," "nasty," or refer to their child as "bad" when he soils himself, the child might transfer these negative attitudes to the genitals themselves.

Boys and girls should be fully prepared for the advent of menstruation and nocturnal emissions so that such experiences will symbolize for them prideful evidences of new maturity, and not fearsome mysteries which must be puzzled out amid evasive explanations and garbled half-truths.

Parents can teach their children to use the proper, dictionary vocabulary when referring to sexual organs and processes of elimination, which are so often described only in baby talk. *Penis, vagina, bowel movement, urinate*—these are words which the young child can be taught to say as easily as any others. The fact that in this one area parents feel the need for "a special vocabulary" can further confirm the child's suspicion that there is something mysterious, unusual, and somehow undesirable about these parts of the human anatomy and their function. When such words are coupled with "dirty, nasty, not nice," the harm is greater still. (The language of moral theologians, when used by the uninitiated, isn't always helpful either. Words such as *pollution* for orgasm, *indecent parts* for the genitalia, *self-abuse* for masturbation, *impure thoughts* for sexual thoughts, and *rendering the debt* for intercourse overemphasize the negative and undesirable aspects of phenomena which—with the exception of willful masturbation—do not involve sin at all.)

IMPORTANCE OF PARENTAL ATTITUDES

We cannot overemphasize the importance of the attitudes of parents towards their own masculinity or femininity and toward the functioning of their sexual powers. The mother, for example, who speaks drearily and resentfully of her monthly period as her "sick time," referring to her menstrual cycle as "the curse," is liable to hand on her negative feelings about being a woman to her daughter. The ability of a child to prepare to be fully and gladly a man or a woman has much to do with the sort of confident and fulfilled wife and mother, husband and father the youngster is to become.

The inability to relate healthfully and wholeheartedly to the opposite sex, in or out of marriage, begins in these very early years. It is at this time, for example, that the seeds of latent or overt homosexuality are sown. As Dr. Howard Davidman has written:

The feeling of clear and undeniable sexual identity—which is established in healthy children by the age of two or three—is defective in the potential homosexual. And it is defective because the parents have sexual conflicts of their own. Such parents severely limit their child's chances to develop an accurate understanding of his sexual role. Daily, in countless ways, mother and father indicate "what a delightful little girl their son really is." In extreme cases, the parents may delight in dressing the child in clothes of the opposite sex. In less extreme cases, parents may be excessively pleased in a girl's athletic prowess and stoicisms, in a boy's sensibility, gentlemanly qualities and grace. At the same time they condemn the skills appropriate to the sex of the child. Such parents do not really understand their child's needs, nor do they realistically perceive his growth to sexual maturity. Their own immaturity . . . stands in the way. Fear and anger at the child's budding sexuality, his sexual assertiveness and curiosity, hamper their effectiveness as parents. Perplexed and confused themselves, mother and father are inconsistent and unreliable when it comes to providing healthy sex images on which the child can pattern himself. They project their secret fears and desires on the child, unconsciously approving behavior which can only lead to sexual inhibition and deviation. In a way, the child serves as a kind of scapegoat to act out the parents' neurotic fantasies.[2]

The ability of parents to communicate, by word and attitude, a healthy and positive evaluation of sex to their children is hampered by confusion in the minds of many American Catholics as to the place of sex in the Christian life. Father John L. Thomas, S.J., has written eloquently on this whole problem:

The Christian's natural disgust and hatred for an offense against God has been misdirected. In regard to sex, this error stems from a confusion between sins against chastity and the physical manifestations of the reproductive drive. The quality of sinfulness has been mistakenly extended from the prohibited act to the physical phenomenon. Because the conscious, deliberate consent to venereal pleasure under prohibited circumstances constitutes sin, some have erroneously attributed the quality of sinfulness to the venereal pleasure itself and to the physical organs which give rise to it. As a result, there is a tendency to look upon the physical aspects of the reproductive drive as sinful and to lose sight of the fact that the sinfulness of unchaste actions is a quality of the act of consent, not of the venereal pleasure involved. . . . Thus by attributing sinfulness to the physical aspects of sex, one perverts Catholic doctrine regarding the nature of sin and promotes the essentially unchristian attitude that bodily or physical phenomena are evil.

This error leads to a distorted view of chastity. Because the physical elements of sex are considered evil, there is a tendency to consider the chaste person as some type of sexless creature, a person who never experiences the physical manifestations of sex rather than one who always uses his sexual powers in accordance with God's plan. . . .

Doubtless well-intentioned people have initiated this "smear campaign" against sex in the hope that they could dissuade people from sinning against chastity and in order to strengthen personal self-control. Paradoxically, experience shows that they have accomplished neither of these purposes, for their approach deprives the sexual drive of none of its force while destroying its human significance. We do not eliminate reality by denying its existence or by giving it a dirty name. . . . This error has resulted in an unbalanced stress of what might be termed the negative aspects of the virtue of chastity. Major emphasis is placed on what not to do. Chastity comes to be regarded as a series of "don'ts." . . . Because the nature and function of sex seldom receive a positive, integrated treatment, everything connected with sex becomes rather vague, indefinite, a source of worry and anxiety if not of actual disgust.[3]

Enlightened sex education is but one example—a very important one—of the more general principle this chapter attempts to expound; namely that the character traits of the adult, his strengths and weaknesses, his self-control or lack of it, his temptations and many of his talents are to a large extent rooted in the experiences of childhood. As the infant grows, some specific emotional needs are replaced by others. If these needs are recognized and understood by the parents, and the environment is reasonably congenial, the child should have no serious difficulty in developing into a happy and self-reliant adult. But where these needs are distorted, or misunderstood, or ignored, there the seeds of frustration, confusion, and compulsion are sown.

THE SEARCH FOR SELFHOOD

The needs of the very young child are very few and uncomplicated. He wants to be fed, changed, cuddled and loved. As he grows, he will begin to make his first bid for independence, a relentless challenge which continues in intensity until complete individuality and autonomy are reached. This striving for selfhood and independence is perhaps the greatest single concern of the conscientious parent. The human personality is not invested in a sudden, magic moment with maturity and self-reliance. These qualities unfold gradually and imperceptibly as the reins of parental control are slackened and the directives of parental authority become less and less necessary.

As the young infant learns to walk and talk he becomes increasingly aware of his individuality, his separateness from other people and other things. Very early in life he tests his independence; he will experiment with self-assertion by saying "No" and "I won't," by occasional defiance and even rage. The way in which the parent responds to these earliest testings of selfhood will mean much to the child's later development. If the emotions and activities of the growing child are completely unbridled and undirected, he is very liable to have difficulties with self-control, social adjustment, the management of his more primitive passions, and with his general capacity for mature self-direction. If, on the other hand, normal ventures into independence and the testing of feelings are stifled and rebuked, the child might become increasingly timid, anxious, uncreative, and inhibited.

The National Association for Mental Health has outlined in brief and concise language those things which every child needs for good mental health and growth:

All children require . . . *love:* Every child needs to feel that his parents love, want and enjoy him; that he matters very much to someone; that there are people near him who care what happens to him. *Acceptance:* Every child needs to believe that his parents like him for himself, just the way he is . . . that they like him all the time, and not only when he acts according to their ideas of the way a child should act; that they *always* accept him, even though often they may not approve of the things he does; that they will let him grow and develop in his own way. *Security:* Every child needs to know that his home is a good safe place he can feel sure about; that his parents will always be on hand, especially in times of crisis when he needs them most; that he *belongs* to a family or group; that there is a place where he fits in. *Protection:* Every child needs to feel that his parents will keep him safe from harm; that they will help when he must face strange, unknown, and frightening situations. *Independence:* Every child needs to know that his parents want him to grow up; that they encourage him to try new things; that they have confidence in him and in his ability to do things for himself and by himself. *Faith:* Every child needs to have a set of moral standards to live by; a belief in the human values—kindness, courage, honesty, generosity, and justice. [A Catholic child integrates these values into his thinking, feeling, and living through the example of good Catholic parents and an adequate Catholic education.] *Guidance:* Every child needs to have friendly help in learning how to behave towards persons and things; grownups around him show him by example how to get along with others. *Control:* Every child needs to know that there are limits to what he is permitted to do and that his parents will hold him to these limits; that though it is all right to feel jealous or angry, he will not be allowed to hurt himself or others when he has these feelings.[4]

As the child grows, some of the characteristics of a good environment mentioned above become more important, and others less important. Love, acceptance, and faith remain necessary throughout life. Protection, guidance, and control from outside become increasingly less important as the individual develops inner strengths and direction. We have already seen how increasing independence is the hallmark of healthy human growth.

It is not only important that a child grow away gradually from the dependence and support of the parents and home, but equally important that this venture into independence should be a progressively successful one. Children and young adults alike must feel that new undertakings and experiments in self-direction are essentially worthwhile, positive, satisfying experiences, even when there are occasional failures and mistakes. If experiments in self-reliance and independence on the part of a young person are met with objections, interference, ridicule, or downright opposition, then the initiative to test personal judgment and independent behavior is stifled and aborted. Adults who in their earlier days were thwarted in their attempts to grow and were kept dependent by their parents are often found to be withdrawn, timorous, self-protective, miserly, and uneasy with other people. Or the same kinds of early frustrations and insecurities may produce the defensive, hostile, cynical or cruel braggadocio, who also resents his inability to relate confidently and satisfyingly with the world around him, but shows it in a different sort of way.

We have been outlining some elementary concepts of human psychological development. A central thesis would be this: experiences and attitudes of early life determine to a significant degree the kind of personality, the type of character, and to some extent the degree of free choice which the adult will possess.

THE HUMAN PERSONALITY

Early experiences and attitudes influence the balance or lack of balance of three essential aspects of human personality distinguished by dynamic psychology. How emotionally healthy or unhealthy the individual is going to be depends on the degree to which (1) primitive urges, drives, passions, and desires, (2) the automatic, built-in do's and don'ts of man's "unconscious conscience," and (3) the conscious and more-or-less responsible self interact. We shall briefly discuss each of these components.

(1) At the very core of man's personality there is a *primal surge of living energy or force* which is without consciousness, beyond

rationality and will, outside of place or time.* These drives, urgings, and desires are making themselves felt in varied and perpetual kinds of activity. These forces are healthily expressed when they are chan-neled into manifestations of love, conjugal sexual interchange, healthy aggression and ambition, creativity and zeal for worthwhile causes. The same substrate of primal energy can be less desirably channeled into expressions of hate, hostility, libidinal excesses, sa-distic and masochistic behavior. In themselves, however, these primi-tive drives are neither good nor bad, right nor wrong, productive nor sterile. The manifestation of these basic drives depends upon the two other components of human personality.

(2) Offsetting, as it were, the chaotic and unfettered quality of the primitive urges is that part of man which we might call the *"un-conscious conscience."†* The unconscious conscience in each man develops long before his use of reason. Very early in life the young child subtly discovers that there are both acceptable and unaccepta-ble things associated with human behavior. He begins to hear "No, no" from a parent as well as "That's a good boy." Depending on the kind of world in which he lives, and the kind of attitudes which his parents gradually, relentlessly, and often unwittingly inculcate in him, he develops an "instinctive" kind of response to the desirable and undesirable aspects of his thoughts and behavior.

This is largely a quasi-automatic, unconscious process. The child seems to absorb, without a great deal of conscious reference, the kinds of attitudes to certain modes of thinking, feeling, and behaving that his parents transmit to him. If, for example, a girl comes from a very meticulous household, where she has perhaps been toilet-trained too early, she may develop automatic, exaggerated responses to dirt and disorder in her adult life. The child whose family main-tains a very "hush-hush" attitude toward sex may never feel quite comfortable and "right" about legitimate sex experiences in his or her own adult married life. The infant who has been stifled in its natural inclination to indulge in exhibitions of deep feeling, such as rage, rebellion, or an open show of affection, will find it difficult as

* The *id* in Freudian terminology.
† The *superego* in Freudian terminology.

an adult to give healthy and uninhibited vent to valid emotional expression. The vague impression, deep in the unconscious, that a show of feeling is an undesirable thing makes it difficult for many to express their feelings freely as adults.

When we examine our conscience in the sacrament of confession we should not consider the dictates of the superego, the unconscious policeman we have been describing. We have little control over the kinds of automatic do's and don'ts that form this part of our personality. We are going to be timid about some things, inhibited and fearful about others, and the roots of such responses are deep in the past.

The *conscious* conscience, on the other hand, is that faculty by which we make a judgment about a kind of behavior over which we have definite control. When we "examine our conscience," we decide that there were certain thoughts, words, or actions which involved conscious choice, but which were not worthy of us. Such self-blame presumes responsible and healthy guilt. Other kinds of *unconscious* guilt, often troublesome and quite painful, have to do with the unconscious conscience of the preceding paragraphs. The chronic hand-washer feels sure his hands are never quite germ free; the sexually inhibited person is certain that each sexual thought is an impure thought, no matter how spontaneous it might have been; certain individuals feel compelled to confess that they have missed Mass even though they were sick or snowed in. In these cases, and in many others, there is a residue of unreasonable and basically unconscious guilt which is attached to an oversensitive and malformed unconscious conscience.*

(3) The third and final component of human personality might be called *The Self.*† This is the conscious, rational, free component of the human being which makes decisions, is in touch with reality within and without the human organism. The unconscious conscience, the automatic policeman with its built-in do's and don'ts,

* See chapter 7.

† The *ego* in Freudian terms. The conscious conscience, examined as a preparation for confession, can be considered as belonging to this facet of our personality.

serves to restrain, control, and direct the nebulous, undefined, yet tremendously powerful demands of the primitive forces and surgings described earlier. A healthy personality is one in which adequate balance exists between these three components, namely the primitive drives, the controlling unconscious conscience, and the aware and judicious self. Perhaps the dynamics of human personality can be described in terms of a rubber ball with three interacting layers. (See diagram.) The undifferentiated urges and desires (the id)

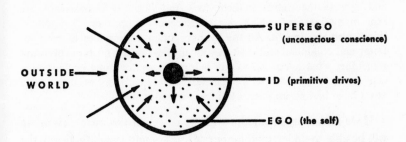

serve as the center of the ball. The ego (or self) is seen as a resilient mass surrounding this core. It is contained by an enveloping outer layer, the superego (or unconscious conscience). As this sphere tumbles about in the big world, the core of inner drives, under the impact of outside persons, things, and events, acts and reacts with the pliable yet protective surface of the superego. If this unconscious conscience is too firm and thick a layer, the internal urges and desires will not find adequate expression, nor will the outer influences of the environment be able to make an appropriate impact on healthy personality formation.

THE ROLE OF THE UNCONSCIOUS

An important corollary which dynamic psychology has taught us is that there exists something within the personality we call the *unconscious*. By this we do not mean a place in the brain, or a container

of any kind, but rather a particular function of the human mind
which does not involve the quality of awareness.

The unconscious [as Dr. William C. Menninger has described it] is the
mental activity that goes on without our knowledge, over which we have
no control. It's by far the larger portion of our personality. It is like the
remaining eight-ninths of the iceberg that lies under the surface of the
water where no one can see it. The unconscious is the power behind the
throne. From it come the forces that make you go; that make you love
or hate. The unconscious furnishes the energy for your thoughts and
feelings. From the unconscious, forgotten desires try to push forward
and express themselves in behavior. And into the unconscious are
sent many ideas of which our conscience disapproves. "Forgotten"
things also slip into it. All the long forgotten experiences of your infancy and childhood still exist in your unconscious. You probably can't
remember what happened to you before the age of three or four—except for a few incidents. Nevertheless, the experiences of those early
years have had an important influence on your personality.[5]

   If we understand something of the power of the unconscious we
will be able to understand more realistically and sympathetically the
puzzling, blind, irrational, and weak behavior of the human being.
The unconscious is the source of our dream fantasies; it explains
why in hypnosis an individual is suddenly able to revive memories
and feelings which otherwise would remain forever buried in the
forgotten past; it explains why different people behave in entirely
unpredictable ways under sudden tension or passion or fear; it explains in so many ways why we are what we are, feel as we do, are
tempted by this and not that, develop interests along certain lines
and not others, and are unable to see the real reasons for many of
our own private prejudices, anxieties, and enthusiasms. (It is the
uncovering of the unconscious in the process known as psychoanalysis that may enable the individual to revive experiences and
feelings of the past, in particular the painful ones which have been
most effectively repressed.)

   The counsellor and/or confessor who understands something of
the unconscious and its role in human emotion and behavior is in a
good position to go beyond some surface problem that is brought to
him and try to see those aspects of it which reach into the uncon-

scious. The existence of the unconscious does not disprove the existence of free will. However, there are many subtle areas of human activity which are touched by unconscious motivation. Perhaps St. Paul had something of the sort in mind when he wrote, "For I do not that good which I will; but the evil which I hate, that I do."[6]

Self-knowledge, the key to the exercise of maximum freedom in human behavior, is often clouded and hampered by these deep and complicated influences of the buried past upon the present. The human personality, like the human mind, began in the psychological sense as a *tabula rasa*. Each personal experience, as it occurs, makes its mark and is indelibly registered. The vast majority of these experiences, especially the unpleasant ones, fade from the conscious present into the unconscious past. But they are not gone; their influences remain at work. The more powerful the original emotional incident, the more powerfully can the present be affected by it.

The unconscious reveals itself in a particularly significant way by determining some of the common procedures by which human beings meet conflict, crisis, and frustration. The various components of human personality which we have been describing are all working at once. We must not think of them as separate entities, describing in a kind of anatomical way separate "compartments" of the mind. Rather, the primitive drives, the unconscious conscience, and the self—as well as the unconscious—are topographical descriptions of the nature of personality. Their influences overlap, emphasizing now one, now another priority of impact.

In what way do these psychic elements contribute to certain kinds of behavior in this or that individual? To begin with, the interaction of these interior forces with the external world produces situations of frustration or conflict which demand compromise. The manner in which we usually react to crisis or conflict depends to a large extent upon the early pattern of our personality development. Some of us respond to these challenges with a "flight reaction." We leave the scene of conflict and withdraw into some neutral or less threatening environment, perhaps into the land of daydreams or make-believe. Others of us resort to the "fight reaction"; we prefer to battle against everything and everyone in the environment, sometimes including the "stone walls." The method we choose depends to a large extent on the kind of childhood we had, on the ways in which we were prevented or encouraged to meet the petty but highly significant challenges and frustrations of infancy.

MENTAL MECHANISMS

The unconscious is at work in many day-to-day responses to that unending series of struggles which is life. In many ways our predictable reactions form as regular and distinctive a pattern as our handwriting. These patterns are technically called mental mechanisms.* They are the devices that make it easier for the personality to adjust to the environment. They are weapons of defense against feelings of insecurity, fear, or anxiety. The use of some of these mechanisms is essential to good mental health. The use of others may be a sign of emotional immaturity. Some of the chief mental mechanisms are:

Introjection. By this process a child automatically takes in ideas, attitudes, prejudices, likes and dislikes and a host of other personality traits which he admires in his parents, and later on in others around him. Introjection accounts for similarity between family members (e.g. politics, religious beliefs, cultural tastes, etc.); and in cases where the child does not love his parents, it may account for his rejection of all the distasteful standards, hopes and teachings for which they stand.

Identification. Identification is the device by which an individual automatically imitates the behavior or mannerism of someone else, putting himself in his shoes. It works hand in hand with introjection, in the sense that the individual identifies with a person or a group whose ideals and attitudes have already been crystallized. A little girl imitates her mother when she plays or talks to her dolls; the teen-ager imitates his movie hero by using the same language, wearing the same clothes, etc. It is important, therefore, that young people, especially, have worthwhile heroes and heroines to imitate.

* It is obvious that these mechanisms are not as neat and definite in their operation as our brief treatment here might suggest.

Sublimation. Sublimation is the mechanism by which one converts the primitive drives of love and hate into activities of which the conscience and other people approve. The sportsman cracks the golfball instead of his boss's cranky head; the celibate sublimates his basic sexual energy in creative and altruistic activities. Sublimation is a vital and frequently employed device for managing the more irrational and uncontrollable elements in man.

Compensation. This refers to the way an individual makes up the lack of some specific ability. Thus a physical handicap is compensated for in some way by another part of the body. Paralysis of the legs is often balanced by unusually powerful arm and chest muscles. Psychologically, too, the same process is at work in all of us. People who feel outclassed in one field of endeavor make up for it by becoming expert in another. Fathers who feel inadequate in the home or in their marriage will spend long hours at the office, becoming efficient in making more money. The poor athlete compensates by becoming a proficient scholar, and vice versa. The housewife who is bored with cleaning and cooking at home becomes interested in community projects or gardening.

Rationalization. This is the personality's device for justifying ideas and behavior so that they seem reasonable to oneself. Regardless of appearances, this is essentially an unconscious process, even though other people see through our own rationalizations much quicker than we do ourselves. We often rationalize our prejudices, our preferences, our daily mistakes.

Idealization. This means simply to rate something far beyond its actual worth. Parents do this when they speak of the intelligence, talent, or beauty of their children. Most of us, to some extent, idealize ourselves. Within reason, this need not be an undesirable device; if our view of ourselves is not too distorted, a somewhat idealized version gives us a goal to aim at and encourages a certain degree of confidence in our own abilities which is very necessary for placid functioning and growth.

Reaction Formation. This is behavior which is directly contrary to our unconscious wishes. Some individuals who are too fussy about orderliness and cleanliness are probably repressing unfulfilled desires carried over from childhood to smear and splash and mess in dirt. Many an old maid who shrieks at the possibility of finding a man under her bed may secretly relish the prospect. Often when the true but buried wish is very strong, the individual will bend over backwards to do the opposite. Thus, a secretly hostile personality may mask his true inclinations by being consistently "too nice," oversweet and complimentary to everybody around him. Or, the mother of an unwanted child may be so uneasy about her hidden feelings (which her guilt will often not permit her to acknowledge) that she will become over-protective and anxious in her relationship with her child. (In extreme cases, it is as if she must somehow protect her offspring against the desperate, negative feelings which she dares not admit she has for him.)

Displacement is the unconscious at work in a particularly obvious sort of a way. By this device the personality quite unknowingly transfers emotion produced in one situation to another, unrelated situation. The housewife who has burned the roast finds herself scolding her children or finding fault with her husband. Or husbands and wives often take out the resentment they feel toward each other on their children. We will usually deflect our stronger feelings upon objects or people who are less of a threat to us than the original source of the emotional disturbance.

Projection. This device defends the personality against our unacceptable ideas or wishes by attributing them to someone else. There are some people who are constantly blaming others for their own mistakes or shortcomings. They are quick to read into others the motives that secretly they themselves hold. Thus the chronic liar feels everyone around him is lying; the individual who has difficulty in relating warmly to others suspects that he is constantly being rejected by his friends and associates.

Conversion. This particular mental mechanism is described in more detail in our chapter on mental health. It is a common process by which an unconscious urge or idea seeks expression through illness or a physical complaint. Aches, pains, stomach disorders, heart difficulties, allergies, skin eruptions, menstrual irregularity can often be traced to conflicts between unconscious wishes and the demands of the environment. It is often easier to go to bed with one or another of these symptoms than to face the conflicts, anxieties, and tensions of an unsympathetic world.*

Two key mental mechanisms which are constantly at work should be carefully defined and distinguished here. They are repression and suppression.

Repression is a spontaneous, irrational response of the mind and emotions to fearful and threatening thoughts, desires, situations, actions. If you have grasped the automatic functioning of the superego, you will understand how repression works. Through insistent parental overemphasis, certain subjects (e.g., sex, loss of temper, resentment of authority) are made "taboo" in the life of the child; these deep and powerful attitudes then continue to exert their influence in adulthood. Whenever such forbidden or threatening subjects or feelings confront the individual, whether in fact or in fantasy, they immediately trigger fear, anxiety, and tension. The mind responds at once by pushing out the undesirable or threatening image, *usually before it has even intruded into consciousness.* The more threatening the image or object, the more automatic is the "pushing out" response. "Pushing out," however, is not an accurate phrase. The threatening image or emotion is rather *thrust deep down* into the unconscious, where it does not disappear but remains to exercise its influence in a powerful but disguised fashion.

Repression of one emotion often leads to the emergence of another emotion equally undesirable, though perhaps more tolerable to the individual. Thus a man who is never able to permit himself to feel angry may ease his tensions by sly and vicious verbal sniping and uncharitableness. Another man, whose psyche flees fearfully and at once any hint of sexuality, may hide behind a forbidding, authoritative pseudo-ascetic façade, often imposing stern and severe controls on others over whom he may exercise authority. Genuine repression is always harmful. The personality is like a balloon: depressing one section will inevitably cause a bulge to appear elsewhere. The indi-

---

* The foregoing schema has been derived from the classification of mental mechanisms according to William C. Menninger, M.D., developed in several of his publications.

vidual who, by repression, is continuously and powerfully stifling many significant emotional outlets will often break down and develop a severe mental illness. Or the dam may break in another way, and lead the individual to abandon all semblance of restraint. The rigid controls no longer hold and the seeming ascetic becomes a libertine, abandoning himself to heretofore unthinkable excesses. (Thus some inhibited ex-seminarians develop sexual or alcoholic problems; rigidly brought-up convent girls may marry outside the Church; overpious, super-docile youngsters often become cynical, rebellious iconoclasts in adulthood.)

When Freud insisted that repression was harmful and to be avoided, he was at once misunderstood to say that the psychologically healthy individual was one who had the freedom and courage to act on every pet impulse, indulge in every gratification, flaunt all traditional concepts of responsibility and guilt. The alternative to repression was falsely presumed to be unbridled self-indulgence. But Freud, whatever his differences with the moral theologians, was quite in favor of self-restraint and self-control. Man's need to curb his primitive urges and more irrational instincts was clearly acknowledged by him. The method by which this was to be done is called suppression.

Suppression is the chief psychological technique by which moral man, whether Christian or otherwise, can safely and effectively control the potentially sinful or harmful tendencies of his imperfect nature. Both repression and suppression restrict and subdue man's instinctual life, but in entirely different ways. Repression is a blind, irrational, relentless, and largely irresponsible process which functions automatically along deeply ingrained reflex patterns developed unconsciously in childhood. Suppression is a mature control of man's instinctual life through a conscious choice of what the mind and the imagination should or should not dwell upon.

A simple example might illustrate the difference between repression and suppression. Two young people are reading the same popular pictorial magazine. Each comes upon a suggestive photograph which, for him, might prove to be an occasion of sin. The first youth is a victim of repressive reaction. From his earliest years he has been fearful of sexuality. He carries with him a sort of permanent anxiety that he may be confronted with the terrible subject at almost any time. He is at the moment unconsciously apprehensive that something sexual may appear on the magazine pages he is turning. Suddenly he is face to face with a suggestive photograph. His heart leaps, his hand flashes, and the offending page is turned at once. Even with the relief which comes from such spontaneous self-protection, there is frequently a persistent dissatisfaction with the immature and compulsive control he has exercised but not really chosen. Often, frustration and curiosity have already begun to build up again, to be met at each fresh encounter with renewed fear and precipitous flight.

What of the reader who has learned to suppress rather than repress? He has, to begin with, a healthy, open, confident attitude towards sex. He has thought through deliberately, without fear, the place this important instinct* is to have in his life. He is enjoying his reading and has no anxiety about what he might encounter. As the potentially stimulating picture presents itself, his emotions do not throw him into panic. He takes an unhurried look—perhaps a momentarily admiring one!—and makes a calm evaluation. He becomes aware that the subject matter may be stirring his passions, may be leading to possibly troublesome fantasies. Without anxiety, and with full deliberation, he placidly decides to turn the page and distract his mind and imagination with something else.

The difference between healthy suppression and harmful repression should be obvious. Repression is blind, inexorable, automatic, with roots deep in the unconscious past. Suppression is conscious, reasoned, the result of deliberation and choice—the substitution of a more wholesome in place of a less desirable thought or object for clearly understood and accepted motives. Repression is the device of a frightened, insecure, and shackled human being. Suppression is

* The authors use the word *instinct* here and throughout this work in full realization that the term is no longer used by most specialists. It has seemed helpful to retain it in this present work, however, which is intended for the non-specialist, for whom *instinct* still seems a broad but meaningful term.

the valuable tool of the mature person, who through its good offices freely determines the direction of his thinking and feeling.

Remember that most mental mechanisms are not good or bad in themselves. When properly developed some are indispensable to healthy and mature living. Among these are introjection, sublimation, idealization, and suppression. These and others can not only help us understand ourselves better, but can cushion the more painful shocks which sooner or later touch every life—severe illnesses, death of loved ones, keen disappointments, etc. In the following chapters we shall see how some of these rather obscure and abstract mechanisms operate, for good or for ill, in the case histories which the priest or counsellor hears each day.

NOTES

1. *The Proceedings of the Institute for the Clergy on Problems in Pastoral Psychology* (New York: Fordham University Press, 1956), pp. 49, 50, 144.

2. "What You Should Know about Homosexuality," *State of Mind*, II, No. 4 (1957), p. 8.

3. "The Place of Sex," *The Catholic Mind*, LVI, No. 1135 (1958), pp. 31–32.

4. *What Every Child Needs* (New York: National Association of Mental Health Pamphlet, 1954). The brackets in the quotation are those of the authors of this present volume.

5. W. C. Menninger, *Self-Understanding* (Chicago: Science Research Associates, 1951), p. 7.

6. Romans VII, 14.

ETHEL MARBACH

The Power Of Positive Listening

MUCH IS WRITTEN these days about the lost art of conversation, the reason for it and the deploring of it. You may even spend an entire argumentative evening discussing the lost art of conversation. Our seeming lack of communication stems, we are told, from the pressures of fast-paced modern life, automation, and plain laziness

ment of torture (or procrastination) for the busy mother, but it is also an indispensable teaching aid for the novice listener. You develop self-control and middle-age spread; you combat tingling legs which have fallen asleep and massage a paralyzed telephone ear as you relive (again) the true-life saga of Sadie's bout with an unsympathetic

hearts) But there are also serious problems laid in our laps; they come with creased foreheads and wide eyes and you are sure it's going to be Where Did I Come From, Mommie, but it is, "I win the cornflakes sweepstakes and \$110 a day, will I get Sunday's money on Saturday, or will they hold it over til Monday?" Only by being the *compleat* listener can a parent realize the

SEAN MARTIN

THE FROG

2

THE PRIEST AS A LISTENER

The priest as a counsellor makes a unique and valuable contribution to the spiritual and mental health of his people. Perhaps no other vocation makes more urgent or varied demands upon the consultor's role. The occupational possibilities faced by a newly ordained priest are as varied as life itself. He may eventually become the head of an educational institution, a dean of men, or a teacher in the classroom. He may be appointed a seminary professor, a spiritual guide to a convent of nuns, a director of a group of working brothers. He may serve as a superior over a house of priests, a pastor responsible for the multiple activities of a large parish, a chaplain in a hospital, prison, or sanitarium. The average priest, sooner or later, will have to deal with the guidance problems of his parish school, manage various clubs and organizations, supervise youth activities, evaluate and instruct prospective converts, give premarital and postmarital guidance.

The pastor's guiding influence is involved in many of the living problems and crises of his parishioners. In the confessional, in the rectory parlor, and in the home, the conscientious priest shares, as no other man can, the unhappiness of tortured souls who are plagued by severe depressions, overwhelming and unreasonable guilt complexes, soul-searing scrupulosity, terrible fears of illness and death, irrational doubts, blind and vicious hostilities. Such afflictions are at times morally indifferent; often they involve deeply rooted and compulsive weaknesses. In any case, the concerned priest is coming to rely more and more on psychological insight as a help to the just and fruitful application of his moral theology.

Counselling, implies St. Thomas, is primarily concerned with those methods and skills which facilitate self-directed choices through personal reorganization, furthering thereby the development of the virtue of counsel and ultimately of prudence. Psychological insight plus the salutary exposition of the external Christian truths and the unfathomable influence of God's grace—when applied to the confessional- or rectory-problems faced by the priest—is what we mean by pastoral counselling.

The priest-counsellor often wears two hats: that of the therapist and that of the instructor. On the one hand, the effective counsellor must be accepting, often nonjudgmental, sensitive to the deep flowing emotions of his clients,* hesitant to impose his own views and solutions. On the other hand, a client usually seeks out a Catholic priest precisely because he *is* a Catholic priest. He expects information and guidance within the framework of his Faith and consistent with its teachings. There are surely times when the religious counsellor is not only obliged to attend to troubled feelings which underlie a problem, but must also help clarify or redefine those religious and moral involvements which puzzle or mislead his clients.

However, recent research has confirmed the long suspected theory that the imparting of information is likely to be the least important and least effective of the counsellor's techniques. The Rogerian

---

* It is not possible to find one word which will always accurately describe the various individuals who come to a priest with a problem. *Parishioner, penitent, counselee, client,* and (where the priest is a psychotherapist) *patient* are all appropriate, depending on whether the nature of the problem is primarily spiritual, moral, psychological, etc. We have tried in each instance to choose the appellation which best describes the problem person, but we realize that we have not always succeeded. *Client* is most frequently used when the personal difficulty cannot be pinpointed as either purely spiritual or purely emotional.

psychologist Father Charles A. Curran* has suggested in his book, *Counseling in Catholic Life and Education,* that the troubled soul who seeks counsel is rarely seeking factual information or "advice." Rather it is the counsellor's task to help the client himself to "uncover the means for personal and responsible individual life action" in the ever-changing daily living unique to him.

The counsellor may often be tempted to "hand out" a solution for the client's problem in the light of "logic and common sense." In our counselling experience, however, we find so many conflicts stemming not from faulty logic, but from deeply rooted and highly irrational emotional perplexities. For Father Curran, a counsellor's objective goes far beyond the initial imparting of logical information. In his words, "The individual on his own personal responsibility must be able to carry out the principles and practical information he has received. He must have acquired individual integration both in his ability to cope with the disorder within himself, the unreasonable impulses of his emotions and instincts, and the disorder in the world, in other personalities, and in reality itself. Knowledge must become activated in each individual's life as he copes with the single events in his daily actions."[3]

THE ART OF LISTENING

Is there one technique which best suits the priest who is constantly confronted with new and diverse counselling problems? Occasionally, he can use his authoritative position in the community to per-

* Carl R. Rogers is the founder of the systematized school of nondirective or client-centered counselling. His theories and methods are outlined and demonstrated in his book *Counseling and Psychotherapy,* [1] a valuable text for the priest who wishes to develop sound guidance techniques. Father Charles A. Curran, who studied with Rogers, shows, in his book *Counseling in Catholic Life and Education,* [2] how Rogerian theory and Thomistic principles complement each other. He makes an excellent case for the application of client-centered techniques to Catholic counselling needs.

suade or even direct others to change environmental factors which he feels contribute to a problem. Every priest should, of course, be familiar with all the local community agencies which might co-operate with him in his guidance work. (See chapter 9.) He can also try to keep up with some of the latest psychological theories pertinent to the various troubles which people bring to him.

But all these are aids to counselling, and do not properly touch the counselling process itself. Most priests are quick to acknowledge a lack of information and skill in handling many of their parishioners' personal difficulties. In one morning, a parish priest may be called to the school to handle a discipline problem, attempt to soothe the fears of a seriously ill person, accept the responsibility of supervising a juvenile delinquent, try to patch up a disintegrating marriage, confer with an alcoholic, and give spiritual direction to a highly sensitive aspirant to sanctity. He cannot be master in all these areas. Time and again he dreams of some simple formula, some common procedure which might with some success be applied to all these cases.

The device which comes closest, perhaps, to this magic talisman of counselling is the art of *listening*. The priest may know nothing about the problem area to which he is called for consultation. He may have little or no idea of the dynamics behind certain types of emotional or moral disorders. He may not have the faintest idea of what to say to this scrupulous penitent or that irate parent. But he can always be a good listener. He can learn to hold his tongue. He can learn what *not* to say. He can show interest. He can reflect an understanding of the person's feelings. He can accept the individual as a fellow human being with a problem.

The priest as a listener can create an atmosphere of solicitous permissiveness in which the troubled client feels free to share the burden he is unable to carry alone. This is the true meaning of *compassion*. The compassionate counsellor touches the emotional pulse of his client by identifying in some personal—though not in any overtly emotional—way with his anguish, his bewilderment and his interior conflict. Thereby the counsellor shows that he understands. The priest need say hardly a word. The fact that someone is interested, someone understands, someone is in no hurry to belittle or disparage or explain away the worry, temptation, or failure of the moment has tremendous value. The ability to listen well is, for the average priest, the safest and soundest of techniques.

No advice is better than wrong advice. Older guidance techniques, such as ordering, forbidding, exhorting, and suggesting are being recognized as often ineffective. Advice, persuasion, and intellectualized interpretation are still considered by some priests to be productive techniques, but many feel they do not have the skill to use them. By trial and error, then, by elimination and experimentation, many priests have settled down to being good listeners. Instinctively or consciously they have become more and more aware of the essential "rightness" of this approach.

The "talking-out process" has the obvious value of catharsis, that indispensable "get it off your chest" ingredient of every successful counselling relationship. In addition, priestly counsellors can feel safe and secure, confident that by their silence they are at least safeguarding the client from the harmful, inopportune, or miscalculated advice they *might* have given.

Obviously listening is not the only effective tool of the priest-counsellor. Often, when a solution to a problem is quite clear to both counsellor and counselee, proper exhortations which strengthen the will and facilitate the action of grace are the best contributions the priest can make. Other times the stirring up of compunction and new resolves to amendment must be the priest's chief duty. The listening technique is best used in such cases where a solution to a complicated and largely unresolved human problem is far from clear to the client. These are emotion-tinged difficulties not grave enough to warrant psychiatric help, yet puzzling enough to resist the resolution which will power and supernatural aids would ordinarily effect. The priest should be slow to presume that most human problems are resolved by purely logical and "common sense" solutions. Often even the most intellectual difficulties have deep emotional underpinnings which can best be dispelled through the nondirective, listening process described here.

It should here be pointed out that the priest who is a good listener is certainly employing a "nondirective" technique, but not necessarily a Rogerian one. The Rogerian counsellor is a true specialist. He is skilled in reflecting both the overt and disguised feelings of the client; he makes judicious use of interpretation; he presides over the largely self-directed growth of the patient. With years of experience and study the priest may achieve some success in these specialized techniques. But initially he is *chiefly a listener* whose primary contribution is a wholehearted acceptance of the client who is made to feel that he may speak, without fear, of any deeds or feelings which may be troubling him.

It is interesting to note that in almost every community there are certain priests, often well along in age, who have gained a solid reputation as wise, considerate, and effective counsellors. Years of experience, coupled with a kind of native insight, seem to achieve skills which take others many semesters of hard classroom study to acquire. In every case, one characteristic of their approach stands out—they are good listeners.

The conscientious priest is sometimes handicapped by his own lack of conviction in the efficacy of this counselling procedure. He may have little confidence in the positive values of listening as such. He is more at home solving problems on a rational plane and frequently waits rather wearily for the first moment of silence in which to inject an intellectual solution as "advice" for his client. Often, unfortunately, advice is neither what the individual wants nor what he needs or can use at the moment. If the problem is a personality problem involving the emotions, the person probably has received good advice many times before, has acknowledged its truth, but has found himself unable to follow it through. This puts him in a further state of inferiority, frustration, and resentment, increasing his resistance to the counsellor, who seems to be giving a quick solution to difficulties with which the one seeking counsel has been wrestling for a long time.

Sometimes a penitent may hear the priest say: "Look how stupid the thing you've done is. The simple answer is obvious. . . ." Such advice will not generate encouragement, or the desire to return for further help. If a person with a deeply rooted and vexing problem is told he is stupid, and that the solution is really "quite simple," he will say to himself: "Father either doesn't understand, or I'm just plain hopeless! In any case, it's no use going back."

Giving advice or help when the client could have thought it through himself deprives the client of the satisfaction and self-esteem of having solved his own problem. The cardinal principle of Rogers' theory is that there is inherent in the individual a drive toward growth, health, and adjustment, as well as toward concupiscence. Rogers further feels that in the long run only the individual himself is able to make valid judgments about the day-to-day experiences which he meets on his own, since the problems of each person's life are so interwoven with myriad factors in his own past and present that a completely prudent judgment about them could hardly be made by anyone but himself.

For these and similar reasons, the priest can readily learn to recognize the wisdom of simply listening at times to the troubled person. The mere fact that he is heard through by an accepting, kindly, impartial individual has many values for the counselee. To begin with, strains of nervous tension are released as he finds himself expressing things about himself which have worried him. This reduction of tension, while no cure for his problem, brings him genuine reassurance, naturally encouraging him to utilize the healthy forces of his personality to cope with his difficulty. Moreover, when the intense pressures of the internal conflict are momentarily diminished, the burden is often lightened at a critical moment. Courage is restored and tensions arising from his inability to identify with others in the world outside himself are cut down.

This may be only symptomatic relief, but even as such it is highly desirable. The resulting emotional calm can give the individual the freedom to see his own situation more clearly. Talking out a problem with a sympathetic listener who avoids comment frequently brings greater insight. "I talk so that I'll know what I think" is the way one counselee phrased it. Talking helps to clarify thinking; by this process the individual may actually come to see his problem in its present setting, and express things about himself which he has heretofore been unable to admit on his own. How often have we found that the "presenting problem" (the initial problem brought by the client) melts into insignificance while deeper and more complicated difficulties unfold as the client speaks.

Intelligent listening is not easy. Beginners are often deceived in thinking that just learning to *remain silent* is the essence of the process. This is far from true. Intelligent, active listening means that the counsellor is not only listening but is understanding—he is giving his full attention not only to what the client is saying but to what he is *feeling*. He responds by encouraging replies, nods, smiles, monosyllables, etc. Communication involves *two* persons, even though one person is doing most of the talking.

Especially difficult is the important technique of reflecting significant feelings subtly revealed by the client. The intellectual content is not nearly so significant as is the emotional tone behind it. "This disturbed you, didn't it?"; "You were frightened at that, weren't you?"; "That made you mad!"; "You feel pretty good about this, don't you?" . . . These are kinds of "identification with feeling" important to the counselling process. To capture and "reflect" your understanding of these tell-tale emotions is another reason for careful listening.

If such *active* communication does not take place, the client will not respond positively to the interview, will leave frustrated or hostile, or will feel guilty in taking up the priest's time. He must be helped to want to return, to feel that by airing his feelings something is happening. He must not feel guilty because he senses that the counsellor thinks nothing is being accomplished. The counsellor must make sure that the client understands that he is welcome to return, not only by inviting him verbally, but by responding positively to the kinds of information the client brings to him.

When troubled souls feel accepted and are listened to without rejection they begin to acquire some of that healthy self-love and self-respect which has been damaged by their interior conflicts. With greater feelings of self-acceptance come the energy, will, and insight to improve the functioning of their real selves. The patient, unruffled listener not only represents the watching, interacting world outside but can come to symbolize the individual himself. When the client is accepted by another he is more able to accept himself; he is freed from lacerating self-criticism and self-deprecation. "Perhaps I'm not so hopeless after all" is a first step to the gradual realization that a problem or a sinful habit is but one aspect of the total personality picture and does not represent every element in that personality.

The will-to-health and to holiness and the beginning of insight are built slowly and cautiously upon just such self-acceptance. The individual cannot release the defenses which may cause his conflict until he senses with reasonable emotional security that a different adjustment is actually possible to him. Self-acceptance is very important for such a feeling. If the attitude of the listener is friendly, tolerant, understanding, this may stir up first the hope, then the conviction that improvement is possible. The client begins to realize that his or her problem is not so unusual or bizarre as to put him outside the pale of humanity or to necessitate self-hate.

It is often through such listening that an awareness of the general lines of the solution will become clear. When the client is really convinced that the counsellor has not rejected him as a person, he may be more ready to drop the defenses against his own self-rejection. This may clear the stage for an unclouded perception of the client's total problem which enables him to sift and weigh the advantages and disadvantages of various solutions in a calm, unemotional atmosphere and arrive at essentially self-directed choices. The priest, then, can find the slow but necessary process of sympathetic, judicious listening a valuable counselling technique, and far from a waste of time.

It is interesting to see how over a century ago a prominent spiritual director, the Venerable Libermann (along with many others before him), anticipated the nondirective technique when he wrote about spiritual guidance: "The spiritual director having once ascertained God's action in a soul, has nothing else to do but to guide it, that it may obey the promptings of grace. He must never attempt to inspire a soul with his personal tastes and individual attractions, nor lead it after his own way of acting or his own peculiar point of view. A director that would act thus would often turn souls from God's own guidance and oppose the action of divine grace in them."[4]

OBSTACLES TO UNDERSTANDING

One obstacle to an effective counselling relationship between priest and parishioner is the special symbol of *authority* which is attached to the priesthood in the minds of the people. There are many layfolk who deal face to face with a priest only at important or solemn occasions in their lives, such as baptisms, weddings, and funerals. Such parishioners are inclined to associate the priesthood with the didactic religious instruction of their school days, moral admonitions from the pulpit and confessional, and other rather remote and directive roles which the priest is often called upon to play. The Roman collar, the cassock, or religious habit may be in themselves rather formidable symbols of authority, and may have to be reckoned with as possible resistance factors in person-to-person counselling relationships.

It is important that the client understand from the outset that the chief objective of the counselling process is not to make censorious judgments or to determine the degree of guilt and responsibility of the client's actions. It is the counsellor's task, rather, to create an accepting, unthreatening atmosphere in which the client can feel free to reveal the emotional undercurrents from which his difficulties spring. In other words, the client in counselling must become interested not so much in *what* he is doing as in *why* he is doing it. He will not risk fully exposing his deepest feelings—the first step to control over them—until he is sure that he will not be censured and rejected because of them.

The silent *acceptance* of the client and his shortcomings by the counsellor does not mean *approval*. There is little danger that the client will confuse the two. He may have been wrestling for some time with a problem which he knows to be morally wrong; the unwillingness of the counsellor to limit discussion to morality will not suddenly make him feel free to do as he pleases.

Says Father Curran of the counselling process:

Growth is not so much in knowledge of what they should do. Generally, they had this knowledge before they came and it was one of the causes of their conflict. We see, rather, a slow change from discouragement, hostility, dependence, insecurity, and immoderate compensations to a more positive attitude about themselves and their ability to change. Simultaneously, as negations are expressed and thought through, they begin to see why they are failing. With this come, sometimes at an almost imperceptible pace, sometimes suddenly, insights which relate problems to each other and to factors in the past and present environment. This relating process leaves them finally to see fundamental causes that are at the basis of their difficulties. At the same time, there is an increase in the number of factors which indicate a growing courage and confidence in their ability to overcome difficulties and reach a more adequate solution.

At this stage new solutions begin to appear, are tried, and usually are found more successful, since the person now takes many more factors into consideration before he makes his decisions. These new solutions are, however, not always successful. The interview then offers a person the opportunity to re-examine the reasons for failure. In this way counselling helps him to achieve happier and more virtuous living. The final stages of a successful counselling process, therefore, show a greater integration and coördination between the person's reasonable judgment and his emotional and physical urges. As a result, the person can make better choices and, when he acts on these choices, he finds he is more consistently able to reach what he is seeking.[5]

While the authoritative aura surrounding the priest is often difficult to undo in the mind of the client, it can also work to great advantage. When a client finds that a priest can be quite nondirective, playing essentially the role of the good listener, such a turnabout can give the client new confidence and impetus to express his feelings freely. In a sense, the authority of the priest sometimes helps to give a doubtful and timid soul courage to reveal frankly and freely the "unlovely" urges and pressures of his disorganized self. "If *he* says it's okay to 'let go' it has to be!"

Another problem, not uncommon in other areas of counselling, is the handicap of *prestige* enjoyed by the counsellor. The priest occupies a position of prominence in the community. He is generally respected, looked up to, treasured as a friend. Because he is a champion of what is "good" and "right" and "respectable," his people in their dealings with him are anxious to be on their best behavior, hoping to present themselves by their words and deeds in the best possible light. In the intimacy of a face-to-face counselling relationship the process of revealing themselves as they really are, disclosing what they feel to be hidden flaws and failings, is a hurdle often very difficult to surmount. The counselling process is seriously impaired when the client, with best foot forward, is eager to say what he thinks the counsellor would like to hear. And yet, when this "prestige figure" has no difficulty in accepting a troubled, guilt-ridden individual placidly and wholeheartedly, when he finds that the priest-listener remains unruffled and unshocked as deep personal disclosures are made, then this new relationship based on tolerance and understanding can have tremendous therapeutic value.

Another initial handicap, also not unique to clerical counselling, is the impression in the minds of parishioners that the priest is the "man with the answers." He is the Shepherd, the father of the flock; he represents the Teaching Church, and has had years of training which supposedly fit him in a special way for making decisions. It is often a major revelation in an early counselling relationship to find that the priest is not going to propose any directive solutions, but is there principally to listen. With tact and experience this adjustment can soon be made.

The *priest himself* has many "built-in" handicaps which may interfere with his effective functioning as a counsellor. In many cases, the very nature of his office mitigates against the nondirective approach to problem solving. He is accustomed to giving answers; he *is* the representative of a Teaching Church whose mission it is to inform, persuade, and defend. Much of every priest's time is given to just this type of activity, whether from the pulpit, in the classroom, or in private instruction.

Most priests, too, live lives rooted in authority. Daily, they respond promptly and unquestioningly to directives from the Holy See, their Bishop, pastor, religious superior, or spiritual director. It is quite understandable, then, that priests are often inclined to expect the same kind of spontaneous acquiescence from their penitents that they themselves attempt to offer their superiors. For the muddled counselee, however, insight must sometimes come before compliance is possible.

This problem of authority is one of the undeniable difficulties of priestly counselling. The clergyman can never forget that he is a priest first and a counsellor second. As we have indicated earlier, there are times when he *must* give positive information. The client who asks for the teaching of the Church on this or that subject has a right to a direct answer. Furthermore, a priest cannot remain non-directive with every sinner at any price. He has a task to acknowledge sadness and valid guilt in the penitent who should obviously have such feelings. He has a right and duty to speak against injustice.

It is the priest's prerogative to develop moral and spiritual values in the lives of his people, which can include a healthy sense of shame. Therefore, the priest must at times suspend his role as counsellor and assume that of instructor and admonisher. In some cases, to avoid a needless and confusing duplication of roles, the priest-counsellor may suggest that the client consult another priest for answers to purely religious and moral questions. It might also be advantageous if a timid or embarrassed client makes his confession to someone other than the counsellor.

In other cases, however, the priest can, and should, be counsellor, confessor, and instructor. There are right and wrong ways of answering questions and giving information. In some instances, facts alone may solve much of the problem. There is a certain type of anxiety which is soothed with a simple statement by the priest: "You misunderstood. You thought this was a sin, but it isn't. Let me explain what the Church really teaches. . . ."

There are other requests for information which are more delicate. There is a right and wrong way, for example, to answer a troubled teen-ager who wants to know the morality of dwelling on an impure thought or sexual gratification. The priest can announce curtly, "This is a serious sin!" and send the questioner away more disturbed than when he came. Or he can answer the question in such a way as to open up new opportunities for self-understanding and growth by saying, "The Church believes it is wrong to indulge *deliberately* in impure fantasies for the purpose of encouraging stimulation and gratification; this does not mean, however, that you should be disturbed or ashamed because fantasies of a sexual nature pop in and out of your mind. A healthy interest in such matters is normal and to be expected; you need only learn to evaluate these newly awakened instincts, to face them comfortably, and to give them their proper, proportionate, and controlled place in your life." An even better way to answer the original question might have been "What do *you* think?" Thus, in the role of listener, the priest could help the youngster examine his own feelings and arrive at similar conclusions for himself.

Occasionally the counselling priest may be too inclined to see himself as "*the man with the answers.*" There are some realistic reasons for this self-concept. He has had a minimum of eight years of specialized college study, and very often more. Furthermore, he is able to draw upon a vast treasurehouse of wisdom and experience with which the Church has been guiding and encouraging her members for almost two thousand years.

Some priests forget, however, that their training is largely in the highly specialized fields of philosophy and theology. The priesthood is becoming increasingly aware that the great sciences of theology and psychology are, in truth, separate entities, and that proficiency in one does not assure proficiency in the other. Regrettably, it takes a lifetime of study to become a specialist in either theology or psychology. It is the rare scholar who achieves a mastery of both.

The holy oils do not confer a charism which of itself enables the ordained to diagnose, treat, and cure mental and emotional ills, regardless of their moral overtones. The realization that a penitent may also be a *patient* is the first great step toward the happy and holy rehabilitation of distraught, suffering human minds. Furthermore, the "right" answer may not always be the effective answer. Time and again, the solution, though objectively the correct one, does not take hold for this or that client because he is not yet ready to perceive it, accept it, or make it operative in his life. Clergymen are finding that "capsule counselling"—short, newspaper column, "slot-machine" answers to complicated personality problems—just is not satisfactory.

In addition to the priest who occasionally "tends toward omnipotence" there is the *impatient* and sometimes even *prejudiced* consultor. He becomes uneasy, irritated, or discouraged when his pat answers, "fervorinos," and stockroom solutions are rejected or do not work. Nine times out of ten the impatient counsellors are not the "good listeners." They feel their clients are "unco-operative," "do not want to reform," are "willfully rebellious," or "a waste of time."

Some priests really feel they cannot spare the *time* for extensive counselling. For many, perhaps even for the majority, this is literally true. The average parish priest often has difficulty in limiting his work to eighteen hours a day. On the other hand self-examination may reveal a preoccupation with some time-consuming duties which could be handled by others. Occasionally we all substitute relatively unimportant activity for the more subtle challenge of a counselling task. Sooner or later most of us, when confronted with an "odd ball," or "scrupe" or alcoholic in the rectory parlor, have one conscious or unconscious concern in our minds: "How quickly can I get this person on his way?" We are threatened by the prospect of protracted conversation. We feel helpless and impoverished as we search our minds for salutary solutions. Again, the clerical counsellor can solve many of his own misgivings, fears, insecurities, and inadequacies by cultivating the art of listening. As we listen, we are required to provide no pat answers, no quick solutions, no magic cure-alls, but only sympathy, patience, warm understanding, and a total acceptance of the client as a person.

AIDS TO UNDERSTANDING

There are many advantages inherent in the priest-parishioner counselling relationship. The priest, precisely because he is a priest,

brings a certain innate competence to his counselling if he is prepared to be a good listener. The traditionally authoritative position
of the priest can reinforce the *permissive atmosphere* of the counselling relationship, once the client is aware that free and uninhibited
expression of his innermost feelings is to be the order of the day.
We have already discussed the positive values of this "permission
for permissiveness."

While his "official" status is often an initial problem, the priest
also has an *independent status* remarkably free of certain com-
mitments which hamper the effectiveness of other professional
counsellors. Unlike the psychiatrist or the psychologist, he need
charge no fees; unlike a teacher or a dean of men, he need not
concern himself with discipline or directives; unlike an employer, he
has no responsibilities involving the client's vocational future; unlike the probation officer, he has no penal control over the counselee. His unique, "free floating" position obviously eliminates a
great many superfluous and impeding responsibilities involved in
other counselling situations.

Another favorable aspect is the absolute *confidence* a client has
in the integrity of the confidential relationship established. The
sacredness of the "seal of secrecy" has been a source of enormous
consolation and reassurance to Catholics over the centuries. The
client is absolutely certain that his problems will not be discussed
with a wife, colleague, or friends—in short, with *no one*. This conviction, coupled with many other subtle factors, may be the reason
why so many Catholics will tell a priest things they will tell no one
else. From their early years they come to learn that a priest can be
told nothing new, cannot be shocked; and they know that he will
defend with his life his duty to keep their confidences a secret. More
than once a psychiatrist has said, "Some patients will divulge secrets
to a priest in three minutes which would take six months of therapy
to uncover." It is a sad fact that so much meaningful information
is sometimes revealed to priests who have so little knowledge of how
to respond to it.

In its strict sense, confession is not intended to be primarily a
counselling experience. This sacrament was instituted to forgive

sin—conscious guilt. All that is necessary for a good and valid confession is that the penitent tell as best he can the serious sins he has committed since his last confession, express his sorrow for them, and make a serious resolve to avoid these sins in the future. However, theologians and spiritual writers have pointed out that the priest is not only a judge in the confessional but also a teacher and a healer. It is obvious that in exercising all three of these roles, some knowledge of the dynamics of human personality can make this ministry much more fruitful.

There is usually little time to devote to the individual penitent in the confessional. A word or two of caution or encouragement are all that most priests manage. However, the confessional can be a sensitive listening post for spotting emotional difficulties. When the priest meets an obvious behavior problem or suspects a neurotic pattern in a patient, he can suggest that they meet at some future time to talk over the difficulty in greater detail. Often the penitent is delighted to find someone who will give time and thought to working the problem through. From then on the individual can be handled in a regular counselling situation. This is not to say, however, that the counselling procedure we have described cannot be used effectively in the confessional. In parishes which have large staffs or small congregations, penitents can often build fruitful counselling relationships with permanent confessors or spiritual directors.

PRACTICAL SUGGESTIONS

In conclusion, here is a list of what seem to be the essential principles of sacerdotal counselling. There are many variations of these, of course, depending on the opportunities, the training, and the time at the disposal of the priest-counsellor.

The external details of the counselling setting should be carefully planned by the priest. If possible, a comfortable room should be set aside for this purpose. It should be in a quiet corner, away from the hustle and bustle of rectory traffic. Priest and client should set a definite time limit to the counselling session. With few exceptions, little is to be gained by prolonging individual meetings beyond an hour or so. The priest should make sure that he is punctual, that he is not interrupted by other duties during the scheduled period. The client should feel that this time is his and his alone, to do with as he chooses. Soft lights, an easy chair, an ash tray, a box of Kleenex (emotions sometimes spill over into tears), and a generally informal atmosphere are appropriate to the counsellor's parlor or office. It is less forbidding, especially in early interviews, if the priest does not sit behind a desk but rather in an easy chair at an angle to the client, so that each may glance easily, without staring face to face, at the other.

Time, undisturbed by outside interruptions, is an important factor in healing emotional difficulties as well as physical ills. It is often most important that the time set aside for counselling be fairly protracted and on no account interrupted. If the priest does not have such time at his disposal (it is his duty day, perhaps) he should say so, and arrange then and there for a leisurely interview with the client at an early future date. There are very few emergencies so urgent that a problem must be gone into immediately. There is rarely a reason why the priest counsellor cannot follow the interview procedures of other professionals in similar situations. Those who come to a priest for help will almost always understand the necessity of fixing a future appointment in the priest's busy schedule. Often the client is relieved to see that the priest is not going to attempt a solution of a personal problem in ten or fifteen minutes; rather he will be pleased to find that the priest thinks his problem important enough and complicated enough to warrant a protracted counselling session.

The counsellor often finds it helpful to take notes either during an interview or immediately afterward. These can include personal statistics, family background, and a summary of the general direction each counselling interview is taking. A brief refresher glance at the notes (on file cards, perhaps) before each interview can keep the counsellor up to date, and more alert to facts and emotional trends which often repeat themselves in successive sessions. These records, needless to say, should be carefully protected from scrutiny by anyone but the counsellor and the counselee.

The priest must be especially careful to respect the confidential character of a counselling relationship. This refers not only to the ethical pledge of secrecy but also to the kinds of communication the priest may have with relatives or acquaintances of the client. The counsellor's first loyalty lies with his client. Generally speaking, parents, relatives, employers, etc., should be involved in the counselling process only if the client gives his clear consent. Even then it is often advisable, unless he prefers otherwise, to have the client present in the room while third parties are consulted, in person, or even on the telephone. It is important for the client to feel that "nothing is going on behind his back," that he has control over his own counselling experience.

The priest, whose time is limited, must be selective in his choice of counselees. He should have at least a minimal training in recognizing personality disorders, so that he will be able to refer serious problems to special and more competent help. (See chapter 8.) This is very important. There is always a temptation to pursue a counselling relationship with an especially interesting or bizarre person who in reality needs concentrated psychiatric treatment. Amateur experimentation with psychotherapy is definitely unsound from both a medical and ethical point of view. The priest should be well acquainted with appropriate referral agencies in his neighborhood who can assist him or take over serious cases.

The priest should be aware of the effectiveness of environmental manipulation in solving certain emotional problems. Outside factors, such as family misunderstandings, lack of adequate social contacts, or a poor job are often so painful that the pressured individual is unable to tackle the more complex problems within himself. The priest can reduce tension and ease these external conflicts by using his prestige and authority in helping the client to improve his relations with the world around him.

The priest should also remember that at times he must perform the instructor's role. He should devise means of imparting necessary information in the least threatening way. Often he can use his instructor's role as a wedge for establishing a less directive counselling relationship.

Terminating the counselling relationship can be abrupt or (more often) gradual, depending on the feeling of the client. In most cases, it seems appropriate to schedule the interviews less and less frequently, in keeping with the client's growing readiness to venture on his own. These longer periods between sessions test the confidence and self-reliance of the client, who finds himself increasingly capable of making independent and satisfying judgments and choices. At the last, an occasional "check-up" interview can be arranged. Counselling is finally terminated with the understanding that the client may always return if new problems arise, or some aspects of the old problem revive.

This, then, is a bird's-eye view of the priest as a counsellor and listener. The special place he holds in the minds and affection of his people make him a vital instrument for potential good. "Grace builds on nature" is a fundamental axiom of Catholic theology. If one of the principal works of the priest is the development of virtue in his people, then his concern for their mental and emotional health should be very real. The counselling priest can help weak and troubled souls gain new insights and new strengths. Clearing away the clutter of fear, indecision, and compulsion can be a sure way of opening new channels through which God's grace is better able to take root, flourish, and produce rich fruit.

NOTES

1. Boston: Houghton Mifflin, 1942.
2. New York: Macmillan, 1952.
3. Ibid., p. 21.
4. Quoted by Adolphe Tanquerey in *The Spiritual Life* (Tournai: Desclée, 1930), p. 266.
5. Op. cit., pp. 9–10.

3

THE PSYCHOLOGY OF
HUMAN WEAKNESS

This book, and in particular this chapter, considers only one aspect of human activity and human motivation. We are very much aware that there is danger in viewing any one part of man as an isolated entity. We know that it is just as artificial and misleading to study man only from the point of view of his emotions and his unconscious drives as it is to view him only as a creature of intellect and free will. The mind, the will, and the emotions are inseparably bound up with each other and exert a mutual influence which can help or hinder the adequate functioning of each.

Many Catholic counselling books rightly emphasize the roles which the intellect, the will, and grace can play in man's conscious attempt to live his life in accordance with the precepts of God and of His Church. They stress the aid these superior faculties can give to man's growth in merit and perfection.

It is important, therefore, to remember as you read that there is more to human behavior, choice, and insight than the particular aspects which we shall study here. This book attempts to highlight the necessity of applying psychological insights to behavior which we judge objectively good or bad. In other words, we are suggesting that purely rational and supernatural explanations and admonitions will in many cases be insufficient to change human behavior, wipe away sinful habits, and motivate man to the higher life. The saints and spiritual writers have long been aware of this extra dimension.

They have sensed that human emotion and passion in many cases precede, underlie, and often influence the effectiveness of the higher faculties, interfering with, and indeed crippling, the most desired and lofty aspirations of man. These great spiritual "psychologists" of the past would welcome the confirmation by modern dynamic psychology of many of the insights and hunches which they had more intuitively and vaguely sensed.

Apropos of this, Father Robert Gleason, S.J., in his comments on grace and liberty in *Christ and the Christian,* writes:

It is well here to recall what psychology teaches about the human conscience. The moral strivings of the individual do not spring from an autonomy so total that everything which appears in clear consciousness is automatically free. This is an outworn idea of human liberty, no longer able to help us in judging the responsibility of the sinner. If we believe that man is possessed of a personal conscience, and therefore is free in every situation that reaches the level of consciousness, we are dangerously close to the illusion of false independence. . . . Without exaggerating infra-conscious determinisms, we must clearly grasp that freedom, liberty, responsibility are not automatically to be equated with clear consciousness. Man's liberty is conditioned by many factors which precede his liberty and which he can mold, alter, and guide only indirectly [e.g. heredity, environment, sociological situation, psychological make-up]. . . .

Two extremes must be avoided if we are to make any realistic judgment concerning the sinner's situation. One is the tendency to consider the conscious self as only a small segment of the person, the least important, one completely dominated by self-conscious urges. The other is to believe that the conscious is the only real personal self and that it suffers little or no influence from what lies beneath it, thus exaggerating liberty and giving the sinner a false sense of responsibility and independence. As a consequence he is sometimes forced to bear the entire burden of an unconscious life for which he could not possibly be responsible. We should not forget that there are structures existing within us (as St. Augustine puts it, "in us without us") which, while they do not necessitate our choices, do influence them more or less strongly. Nor can we avoid the conclusion that certain psychological types seem to be less fitted by nature to lead stable, balanced and responsible moral lives. Such people should be encouraged to hope in the understanding love and mercy of a God aware of the personal environmental and hereditary factors of their total history. . . .[1]

In the first chapter we attempted to outline several of the basic emotional components within man which significantly influence his behavior. We insisted that these various components of human personality were neither separate nor tangible entities, but were, rather, highly complex interactions within the human psyche. We isolated each for the sake of description, but stressed the impossibility of clearly distinguishing one from the other in the practical evaluation of at least some human actions.

Herein lies the challenge to the confessor or counsellor, who must not only attempt to make a judgment about the responsibility of human behavior, but must also present specific remedies which will help the individual to change and improve. Which individual motives, choices, and behavior are rooted in irrational drives and urges? Which are rooted in automatic and largely unconscious compulsions dictated by the do's and don'ts of an overdeveloped superego? which in relatively free and intellectual choices?

Referring to this major dilemma of the confessor, Father Gustave Weigel, S.J., makes these comments:

. . . Superego and conscience are closely and tightly interwoven when the intellect makes its practical judgment. [This] must be kept in mind lest we speak and think as if conscience and superego were distinct, readily distinguishable dictamina, so that all that need be done by the spiritual director is to make his penitent concentrate on conscience and ignore the superego. If this were our technique we would be missing the point which modern psychology has so successfully made. In the concrete moment in the concrete person the voice of superego and the voice of conscience fuse; nor is there any awareness of which is which. Only an analyst could extricate the different threads. Moral theology gives us the content of conscience but it does not give us the content of the superego. In the direction of human beings moral theology alone cannot be an adequate guide, just as dynamic psychology cannot be an adequate guide. The two together must be used in the guidance of the concrete human person.[2]

In these pages we hope to direct our attention in particular to those aspects of human behavior which are intimately related to the unconscious, emotional, superego-tinged influences of psychological motivation. We shall do this by considering each of the

Commandments and shall then discuss very *briefly* (hence, often, inadequately) the more common sins and faults met with in the confessional.

First Commandment. "Denied or doubted faith—Murmured against God—Spoke irreverently of holy things or persons."

Strange as it may seem, these difficulties are often related in certain ways to the Fourth Commandment. Both involve a negative concept of authority, one of the most significant and troublesome of psychological attitudes.

We have already seen how each individual tends towards independence, yearning for the opportunity and the capacity to stand alone, self-sufficient and self-reliant. There are limits, of course, to the possibility of life without authority or dependence. Some of both is appropriate in every life. The healthy way in which an individual can accept useful and necessary authority depends upon the degree to which he has been allowed to mature, to develop independence in all possible and desirable areas. The child who is never permitted to make a decision on his own, to express an opinion of his own, to indulge in feelings of his own, will become more and more resentful, more and more rebellious, more and more disdainful in his relationship to those who needlessly impose their will and their way upon his life.

Authority can be most significantly misused by parents. Teachers, too, as well as officers of the law, employers, and the clergy can abuse their prerogatives by making blind and superfluous demands. They are often identified in the mind of the rebel with unreasonable and dictatorial parental figures. The tragedy is, of course, that in repudiating the evil aspects of misused authority, the youngster, in his blind hostility, is liable to "throw out the baby with the bath" and rebel against authority *per se*. The Church, her priests, and even God Himself may become symbols of the unreasonable, imperious, vengeful parent-figure from whom the resentful offspring turns in protest.

Misgivings and disillusionment associated with childhood authority figures are occasionally at the root of denials and doubts of faith. Children who are permitted to think that their parents are all-good and all-wise are often rudely shocked and disappointed to discover that their parents have shortcomings and are far from perfect. Such disillusionment may extend unconsciously into adulthood. Thus an individual may regard the authority of the Church and its teachings with the same kind of emotional tentativeness he feels towards his parents' imperfections. This is especially true if the early religious emphasis is placed on externals, the nonessential aspects of the devotional life, and the subtle distortions of doctrine which seem so unreal and "magical" in adulthood, as indeed they are. Often the individual is not denying or doubting faith at all, but is maturely rejecting arbitrary devotional practices and near-superstitious trappings overstressed in his early religious education. In practice, the "doubter" can often be congratulated on his perceptiveness and his intellectual questioning. The difference between difficulties and doubts, as elaborated upon by Cardinal Newman, can be illuminating and consoling for such an inquirer.

Finally, doubts against faith can be a symptom of a larger neurotic problem. An individual sometimes unconsciously seeks to punish himself by imagining that the worst possible fate has befallen him, namely, the loss of faith. It is important to point out to such sufferers that their misgiving about God's mercy is essentially an emotional, not a rational phenomenon. It is sometimes helpful to prove the truth of this possibility by pointing out that their "temptations against faith" are keenest when they are upset, depressed, or unusually tense, and that such despair and doubt often ease up in moments of comparative calm and happiness. They can be helped not to be so frightened when such doubting or despairing thoughts occur if they understand there is no guilt or responsibility involved. A few kind words of this sort should help:

You will notice that on days when everything goes wrong, when you're tired and have maybe had a good row with someone in your family, when you are just plain blue and depressed, these religious doubts and worries will be strongest. Notice, too, that on the sunny days, when things are going well, when you are in love with life, enjoying your friends, and looking forward to pleasant things to do, these thoughts and anxieties become much less insistent and troublesome, and Almighty God is able to manifest Himself as the understanding and loving Father that He is. My telling you that these painful, recurring worries belong to your emotional life, and do not touch your intellectual and moral convictions, won't make them disappear. But understanding something about the nature of your fears may lessen their severity and help you to see them for what they are—emotional reactions to stress and tension for which you are in no way to blame.

Such reassurances may be the beginning of a cure for this sort of scruple. (Chapter 7 deals with these matters in greater detail.)

Second Commandment. "Took God's name in vain—Blasphemed."

Blasphemy, profanity, and vulgar language are essentially infantile devices. To use language which is socially unacceptable is the daring, rebellious, self-asserting sort of behavior which a child uses to test his independence and proclaim his autonomy. Often such words are first used by a child because he hears them used by adults. They are soon part of his vocabulary, and eventually become automatic responses to routine situations in daily living.

Blasphemy and profanity are obvious ways of giving vent to anger. Objectionable language is just one of many possible symptoms of other problems. We shall see some of these implications when we discuss temper control. Incidentally, social taboos often prevent swearing by women. At the adolescent level boys often find the sort of emotional release in "bad language" that girls find in weeping (socially unacceptable for men). A first step to correcting profanity is to find out what it symbolizes in the mind of the user, and what emotions he is releasing when he swears. Often the use of certain kinds of language has become so habitual that the possibility of control, and of responsibility, is almost nil.

Sometimes it is important to explain to a young child that habitual bad language is not seriously sinful; often the guilt and hopelessness surrounding his habit can cause him undue concern and anxiety. Eliminating blasphemy and profanity from an habitual speech pattern is one of the most difficult remedial challenges. Both confessor and penitent must be content with very slow progress. What is largely an unconscious pattern must be made conscious, and very often the individual must first learn to use other methods of "letting off steam" and displacing his hostilities.

Third Commandment. "Deliberately missed Mass—Was late for Mass—Inattentive at Mass—Didn't say my prayers."

We have here a prime example of a psychological principle which needs special emphasis: The key to adequate motivation is *positive conviction.* There are of course occasions when fear of punishment and sanctions force a person to observe some code or avoid some misdeed. But this is, at best, a tentative and inferior motive, not alone from the spiritual but also from the psychological point of view. The individual who consistently and willfully misses Mass, eats meat on Friday, barely makes his Easter duty, and fails to pray regularly has a very tenuous and artificial relationship to his Faith.* Attending or missing Mass regularly is not the problem; much more important is the question: What does the Catholic Faith *really mean* to this person? The individual who consistently misses Mass needs both counselling and instruction. His indifference to Mass is but a symbol of his indifference to the Faith itself. Threats and admonitions are poor substitutes for working through the meaning of religion in his life.

There are many reasons why a Catholic misses Mass, or attends Mass only because he has to and not because he wants to. His Catholic education may have been scanty and unrealistic. He may not really grasp the meaning of the Mass and the tremendous treasures of grace and consolation it holds for the attentive parishioner. He must be helped to understand the miracle which takes place at the altar, to appreciate the Missal as an aid to his more intimate participation, to value the Mass as an illuminating and vivifying influence on his daily activities.

* Some nationalities and lower socio-economic groups do not consider the Sunday Mass obligation to be too important or binding. This misconception must be approached as a sociological question, and should be solved on the basis of massive re-education. It is not a problem of reforming and inspiring individual consciences in the sense outlined above.

Occasionally, the individual with a serious moral problem feels hypocritical attending regular Sunday Mass if he is not able to live up to the whole moral teaching of the Church. A teen-age masturbator, for example, feels uneasy and conscience-stricken amid holy, solemn reminders at a church service of what his life should be like. Because he feels hopelessly enmeshed in his difficulty he stays away from Mass rather than be reminded in so poignant a way of his own contrasting unworthiness. Such penitents should be helped to see that particular habits of sin which they are striving to overcome should not be a block to their participation in divine worship, but rather an incentive to throw themselves more completely and hopefully on the mercy of their Eucharistic Lord, wonderfully operative in the Holy Sacrifice.

Other possibilities may explain the cooling of devotion to the Mass and to an earnest prayer life. A too-rigid, external control of a child's devotional life can lead to rebellion in adolescence and early adulthood. Parents and teachers sometimes insist that a child go to daily Mass, lead him in long family prayers, or force him to observe other pious practices without giving him an opportunity to develop initiative of his own in these matters. The youngster may proclaim his resentment and independence later on by dropping many or even all of the earlier religious practices of his youth. The counsellor can help such a rebel see that when he vents his hostility on religion, he is in reality flaunting the bossiness or interference of authority figures he resents.

Routine and boredom can also discourage regular prayer life and devotion to the Mass. Liturgical reform can help to revitalize the perfunctory sort of religious services which so many of our people seem to attend in body but not in spirit. They sit, glassy-eyed and unhearing, Sunday after Sunday, personally uninvolved except for the coins they drop into the collections. No wonder they say "I don't get anything out of the Mass." The active, intelligent participation of the laity in public worship can be a significant remedy for lukewarmness and indifference.

Prayer, too, can become a bore. It is often helpful to explain very precisely that good prayer is not a matter of parrot learning or long repetitious formulas. A counsellor can urge discouraged penitents to set aside traditional memorized prayers and speak to God in their own words about themselves, their daily lives, their loved ones, their problems, ambitions, fears, etc. Variety is often the secret of successful prayer. Too many of the laity have shackled themselves to the recitation of long lists of prayers, a plodding, uninteresting chore and nothing more. For example, it may surprise a pious housewife who is plagued with distractions to suggest that she abandon her "mumbo-jumbo" recitation of the rosary for shorter and more meaningful praying from the heart. She can be helped to see that she may not have the nimble imagination and powers of concentration at the end of a long, wearying day to say the rosary with consistent profit.

The individual who cannot pray and misses Mass often needs protracted counselling help, more so than many other confessional cases. His negligence is but a symptom of a much deeper lack. In general, it is plain that too many Catholics have stereotyped notions as to what ideal prayer is like. The re-education of our people in good habits of prayer should be one of the chief and most consoling counselling projects of the clergy.

Fourth Commandment. "Disobeyed, angered, grieved, or insulted parents and superiors."

This is probably the most misunderstood of all the Commandments. It seems without question that this is the number-one sin most children confess. It is in many ways unfortunate that so much of a young person's examination of conscience should be focused on his negative relationships to his parents. In far too many cases parents and teachers are inclined to protect themselves by stressing the sinful aspect of disobedience in their pupils and children.

We have seen how the struggle for independence is a keystone of the maturing process. It is inevitable that as the child attempts to grow away from the protecting and often clinging arms of parents, differences of opinion, conflicts and frustrations are bound to arise. The sort of behavior popularly called "disobedience" is often a normal, healthy, predictable, and necessary kind of childhood experimentation.

The Fourth Commandment is surely a two-way street. The *duty of parents* to honor and respect their children seems in some way greater than the other way around, since parents should have the experience and foresight and sensitivity to see the importance of affection and understanding in the development of the child. "Honor thy father and thy mother" implies that mother and father are "honor-able" and "respect-able." It is entirely unrealistic to expect children to *feel* respect for parents who are two-faced, autocratic, and insensitive to the needs of their children. If the philosophy of a parent is "Do as I say, not as I do," it is difficult to see how he can successfully demand respect, much less love, from his child.

Parents must be helped to see that their children are engaged in a perpetual bid for independence, often quite irrationally and clumsily ventured. They must be helped to see the value of learning through mistakes, and must be encouraged to minimize their children's inept experiments with self-reliance. Children, on the other hand, must be helped to see that adults often have the wisdom of experience on their side, or at least are so set in their view of things that it is far harder for parents to compromise than for the child.

Sometimes a confessor can point out to an older child or an adolescent the difference between disrespect and disobedience. There are cases when parents are making demands of their children which they have no right to make. When the youngster violates such demands he may not be disobeying, but he can be guilty of thoughtlessness and disrespect not only to his parents but to the family and himself by his ill-mannered responses.

The teen-ager should be seen by himself and his family as a member of a team working together for the common good of the household. The teen-ager may feel very strongly, and with good reason, that his parents have no right to make unrealistic demands of him. Yet he fails on his part if he does nothing but rebel stormily and selfishly without making an effort to communicate his point of view in family discussions and in reasonable attempts at compromise. If the accent is on teamwork, co-operation, and mutual respect for shortcomings on both sides, then disobedience becomes less and less of a problem and family harmony more and more of a pleasant objective.

Fifth Commandment. "Angered, fought, quarreled, or hated— Held a grudge—Desired that harm come to others."

The key to many of these failings lies in the inability of the penitent first to accept and manage his own "less desirable" feelings. The secret of managing hostile, antisocial kinds of thinking and behavior begins with a realistic understanding of our psychological nature. Aggression, anger, resentment, sometimes even leading to homicidal thoughts, feelings, and desires, are a part of the normal man. The very fact that no two people are alike makes for differences of opinion, clashes of temperament, opposing goals, inevitable rivalries. Certain types of personalities and character traits will "get under the skin" of even the most adjusted and mild-mannered of us.

Many antagonisms are perpetuated on the basis of reason, logic, and common sense. As long as human differences are debated on these grounds the hostilities will, in many cases, remain unresolved. The art of harmonious living rests not in every person becoming like the other, but rather in every person coming to respect and tolerate the individual differences of the other. Many personal tastes, irritating whims, and disturbing eccentricities defy the rules of universal logic, propriety and appropriateness. They can be constant focal points of friction in interpersonal relationships within family, business, and social environs. Such individual differences, nine times out of ten, cannot be changed; to learn to "live and let live" is often the only solution worth pursuing.

Moral responsibility lies chiefly in the way we manage our feelings, and the way they affect others around us—*not* in the "goodness" or "badness" of the feelings themselves. So many Catholics are overwhelmed with guilt because they *feel* angry or resentful. To attempt to deny such feelings is to deny a part of human nature itself. It should be a chief concern of the confessor to help the individual see himself and his emotions as they are. With patient self-acceptance comes the desire and the ability to channel the more unruly feelings into healthy safety valves so as not to hurt the sensibilities of others, or interfere unjustly with their lives.

A mother can be helped to accept the negative feelings which every parent sometimes has towards her children. Children can be shown that it is natural to "hate" their mother or father on occasion. Adults, in their relationships with each other, must learn to resign themselves to inevitable clashes of temperaments, opinions, and preferences. A mutual and genuine respect for individual human differences is the key to the resolution of routine personality clashes. So often a person becomes angry at himself for being angry at others. This is a double dose of anger, which makes the problem twice as difficult to manage. (This may explain why a man with a bad temper can almost never laugh at himself.) If an individual is able to accept, and occasionally even smile at, his own negative and hostile feelings, he will be far better able to make allowances for the similar feelings of others towards himself.

Sixth and Ninth Commandments. "Took pleasure in impure thoughts—Had impure desires—Looked at impure pictures—Was guilty of immodest acts."

In our comments on sex education in chapter 1 we have indicated some negative aspects of the prevailing Catholic approach to sex. In so many cases, forbidding and fearful attitudes on the part of parents, teachers, and the clergy toward man's sexual powers create a special kind of anxiety in the mind of the young person so far as this instinct is concerned. We have accused the secular world of overstressing sexual symbols, literature, and entertainment. In another sense, some Catholics have succumbed to the same preoccupation. So often the emphasis of our writers and the tone of our moralists reveal a special and fearful concern with sexual temptation and sin. In reality, it seems quite probable that such sins and weaknesses of the flesh are less deliberate and less significant compared with the more willful sins of dishonesty, discrimination, calumny, and exploitation.

Perhaps the greatest single shortcoming of our sexual attitudes is the lack of a down-to-earth, positive preparation for sexual maturity. For every sentence in Catholic literature which prepares the young person to enjoy and appreciate the sexual aspects of love, there are hundreds of sentences which define precisely and often quite unrealistically the threatening and dangerous aspects of man's sexual life. Catechism questions and answers on purity, chapters on sexual life in our marriage manuals, sermons on sex from the pulpit and in private retreats, magazine articles on sex directed toward the adolescent, marriage courses in our Catholic schools, etc., so often limit themselves to a detailed analysis of such negative aspects as sinful kissing and petting, impure thoughts, immodest language and dress, "dangerous" entertainment, bad reading and pictures, and occasions of sexual sin in general.

The confessor can help the Catholic penitent learn to feel comfortable with sex. He can help the Catholic understand and appreciate the positive aspects of loving and being loved. He can help the young person to appreciate, proudly and joyfully, the sexual capacities which one day will be fully exercised in marriage. Herein lies a tremendous challenge for the clergyman. It will take all the skill and insight at his disposal to safeguard the moral teaching of the Church on matters of consentual sin and at the same time help the young person to think about sex, study about sex, talk about sex—in short, help him to accept this aspect of his emotional life with the same placidity and forthrightness as any other.

This preparation is essential. We cannot expect young men and women who have had basically negative, fearful, or disinterested attitudes toward sex for the first nineteen or twenty years of their lives suddenly to reverse the process and give themselves freely to each other in the uninhibited, glowing, ecstatic, and positive sexual relationship that is marriage. There must be real and prolonged emotional preparation for this aspect of marriage as for every other.

How can confessional technique contribute to this preparation? To begin with, penitents who confess to "impure thoughts" can be helped to make some very careful distinctions. The reasoning can be phrased something like this: Sexual thoughts are *not* impure thoughts. Thoughts about sex and fantasies about sex are inevitable characteristics of emotional growth and development. The normal individual will be as intellectually curious and emotionally intrigued by the sexual aspects of life as he is by other important human concerns. If he is to manage these powerful interests and instincts rightly, he must be taught not to push sex deep into the unconscious but to examine it carefully, value it as essentially good, and orientate himself positively to that kind of sexual life which his religious convictions dictate.

It is important to stress the fact that sexual thoughts are *not* impure thoughts, and that experiencing pleasure in connection with sexual fantasies *need not be sinful either*. The informative process, a right of every young person (which includes appropriate thinking, talking, and reading about sex), might produce stimulating mental images. These are indifferent in themselves, and become sinful only if consciously and deliberately consented to. Many people feel that because they seem to "want" these pleasurable thoughts they are sinning. The fact that these fantasies are enjoyable and attractive means that in one sense they are "wanted"; but it does not mean that the pleasure is being sought after for its own sake and in violation of a law of God which denies direct and deliberate gratification. The meaning of "wanting," "enjoying," and "choosing," especially in a sexual context, are subtle and often difficult to determine. Patience, compassion, and a sensitivity to individual differences are important qualifications for the understanding confessor.

The way in which young people learn about sex, become comfortable with it, and learn to live their lives without a fearful flight from it varies considerably with the individual. It is a great mistake to make specific and identical applications of a general moral law. In the area of sex, especially, there are no "average" human beings. What is an occasion of sin for one may be quite innocent for another. Kissing, dating habits, going steady, various types of clothing cannot be arbitrarily defined as sinful or even occasions of sin. The age of the couple, the length of time they have dated, the particular customs of the locality, and above all the psychological makeup of each individual must be carefully considered before we can presume to say that many of these things are good, bad, or indifferent.

The engaged couple are in a particularly delicate situation with regard to chastity. They are allowed no more intimate expressions of affection and love than are the non-engaged. Yet it seems as though all things conspire to make expressions of affection such as "petting" almost inevitable. The increased freedom which our general culture permits engaged couples—unchaperoned companionship in particular—creates added stimulations. Intense mutual sympathy and the constant real or imagined presence of one partner to the other fosters the development of love on all levels, spiritual, affective, and physical.

This is the normal psychological preparation for the total union which is marriage. Nonetheless, engaged couples must refrain from those expressions of affection which are obviously designed to provoke sexual excitement. In many cases, engaged couples are expressing honest affection which frees them from a wrong intention in these matters. But certain manifestations of affection are so closely related to marital union and its preparation that they must be avoided by the unmarried whatever the goodness of their intention.

Abstention from such forms of activity fosters balance and a healthy attitude towards sex in marriage. It is psychologically unwise to indulge in passionate petting which overstimulates sexual tension without granting it relief. Some wives who formerly engaged in this sort of thing are incapable of satisfactory orgasms since patterns accepted before marriage may tend to dominate their responses after marriage.

Nevertheless, it is possible in some cases to judge these couples more leniently if one considers the concrete details of their situation. In many instances the moralist will recognize a case of "antecedent blameless concupiscence." Not infrequently the mere presence or thought of the beloved will arouse strong sexual desires quite independently of free consent. At such times excitement may even go to the point of involuntary orgasm. Where an intense personal relationship has developed, a day-long, instinctive drawing power is exercised by the other's image, so much so that such penitents speak of an "unfree," seemingly impersonal, attraction to each other's body. When this state of affairs obtains, it is extremely difficult for the individual to avoid the occasions of sin of the textbooks. When patterns of affective physical expression have been set up, they pursue their own dynamisms almost independently of the will. Often such individuals can here be judged as being in what moralists would call "necessary" occasions of sin. They are obliged to use all reasonable means to render these occasions remote (double dating, avoiding parked cars, eschewing liquor, etc.), but it is to be expected that in a culture which prescribes somewhat spontaneous dating patterns these means will, in some cases, fail.

Remembering what is said elsewhere about the mitigation of freedom under psychic pressures and the type of knowledge required for grave sin, the priest will, at times, judge the penitent insufficiently knowledgeable, and free from serious fault. The confessor must avoid creating in the couple feelings of terror, remorse, mutual recrimination, mistrust and fear of each other. God regards the entire course of their engagement as well as individual acts. It can be a new and potentially unnerving experience for a deeply committed soul whose whole life has been lived for God with the freedom and radiance of intelligent purity to find herself or himself in love with the intensity such souls bring to love. He or she may come to see human love as the first genuine threat to union with God and a blameless life. Those who possess delicate consciences and have not passed their early lives in casual sexual experimentation can find the first experiences of physical attraction and affection seriously upsetting.

BIRTH CONTROL

We have devoted special chapters to the particularly complicated sexual problems of masturbation and homosexuality. There remains one final traditional difficulty which the priest will meet fairly frequently. It is the problem of birth control.

The priest should presume that those who come to him with this problem are sincere. For every Catholic who confesses to this weakness there are many, many more who have, in rebellion or despair, severed their relationship with the sacramental life of the Church. To approach the counselling of a birth controller with impatience or antagonism is to misread the complexity of the problem and to overlook the anguish of those involved in it.

At the outset the priest should determine how firmly convinced the counselee is of the validity of this particular teaching of the Church. It is not uncommon to find a Catholic who just cannot accept with his whole heart and mind the Catholic position on birth control. The first task of the priest must then be to re-educate and revitalize the individual in his faith. Often the traditional reasons from the natural law cannot be grasped; in such cases the teaching authority of the Church must be the basis upon which the conviction is evoked.

There are many others who have no difficulty in accepting the Church's argument; they do, however, have trouble with their own weakness. There are many sincere individuals who are often victims of their spontaneous physical urges. Often the priest will find that there is no premeditated attempt to practice birth control, no evidence of mechanical devices kept in the house. The majority of Catholics who confess the sin of birth control reveal that withdrawal is the inevitable technique. In many, if not most cases, such couples have good reason to avoid conception; they have agreed to practice rhythm or abstinence. The essence of their fault lies not in their willful decision to enjoy intercourse and prevent conception, but rather in their *failure* to observe their resolution to abstain totally or to limit themselves to periodic relations.

The following considerations must be kept in mind by both penitent and priest in an effort to help such couples develop more self-control. All concerned must acknowledge the tremendous habitual demand which regular sexual relations create during the early years of marriage. To suddenly bring such enormously gratifying experiences to an end, or seriously curtail them, creates a desire, an almost compulsive need-pattern, which can at times be close to unbearable. Again, even those daily exchanges of conjugal affection so necessary for the maintenance and fostering of family life and love can slip quickly from the realm of conscious and voluntary control into the area of primitive sexual urges.

Couples vary in their ability to control their affectionate relationship without permitting its natural fulfillment in intercourse. Living conditions and household arrangements often create external difficulties which require almost superhuman efforts to surmount. Many families live in crowded apartments or homes in which separate rooms and even separate beds are practical impossibilities. The priest must make every effort to sympathize with the enormous self-control required of two people whose yearning bodies lie side by side night after night, struggling with one of nature's most basic demands.

There is perhaps no greater single challenge to an individual's moral convictions than the self-control required to practice rhythm or abstinence under these conditions. The key to such heroic exercise in chastity is the *deep and convinced living of the full Catholic life.* All the external precautions and arrangements devised by the couple and the priest to make the temptation easier to manage cannot be substituted for a wholehearted interior dedication to great sacrifice for Christ and His Law.*

The confessor must judge the degree of responsibility of those who confess they have practiced birth control, not by the number of falls, but by the intention which the failing partner has to improve. Both man and wife must be helped, in protracted and unhurried situations if possible, to define clearly in their own minds the sexual activity—if any—that is permitted them if they are to

---

* Catholic Marriage Counsellors are awaiting the development of a new fertility test—not yet perfected, but at present undergoing intensive experimentation—which will reveal to the couple practicing rhythm that precise period during which ovulation occurs, thus limiting the period of abstinence to two or three days of the month.

The Catholic attitude toward family limitation and the emotional problems involved cannot be dealt with in a few pages. We highly recommend an extended treatment of this subject by Father John Thomas in his book *Marriage and the Family.*

avoid conception within God's law. Often a confusion of goals and motivations on the part of one or both can needlessly complicate and frustrate the effectiveness of their collaboration. In this instance, as in other observances of Catholic sexual morality, a sturdy and enveloping love of the Faith and its teachings, meaningful consolations from the frequent reception of the Sacraments, a solid confidence in the wisdom and worth of self-control, and a positive, satisfying conviction that one has faced a most difficult challenge successfully—are some of the balancing gratifications which motivate the hard-pressed couple to attempt again and again a more perfect conjugal relationship.

Seventh and Tenth Commandments. "Stole—Desired to possess unjustly my neighbor's goods."

Stealing can be one of the most complicated of the psychological deviations. In adults, a pattern of stealing might imply a lax attitude to this particular commandment, or it can mean a very severe emotional disorder known as kleptomania. The former difficulty requires a careful examination of the sort of satisfactions the individual seeks when he takes things or juggles his accounts. The kleptomaniac needs psychiatric help.

The confessor is most often confronted with the stealing habits of children. Here it is important to have as many details as possible. How old is the child? If five, six, or seven years old, the child has not yet had time to develop clear concepts of property rights. Kindness and patience can help him gradually to appreciate the moral significance of what he does. How long has he been stealing, and how often? "Snitching" candy bars, fruit, or free subway rides seem normal and understandable challenges to most grade-school children. An occasional attempt along this line should not be met with severe and punishing responses. What does he steal? If it is food, he may be genuinely hungry; or his parents may not give him sufficient money to match the allowances of children of his own age.

What does he do with his stolen objects? The child may feel inferior and unwanted, and "buy" friends by giving them treats with

the stolen money. Is there lots of inter-family competition? Is the
child from a large family getting enough love and affection and attention from his parents? Often stealing is a symptom of a kind of
emotional poverty, and the child tries to substitute things for the
affection he is not getting from people. Sometimes a resentful and
hostile child may "get back" at his parents by making himself a
nuisance with his stealing. Perhaps the parents themselves have
given bad examples by bringing home odds and ends from work,
short-changing store clerks, etc. An examination of the child's recreational activities, his school adjustment, both academic and
social, and the kinds of friends the child has are additional areas
which may give the counsellor insight into the real reasons for the
child's problem.

Stealing by adults is much more complicated and unpredictable.
Often "petty theft"—taking little things from the office, cutting
corners on a shopping tour, minor falsification of income tax re-
ports—are merely childhood adventures carried over into adulthood. Pointing out the infantile quality of these furtive little ma-
neuvers often enough persuades the penitent to grow up. Where
stealing involves large sums of money or major deceptions, the
diagnosis might be one either of cold-blooded and premeditated
responsibility, or of a severe character disorder which needs intensive treatment.

The Eighth Commandment. "Told lies—Gossiped maliciously—
Spoke of the secret faults of others—Was uncharitable, envious,
jealous. . . ."

Lying can become a habit much like that of improper language
or uncharitable speech. Adults often lie to avoid involving themselves more deeply in controversial and opposing points of view
which they feel are better left undisturbed. The lying habit usually
begins in childhood. Every youngster occasionally hides the truth
or exaggerates; it is part of the development of an autonomous,
private life of his own, and can be a healthy sign if not overdone.

On the other hand, a child who is a chronic liar is almost certainly *afraid*. Fear of punishment, of disapproval, of rejection or of

ridicule will prompt a child again and again to spare himself more painful feelings by hiding facts which threaten his security. A child who lies consistently almost certainly has a poor relationship with his parents. In other words, lying is the symptom of a much deeper problem, and the counsellor must work to uncover hidden fears and anxieties before the child will feel it is "safe enough" to confide in those he loves.

Self-acceptance can mean the beginning of control of many of the antisocial eighth-commandment failings. Uncharitable thoughts, malicious gossip, detraction, and calumny frequently have their roots in strong feelings of inferiority. The character-assassin, back-biter, or calumniator sees others as a threat to his own deep feelings of inadequacy. He hastens to demonstrate, by his own irresponsible talk, that others have faults worse than his, and are therefore more deserving of censure. His best plan of defense is attack, for in highlighting the shortcomings of others he is slyly keeping the spotlight off himself.

Something similar is true of the envious and jealous person. Both see the talents and achievements of others as pointing up the lack of such excellence in themselves. Deep down, they are not so much resentful of the talents, privileges, and good fortune of others as unhappy because they feel they themselves fall far short of similar desirable goals.

The first task of the counsellor is to build up true self-esteem in the uncharitable, envious, or jealous penitent. The counsellor must help such a person understand not so much why he demeans his rivals as why he demeans himself. The counsellor must lead him not so much to love his enemies as to have a healthy respect for himself. He must be helped to face his own basic feelings of inferiority and impoverishment. He must become convinced of his own worthwhile, God-given talents (developed or in embryo), convinced that he is capable of love and worthy of admiration, convinced that he has certain talents and qualities, in a sense unique to him, in which he can take genuine satisfaction.

When an individual is able to see himself as an acceptable person, when he has some reasonable pride and confidence in his own personality and gifts, however modest they may be, then he will not see the abilities and triumphs of others as a threat to his own autonomy. The confessor will often find it salutary to encourage the uncharitable penitent, not so much to seek and find Christ in others whom he cannot love, as to seek and find Christ in himself, whom he will then find worthy of acceptance.

SUMMARY

The foregoing observations are obviously brief and inadequate examples of how complex human motivation can be. They have been included in this volume, not as conclusive and all-embracing solutions to common moral problems, but rather as samples of the sort of inquiry and reservation of judgment the priest must make if he is to help the penitent manage the unconsciously motivated emotional problems so often inextricably bound up with his moral difficulties. There are many other human weaknesses and psychic conflicts which we have not even mentioned. Such complicated disorders as alcoholism and scrupulosity are examples of derangements which are so complex that only separate chapters, and more likely separate volumes, can do justice to them.

NOTES

1. New York: Sheed and Ward, 1959, pp. 121–123.
2. *The Proceedings of the Institute for the Clergy on Problems in Pastoral Psychology* (New York: Fordham University Press, 1956), pp. 25–26.

4

MASTURBATION

Our book devotes two chapters to the consideration of masturbation because of the singularly troublesome aspects of the difficulty.* Young priests rarely fail to be amazed at the frequency and persistence of masturbation, particularly among adolescent males. They are puzzled by the unpredictability and seeming impartiality with which this habit engulfs the lives of all manner of individuals. They are dismayed when they find so many obviously capable, good-intentioned, conscientious young men functioning with normal,

* ". . . It is imperatively necessary to deal with the old problem of self-abuse (onanism) from a modern angle. The helplessness with which parents, educators, and especially priests—together, needless to say, with all those who suffer through it—face this problem, is so striking that we can justly speak of a real tragedy. The measures taken by the uninformed to combat this evil are usually useless and are often quite grotesque. The spiritual trouble and the suffering which overtake large numbers of people through this habit cry out for some remedy. Many priests know this well and are filled with anxiety about the young sufferers who slip away from their control and often end by leaving the Church altogether. . . . Through the experience of the confessional, many priests have been moved to change their own position, but do not feel sure as to the correctness of their courses, for the new scientific knowledge in this field, which forms the basis of a different attitude, is only gradually permeating official circles." These words are found in *The Problem of Onanism*,[1] by the Catholic psychiatrist Baron Frederick von Gagern. This slim, clearly written little volume can be recommended as a helpful treatment of this subject from a psychological viewpoint.

healthy, moral resoluteness in every area but this. A number of observant priests have wondered, along with Dr. von Gagern, whether the seeming hopelessness of this habit has not led to the despair or indifference which induce so many of our Catholic young men to sever their active, sacramental relationship to the Church.

The priest who hopes to be effective in counselling the masturbation problems of his penitents must understand that he is dealing with a most complicated problem. Masturbation is practiced in many different ways, by members of almost every age group, by both sexes, and for a bewildering variety of reasons. Needless to say, the solutions are intricate and diverse. Because the subject is complex, this present chapter will deal only with the psychological aspects of masturbation. The moral aspects are given extended treatment in Part Two, chapter 10.

Dr. von Gagern defines masturbation as "sexual excitement and satisfaction sought either alone or with others as a means to procure pleasure or relief, usually as a reaction brought about by motives in the unconscious." In the following pages distinctions will be made and details will be presented which may help to give further meaning to this statement, although the authors would like here to point out that Dr. von Gagern seems to overstress the role of *unconscious* motives. Particularly in adolescence the motives are often conscious enough, as we shall see.

The phenomenon of infant masturbation need not detain us long. It is quite common; in fact, it is to be expected. The young child has an impartial curiosity about every part of his body and will handle his genitals quite naturally. Such manipulation may be especially evident in the years from three to six. Infantile masturbation in no way involves responsible guilt or sin. The discovery of pleasurable sensations in the genital area must be considered as part of the natural process of growth. Counsellors may have the opportunity to reassure worried parents that masturbatory experience can be a part of healthy child development. It is generally unwise to call attention to the phenomenon by "no—no's," hand slapping, or threatening admonitions. Such concentration upon the genitals can only suggest to the child that this part of his body is less desirable, fearsome, or "bad." In other words, parents should be encouraged to ignore the masturbatory practices of their young children. If a child is constantly or excessively preoccupied with masturbation, a counsellor may help the parents discover why the child is anxious or overconcentrating on self. Feelings of rejection, lonesomeness, puzzlement and worry about male-female sexual differences, lack of wholesome play experiences—these are some reasons why there may be an overconcentration on the genitalia. The older theory that frequent childhood masturbation will lead to a stubborn habit in later life seems quite unfounded.

Fears and worries about matters quite unrelated to sex may cause a child to masturbate between the years of six and puberty. If this habit is frequent, and a child becomes withdrawn and tense, psychiatric help may be necessary. As in the case of the infant masturbator, it is useless and often harmful for a parent or counsellor to concentrate, by admonition and disapproval, on the habit itself. They should seek, rather, to determine the deeper causes and anxieties underlying the symptom.

With the advent of puberty comes a markedly more intense drive to masturbate. Adolescent masturbation, particularly among boys, is a problem which the priest-psychologist is inevitably asked about by his fellow clerics. "What can be done? What shall we say? What should we think?"

To begin with, let us examine the available factual data. Many reliable studies deal with the frequency of masturbation among certain age groups. Dr. von Gagern cites about twenty-five statistical investigations of this kind.[2] We can say without fear of contradiction that the masturbator is the rule, and the abstainer the exception. A conservative estimate of existing studies indicates that ninety percent of boys and fifty percent of girls who have attained to maturity have masturbated once or more than once. The great majority of adolescent boys seem to masturbate with some regularity. The average fifteen-year-old boy, for example, might masturbate two to three times a week. This revival of an infantile practice varies with the onset of puberty, and the habit may continue anywhere from a few months to four or five years. A few cases, more pathological in cause, continue into adulthood, as we shall see.

THE CAUSES OF MASTURBATION

What are we to think of these figures? Considering the near universality of the phenomenon, it is easy to see why some psychologists have confused frequency with normality. It is true that clinical histories of neuroses reveal either a persistent and extreme repression of the urge to masturbate, or severe irrational guilt regarding the practice. On the other hand, though such cases are much less frequent, an individual who has never or seldom masturbated can attain to a healthy maturity. In other words, the moral theologian is quite right in insisting that masturbation is not, per se, an inherent and necessary characteristic of human development.

Still, the overwhelming and universal incidence of masturbation, especially among adolescent males, suggests that this is a special developmental problem which needs further study in our time and culture. It is not enough to say, "This is an evil and cannot be tolerated."

Puberty, by its very nature, presents a pressing and imperious invitation to masturbate. The full flowering of the hormonal glands at this time generates a whoie new set of primitive surgings which are as puzzling as they are powerful. The automatic awakening of the sexual organs in even casual relations with the other sex, in fantasy life, and in nocturnal emissions demands some sort of conscious participation in the release of emotional tension. Just plain curiosity —"What does it *feel* like?"—plus the matter-of-fact encouragement from others of his age will lead the youngster to experiment on his own. We must not underestimate the enormous influence youngsters of the same age and group exert on each other. When today's teen-ager hears his friends talking constantly about their new-found "masculinity" he becomes increasingly more curious about the pleasures described in arresting terms by his buddies. The pressure to be "one of the boys" is powerful indeed.

Finally, the common helplessness, insecurity, and anxiety felt keenly by many a teen-ager, who must live in the halfway house between childhood and adulthood, propels him to seek brief comfort and reassurance from an experience which brought consolation in a vaguely nostalgic and even more self-centered past. Thus, masturbation in the adolescent can be regarded not only as a test of future manhood, but often as a blind return to the refuge of earlier, infantile satisfactions. Also, confident acceptance and encouragement of the youngster by his parents is a symbol of the kind of affection which the adolescent needs most and understands best. When he is not trusted, but is criticized and thwarted in a hundred little ways instead, the tendency to seek momentary solace in self-gratification is very strong.

The preceding paragraph has presented characteristics of human growth which make the drive to masturbate a challenge to any young person emerging through puberty into adolescence. In addition to these inherent pressures, our age and social structure present conflicts which often seriously cripple the efforts of modern youth to control their sexual drives. We shall deal with some of these influences in more detail later on. It will suffice here to list some of them. Transportation difficulties and work schedules deny many young people the kind of close relationship with parents which makes for healthy, outgoing emotional release. In fact, there seems to be a complete absence of affectionate interchange and understanding between so many of today's family members. The failure of parents generally to impart adequate sex education multiplies the aimless, searching, experimental quest for knowledge on the part of children. Clashes of authority between parents and young adults present another impetus, unlikely as it may seem, to the substitution of masturbation for confident, independent kinds of activity that young people dream of but are not permitted to try.

There are other dichotomies. The human male reaches the peak of sexual potency at approximately sixteen. Yet our culture does not permit young men at this age to consider even the possibility of marriage, with its normal sexual release. On the other hand, this same society prods him with the most flagrant sexual symbols in the press, the movies, the billboards, the fashions—in short, in almost every facet of daily living. At the same time, at least in middle-class circles, our culture demands that the high school student devote himself to a course of study involving highly competitive and often endlessly monotonous academic chores. Finally—and this is of major importance—so many of our young people come to adolescence totally unprepared by their parents, their school, their church, or society to face the true and positive meaning of sex in their lives. They are hemmed in by great walls of shame, ignorance, fear and cynicism.

An aspect of masturbation which is not usually given sufficient emphasis should be stressed here. Once the adolescent becomes addicted to masturbation a new compulsive dimension must be considered. The psycho-neurological pattern of this habit is a tremendously powerful factor in temptation. The impact of continual masturbation on the nervous system creates an ebb and flow of demand and release quite apart from voluntary choice and external stimulation. This creates a craving for satisfaction, similar to the need for drink in the alcoholic or drugs in the addict, which puts a tremendous pressure on the psychosomatic organism. The counsellor of the habitual masturbator must understand that owing to these nervous forces working independently of the individual's choice or determination, the client may succumb in spite of himself. (This psycho-neurological need pattern often explains the persistence of this habit into adulthood, affecting the sex life of both the single and the married.)

At this point the reader may begin to see that masturbation is far from being a simple sexual sin. On the contrary, the habit can be a predictable concomitant of complex human development. Masturbation can be linked to depression, insecurity, a lack of confidence in self, difficulties at school, a lack of affection in the home, inadequate boy-girl relationships, an undue preoccupation with guilt and sin, and, above all, an inability to give sex and love their proper and proportionate place in healthy emotional living.

Perhaps this is the place to comment on the psychological implications of sin, guilt, and responsibility involved in masturbation. Such considerations are of tremendous importance to both the counsellor and the client. The priest, especially as a confessor, is naturally concerned with the quality of any moral offense. Unfortunately, characteristic overemphasis upon sexual matters might encourage some priests to stress needlessly and often harmfully the gravity of masturbatory sin and guilt.

We know, of course, that masturbation is always *objectively* a serious offense against the natural law. We know, too, that in individual cases masturbation can be freely consented to, and as such should be judged formal as well as material sin. Having stated this, we must cite two facts which moralists and psychologists are stressing with increasing frequency. First, *habitual* masturbation implies a frequent, and often a significant, diminution of freedom, so that in many cases it would be rash to impute grave moral responsibility to the masturbator. Secondly, it is extremely difficult, and often impossible, for the average confessor to judge whether *this* penitent, in *this* particular instance, has committed a serious sin of masturbation. These statements will surprise only the uninformed or unperceptive confessor. The enormous complexity of the problem, the bewildering variety of hidden causes, the patent good will and obvious dismay of the contrite masturbator reinforce the impression that the will, overwhelmed by the habitual and compulsive demands of man's turbulent physical drives, is in so many cases inadequate and even helpless.

As we shall see, one of the chief tasks of the counsellor is to deflect the masturbator's attention from his habit and his guilt. If the counsellor joins the client in persistent and drawn out soul-searching as to possible degrees of guilt, number of sins, estimates of responsibility, etc., he is liable to perpetuate rather than alleviate the severity of the habit.* The diminution of irrational and excessive guilt, on the other hand, will almost certainly reduce the fearful tension which usually increases the compulsion to masturbate. This will also remove some of the deep and subtle onus which often comes to be associated with orgasm and which prevents wholesome and guiltless sex adjustment in marriage later on. (Often habitual masturbators seem to regard marriage as an opportunity to "sin with impunity.")

Lest the reader feel that the sinful aspects of masturbation have been swept away by the preceding comments, let it be clear that subjective guilt is only one aspect of the problem. Compulsive masturbation is from the psychologist's as well as the moralist's point of view unnatural and undesirable. It is to be combated with all the effective aids at our disposal. We naturally oppose sin, material or formal. More positively, we favor self-development and the struggle for perfection. It should be a major concern of ours to eliminate every obstacle, compulsive masturbation included, which hinders such development.

UNDERSTANDING THE MASTURBATOR

It is important, as a prelude to a detailed discussion of counselling technique, to sketch some general principles which underlie the problem. The counsellor in order to be helpful, and the client in order to help himself, must come to see that masturbation can-

---

* It has been observed, incidentally, that the degree to which the counsellor is preoccupied with the guilt, shamefulness, and enormity of masturbation depends to a considerable extent on his own personal attitude towards sexuality. The counsellor who has himself successfully weathered a troublesome bout of temptation and emerged placidly victorious should be able to approach another's problem with a significant degree of sympathetic understanding and patient hopefulness. Some rigid, condemning, insensitive confessors, on the other hand, might have battled their own adolescent urges with violence and repression, fearfully refusing to face the positive aspects of sexual development, even to a denial within themselves of permissible and important human emotions.

not be dealt with in and of itself. Masturbation can mean many different things to different penitents. It is not an overstatement to say that masturbation by itself is meaningless; we must probe deeper to uncover the myriad psychological possibilities which give the habit meaning. As von Gagern points out, "It becomes obvious that the decisive thing is not the action, which is a *symptom,* but the attitude of mind behind it; not what is done, but the mental state of the doer."[3] And again, "Self-abuse is a symptom of failure in the development of the personality as a whole, revealing weakness in character and in the attitude towards life."[4] And finally, "Threats and stern prohibition—even if they have a metaphysical basis—are not adequate to restore the lost balance of personality; and only when this balance is discovered and maintained will the individual be able to develop and resist temptations that assail him before sexuality can be fulfilled in a genuine love."[5]

What does this mean? It means that the habitual masturbator needs to reorientate his whole life. He needs to re-examine his goals, his concepts of sexuality and love, his relationships to his family, to his peers, and to the world in general. This often implies a process of re-education on an intellectual, moral, and in particular on an emotional level. This leads to a discovery of the positive meaning of sexuality and the pride and hope which the individual then places in its worth. Secondly, it means a revitalization of the individual's involvement in the entire process of living, with particular emphasis on a meaningful and operative appreciation of spiritual and religious values. The Faith must be a deeply integrated conviction, effectively influencing the will to choose values within reach, if the temptation to masturbate is to be minimized and kept under proper control.

We have mentioned elsewhere that ineffectual education within the home, the school, and the church has often stunted and blighted the persuasive influence of religion upon the daily activities of youth. It is the chief task of the counsellor to help the individual relate all the important experiences of life to each other, thus bringing proportion, insight, and self-determination into a disorganized life. A false egocentricity is the basis of all regression. Masturbation is one prominent symptom of this. When a young person is able to go forth and face life with confidence and resolution, consoled and encouraged by many gratifying daily experiences, then the inordinate demands of the flesh subside to controllable levels, and inadequate regressive compensations become unnecessary.

COUNSELLING THE MASTURBATOR

How can these admittedly general and idealistic principles be applied to the practical counselling situation? Since most masturbation problems met by the average confessor concern the adolescent male, let us use the teen-age masturbator as a sample subject for our discussion. The first conviction the confessor-counsellor must have is that there is no such person as an "average" teen-age masturbator. Even when the characteristics and frequency of the habit repeat themselves with monotonous regularity, the priest must remember that each individual stands alone, with family background, personal attitudes, and human relationships which are uniquely his. The priest resolves wisely, then, to make no comments and give no advice unless he is prepared to follow through. He should understand that many—perhaps most—cases of masturbation involve a transitory habit which usually resolves itself as the individual emerges from adolescence into maturity.

It seems a reasonable though a minimal practical goal, especially for the priest who feels inadequate as a counsellor, to be content to keep the young masturbator close to the Church and the sacraments. One wonders how often a confessor's harshness or ineptitude has led a discouraged young man to abandon his relationship with the Church. On the other hand, it is not uncommon to meet an adult who confides, "Thank God for old Father Smith, who helped me over a rough four or five years by hearing my unchanging weekly or monthly confessions with a minimum of praise or blame, merely granting a merciful absolution with the cheery words 'Keep doing your best.'" Many such young people are thus sustained through their adolescent years of crisis. With adulthood and marriage come new satisfactions; the old temptations subside and disappear. These young people are then able to continue their unbroken affiliation with the sacramental life of the Church in a spirit of increased joy, gratitude, and spiritual ambition. Often, in parishes with large student bodies and small staffs, this simple confessional approach is all that is practically possible, tragically inadequate though it may be. At least, in these cases, the wrong things, the harmful things have not been said, and the individual emerges into adulthood, after his uneasy period of conflict, with his dedication to the clergy, his devotion to the sacraments, and his habits of hopeful prayer still vital and intact. He has been encouraged to persevere.

However, the priest with confidence and insight, who has a little extra time to give, can do much more. An initial word of kindness and encouragement can remind the individual penitent that there are ways to break the chain of habit. The priest can suggest that it will take time, that immediate success is not likely. He can recommend that the young man return regularly to the same confessor for help. If the individual is particularly disturbed, or the habit is an obviously compulsive one, the priest may arrange a protracted talk or two in the parlor. A confident, friendly interchange between confessor and penitent is particularly valuable. The importance of a relaxed, understanding relationship cannot be overestimated; it is one of the chief ingredients of the successful counselling relationship.

What next? It is, of course, not enough to tell the penitent that there is hope. He must believe it, and feel hopeful. A counsellor can profitably spend the first few sessions discovering what it is that bothers the penitent most. Very frequently fear and guilt loom large in the client's attitude towards his problem. This might be the time to begin the re-educative process. At the start all misconceptions, old wives' tales, and "sidewalk" information should be carefully clarified. The client should be told in simple terms that no possible physical harm can come from masturbation. This habit does not drain away manliness, it does not cause impotency, fatigue, or skin blemishes. The habit is not revealed by the size of the sexual organs, circles under the eyes, nail-biting, or by any other physical manifestation. Nor is masturbation the cause of mental illness, insanity (though some mental patients are compulsive masturbators), homosexuality or "nerves." (We need not tell the client, but it is important for us to know, that unreasonable and excessive *guilt* about masturbating can produce mental and emotional disturbances.) Finally, it might be wise, especially if the client is a compulsive masturbator, to indicate that the frequency of masturbation has nothing to do with physical or mental health. The only exception is a possible irritation of the genital area, particularly of females who masturbate excessively.

Having allayed fears and doubts about the physical and psychological harm erroneously attributed to masturbation, the confessor might go on to a brief discussion of some of the moral factors involved. It would be unwise to tell the penitent that for him masturbation is no sin. This may not be true, and in any case it will have very little meaning. The important thing is to help the penitent see that to dwell upon degrees of guilt and sin and responsibility will serve little purpose. A confessor can explain how certain temptations, especially those involving strong sexual demands, may sweep over an unprepared or untrained will, clouding judgment and crippling choice. He can further describe the difficulty of assessing responsibility in cases where the aberration has become a habit. Finally, he can suggest—in fact, strongly urge—that the counselling time can best be spent in a search for the "whys" behind the masturbation rather than a discussion of the habit itself and its frequency. The reader will note that this approach does not minimize the difficulty; it does, however, deflect the attention of the client from the act of masturbation itself, and consequently from an overconcentration upon the implied guilt and sin. This is a very desirable, indeed a necessary, step in the counselling process.

Now it is time to begin some positive rebuilding of the ego. This can be done gradually and in small doses. The counsellor must be content with slow progress, and must help the client to be similarly content. For some time, depending upon the individual, there may be no progress at all; there might even be an increase in the severity of the temptation and the frequency of the falls. This is true in all sorts of counselling situations.

The priest who counsels the masturbator can see his task in the light of three objectives. First, he must distract his client from concentrating upon the act of masturbation itself by removing as much excessive fear and guilt as he can. Secondly, he must help his client see what the healthy Catholic attitude toward sex—and towards life in general—is like. Thirdly, he must help his client discover what satisfactions he is seeking through the inadequate device of masturbation.

We have described elsewhere what the objectives and techniques of effective sex education should be. These are especially important here. The young person should be helped to see that the sex instinct is an integral and very important part of human nature. He should be encouraged to look upon this basic instinct with pride. Sex will always be a part of him, and sexual feelings, fantasies, and desires will ebb and flow as naturally as the appetite for food and drink. It is to be expected that the young person will look ahead with keen anticipation to a full exercise of these powers and pleasures in marriage. The period of puberty and adolescence is, therefore, not only a time of turbulent adjustment but also a time of promise.

It is usually helpful, at this point, to discuss the happiness and satisfactions of the marriage state. By so projecting into the future, and relating the concepts of genuine love to dating experiences of the moment, the young person is helped to understand what true, outgoing, giving-and-sharing love is like. He comes to see that his masturbation represents all the shallow, self-centered, selfish and infantile aspects of sexual expression.

In short, then, this part of the counselling process encourages the young person to build a genuine capacity for giving and receiving love. The preliminaries of such growth involve a positive and confident acceptance of self, warm and affectionate relationships with others, including individuals outside the family circle, and many happy, satisfying experiences within the daily life pattern.

Learning to love means learning to sacrifice also. If the young boy or girl develops a real appreciation for the joys and privileges of married life (or for the more difficult, yet richly rewarding dedication to virginity as a single layman or religious in God's service), then he or she will be much better able to sublimate the immediate need for fleeting sexual pleasures. The temptation to masturbate is seen not as an occasion of shame and self-loathing, but as a challenge. Even where there is consistent failure, the young person is not bowed down or obsessed with guilt and sin, but instead sees this time of trial as an opportunity for growth.

If the youngster can see that he is using masturbation as a device for recapturing the solace and security of childhood, then the infantile quality of the act, rather than the sinful quality, becomes the important point. He can be encouraged to concentrate, not on the times he has failed, but rather on the ever-increasing number of times that he triumphs over the temptation. He can rejoice in each new victory as another step towards full manhood, another test of matured adulthood. His spiritual life must be geared to the same emphasis. He must come to see our Blessed Lord and Our Lady not as executors of vengeance, poised to pounce upon and repudiate the sinner, but as benign and encouraging allies who understand the overwhelming power of his urge and view his struggle with compassion.

This new discovery of a positive and optimistic philosophy of sex and love is the key to much of the masturbator's difficulty. Since it is a matter of rebuilding attitudes, both client and counsellor must expect the process to be a gradual one. A number of specific, practical considerations are part and parcel of the pattern.

We have indicated more than once how unwise it is to concentrate upon the masturbatory habit itself. On the other hand, especially in the beginning, it is sometimes helpful to examine the time, place, and circumstances of the temptation. These vary considerably with each individual, and the counsellor must be careful not to assume that similar symptoms have necessarily similar causes. Of real significance, for example, are ways by which the individual masturbator attempts to sublimate his sexual drive. It is not enough to have a theoretical philosophy of love. The primitive drive of sex remains inherent in every man and must be dealt with.

One of the chief tasks of the counsellor, therefore, is to help the adolescent devise effective outlets for his sexual drives. So frequently the young person will describe the time of greatest temptation as a time of boredom, idleness, disappointment, frustration, depression, or failure. In the face of such emotional states, it is not enough to say, "Don't masturbate." Masturbation is filling a need; it is a substitution for other outgoing and satisfying experiences. The adolescent needs many gratifying, pleasurable, compensating events to fill his day. If he is masturbating a great deal, one of the first questions he must ask himself is: "If I stop masturbating, what will take its place? How will I fill the vacuum?"

Some of the more shallow treatises on this subject suggest sublimatory activities which are altogether too pat for universal application. Very often there are additional problem areas quite removed from sex. For example, it is useless to suggest to a boy who hates his father or resents his nagging mother that, to overcome his habit, he become more actively involved in family enterprises and family recreation. Many teen-agers will confess that they resort to masturbation whenever they feel misunderstood, thwarted or "picked on" by members of the family.

Athletics can be a healthful physical release which drains off much excess energy. However, the boy who feels inadequate at sports, or who needs very much to win when he plays, may find himself masturbating whenever he feels he has failed himself or the team.

Frustration at school and boredom with study are very high on the list of important contributory causes. Many a schoolboy finds the temptation strongest at the end of the school day, or in the midst of uninteresting homework. A change in curriculum, a new job, more free time for recreation, or a complete revision of the day's schedule are all fruitful areas for discussion. The priest can often work effectively (without, of course, mentioning the specific reason) to have parents modify some of the unrealistic academic expectations they might have for their son or daughter. In general, any device which will eliminate tension from the daily living pattern can be tremendously helpful. For example, the student who

finds himself masturbating regularly while doing his homework
after school might change his routine by spending his afternoon
recreating, and do his homework later in the day. However, the opposite might work just as well—namely, get homework out of the
way early so that he can have his evenings free if that suits him
better.

Perhaps the single most important clue to underlying causes of
masturbation is the fantasy life of the adolescent. In many cases
the activities of the imagination are concurrent and often contributing factors which lead to masturbation. A reasonable amount of
daydreaming is a very necessary ingredient for psychological
growth. The adolescent, especially, imagines in fantasy future activities which are at the moment not possible or permitted to him.
However, there is a limit beyond which such "fantasy living" is
not healthy. The extreme introvert who is unable to relate well to
family, friends, and members of the opposite sex often seeks imag-
inative consolation in fantasies which are powerfully sexual in
nature. Masturbation is often the inevitable result.

One of the chief tasks of counselling, then, is to help the shy and
anxious teen-ager, somewhat fearful of the opposite sex, to venture
into wholesome social and dating experiences. It is the divine
plan that the young adult be drawn gradually to an interest in the
opposite sex. It is natural that he should concern himself with the
control of the romantic, *heterosexual* stimulations of his dating
life, rather than continue to struggle with the more immature satisfactions of masturbation. The counsellor, in helping the young person make this transition, must be slow to view with alarm the new
temptations towards passionate kissing and petting which naturally
supersede the old difficulties with self.

It is occasionally helpful to discuss ways of managing the emotions when the temptation to masturbate is at its height. The penitent
should be encouraged to have certain positive outlets at hand which
might serve as distractions and sublimations before extreme and
unmanageable tensions develop. Television, a walk around the block,
a telephone call or visit with friends, interesting reading matter or
an absorbing hobby can all be used to drain off excessive libidinal

impulses of the moment. If a boy reads in the bathroom, and often masturbates there, he might stop reading at such times. If he doesn't read, and masturbates, perhaps he should take a book or magazine with him. Note, however, that these are positive methods of distraction and do not involve repression as the chief deterrent factor.

To attempt to conquer masturbation by a method of direct attack only centers the mind on the habit so that it tends to get worse. For this reason certain traditional practices of battling the temptation are to be discouraged. To suggest, for example, that the adolescent wrap a rosary around his hand at bedtime, or make sure that his bed clothes and pajamas are not too tight, merely sets the stage for a frantic and fearful battle which the teen-ager will more often than not lose.

In a great many cases, too, it is unwise to suggest prayer at the extreme point of crisis as an effective deterrent. Prayer should come earlier, and at other times during the day when the mind is clear and the emotions are unruffled. Tense and frantic pleas to Almighty God and the saints for courage and protection at times when the temptation has already overpowered the will create more emotional upheaval and focus the entire attention squarely on the masturbation itself. This is one battle which this kind of prayer cannot win.

These methods of controlling temptation are particularly ineffectual in cases where habitual masturbation takes place just before the individual is going to sleep, or when he is in a state of semi-wakefulness. In such instances the usual forms of distraction which make sense during the day are not available. The individual must rely entirely on his mastery over his fantasy life. As sleep approaches there is less and less conscious control of the imagination. The degree of consent to sexual fantasies released from the subconscious which lead to masturbation is very difficult to assess. Learning to focus the uncensored imagination upon healthy, positive, and nonstimulating images as one drifts off to sleep is, for the bedtime masturbator, a long-range and intricate undertaking. This re-education of the emotions and imagination must take place without nervous tension and anxiety. Most of all, this "hygiene of the imagination" is possible only if one's life experience and attitudes are in their sum total healthily developed.

While the interior attitude toward sex and self-control is of chief importance, certain individuals are benefited by external helps as well. There are types of personalities whose wills are strengthened through the hardening of the body. For them, airy, cool, hard beds, early and prompt rising, sports and gymnastics, cold showers and rubdowns may help the development of discipline in every area of their lives. The avoidance of stimulants, such as alcohol and nicotine, can be experimented with. Finally, certain masturbators should be encouraged to avoid obviously stimulating reading and recreation which make their fantasy life difficult to control.

A special confessional approach can be used to advantage in particularly difficult cases. If the habit of masturbation persists in an obviously conscientious individual who has sought counselling help over a long period of time, there can be good reason to suppose that the habit is compulsive. If priest and penitent come to the conviction that this is not a case of mortal sin, but of, say, more or less venial sin, the penitent can be informed that confession is not obligatory before each communion, especially in the case of the daily communicant.[6]

MASTURBATION IN ADULTS

This chapter, for the most part, has confined itself to an examination of that transitional, adolescent masturbation practiced by many adolescent girls and most adolescent boys. There are other forms of masturbation far more complex in nature, and therefore more difficult to counsel. Some are pathological cases which can be treated only by a psychiatrist.* Occasionally masturbation plagues the immature married adult who has every opportunity for sexual intercourse but is unable for one of many reasons (e.g., inhibition,

* Where compulsive masturbation has been used as an aid to sleep, doctors may occasionally prescribe medicinal sedation which, when substituted for a time, can break the chain of habit. Needless to say, this is to be done only under a doctor's direction.

latent homosexuality, etc.) to obtain adequate sexual satisfaction except through masturbation.

There is also a fairly common type of adult masturbation known as "onanism by necessity." This is a special compulsion which seems to be rooted in physical as well as emotional pressures. (See p. 78.) In many cases, its chief object is not so much sensual pleasure as it is the relief of physical tension. It may be found in single persons who have carried over into adulthood a deeply fixed adolescent habit. It is practiced by married men and women who find themselves widowed, separated from their spouses, or unable to practice intercourse in times of illness or pregnancy. The confessor can usually do little more than soothe the distress of such puzzled and ashamed souls, who often find themselves caught in a web of compulsion beyond their control.

Finally, masturbation is often resorted to by married couples who are practicing rhythm or abstinence, or whose day-to-day relationships are strained or hostile. Masturbation in an adult is usually a far more complex problem for the counsellor. The reasons for the weakness are so much more varied and intricate that he may often have to have professional help. Occasionally, improving communication between married partners, encouraging more uninhibited sexual experimentation, or helping single clients to seek new sublimatory activities will prove successful. In any case, the sort of nondirective, patient counselling outlined in the preceding pages is worth trying here.

SUMMARY

Here, in brief, is a list of questions which the counsellor of a teen-age masturbator can ask to gauge the progress of his client.

Is the client encouraged to see the same confessor or spiritual director regularly?

Does the client concentrate most of his attention on sin and guilt, or does he see the habit as a challenge to emotional growth, and its mastery as an aid to the achievement of maturity?

Is the client content with slow progress and prepared for relapses?

What is the attitude of the client toward sex, love, and marriage in general? Is this attitude positive and hopeful, or fearful, anxious, and negative?

Are his parents too strict and demanding, creating constant irritations and frustrations in the face of which masturbation might be a symbol of revolt?

Is there serious rivalry among the children in the family?

Is the client reasonably successful and satisfied with his work at school?

Does he have a job that he likes?

Does the client have enough satisfying recreation? Has he enough time for the sports, hobbies, and tension-releasing activities that he needs?

Is the client growing heterosexually; does he have adequate social and dating experiences? How are his relations with the opposite sex?

Is the client learning to manage his fantasy life, exercising reasonable control without anxiety? Is he able to avoid obvious occasions of sin which stimulate the masturbatory urge? Does he use prayer and the sacraments positively, or does he expect them to cure his problem automatically, as a kind of magic?

What is the client seeking in his masturbation? What does masturbation symbolize for him—love, hostility, revenge, self-pity, anxiety, depression, curiosity, manliness? The answer to this question may hold the beginnings of a solution.

Is the client as concerned about some of his other moral problems (e.g., uncharitableness, control of temper) as he is about his masturbation? How can his attention be deflected somewhat from sexual sins and focused on other, often more deliberate faults?

Does the client use self-denial and mortification as positive tools to build self-control? as unnecessary frustrations which further block already inhibited legitimate emotional outlets? as "magical" devices which will assure control even in the face of habit?

Is the client able to capitalize on the many positive talents and qualities which almost every youngster possesses? or does the single factor of masturbation assume such proportions in his life as to overshadow all he does and negate his achievements and ambitions until they become as ashes in his mouth?

As the client gains insight, hope and confidence, does he learn with the help of grace, to face difficult things, not choosing the easy path as a matter of course? Is he finding himself gradually striding ahead, cheerful in defeat, proud and confident in the ultimate victory?

NOTES

1. Westminster: Newman Press, 1955, p. 53.
2. Ibid., pp. 66–67.
3. Ibid., p. 64.
4. Ibid., p. 103.
5. Ibid., p. 96.
6. Ibid., pp. 92–93.

5

HOMOSEXUALITY

Most priests approach the counselling of a homosexual problem with mixed emotions. Fear, mistrust, feelings of inadequacy, resentment, and just plain ignorance make the problem an unsettling one. We priests are often as disposed as the next person to accept the stereotype which society has identified as "the homosexual type." Willful depravity, seduction of the innocent, preoccupation with effeminacy, perversion of morality—these, and similar associations, may have prompted many of us to give short shrift to a puzzled, struggling, unhappy soul who has dared to reveal the psychological and moral burden which he or she has heretofore carried alone. Because the problem is so important and so complex, we shall, in this chapter, deal primarily with the psychological aspects of homosexuality. The moral aspects are discussed at length in Part Two, chapter 11.

Homosexual problems are much more common than is generally supposed. Owing to the stigma which society at present places upon the homosexual, accurate statistics are difficult to obtain. Five percent of the total population is an estimate which appears in a number of presumably reliable studies. Other samplings give far higher rates. One might speculate that there are anywhere from two to three million homosexuals in the United States.[1] While some of these figures may be exaggerated, it is almost universally agreed that this form of sexual deviation is a real and present problem. The tragic reception which many a homosexual has received from a well-meaning but uninformed, ineffectual, or sometimes even hostile, priest at least partially explains why so many of these unfortunates leave the Church in frustrated rebellion or deep despair. It is characteristic of the homosexual to feel that society has abandoned him—as indeed it has; it is easy for him then to conclude that the Church has abandoned him too. For this reason a vast number of inverts never even approach the priest with their problem. We must not be fooled into thinking that homosexuality is relatively rare because we do not often meet it in the confessional or the parlor.

Happily, social attitudes are changing somewhat. "Homosexuality" is not quite the dirty word it used to be. In certain circles, at least, it can be talked about quietly and dispassionately. With continued enlightenment of the public, some of the more repulsive, distorted, and judgmental interpretations of the problem will disappear. The parish priest, by informing himself on this subject, can aid society in re-evaluating this much misunderstood affliction, can contribute substantially to preventive educational techniques, and can help the individual deviates in his flock to live chaste, productive, and happy lives.

HOMOSEXUALITY, AN INDIVIDUAL PROBLEM

There are many conflicting opinions as to the nature and treatment of homosexual tendencies. It is a great temptation for most priests, in their threefold confessional role of judge, doctor, and teacher, to jump to quick conclusions, arrive at pat diagnoses, and hand out ready-made solutions. The counsellor must, above all, train himself to proceed cautiously and speak prudently. In these matters, perhaps more so than in any other, it is better to say nothing than to say the wrong thing. The admonition of texts in moral theology to avoid prying into sexual details and motives without sufficient reason is never more in force than here.

The priest-counsellor must, above all else, be convinced that there are few cut-and-dried solutions to this problem. Homosexuality is an emotional, intellectual, volitional, moral, compulsive condition peculiar to *this* man or woman. It is admittedly one of the most difficult of psychiatric challenges. We must begin humbly in the face of such complexity, realize our limitations, and regardless of our sympathetic interest and readiness to help, we must stay clear of amateur probing and speculation for which we are not trained.

The average priest, in his role as confessor or counsellor, should be skilled and informed enough to make an elementary diagnosis. This is a matter of necessity, not prerogative, for in many cases an individual with a homosexual problem will speak only to a priest. It is important, therefore, that the priest should know that the person who engages in homosexual activity is not necessarily a homosexual. To label him as such, to prescribe directives aimed at the solution of a homosexual problem, or to suggest psychiatric remedies might be quite out of place and positively harmful. Here are a few typical examples:

A panicky young mother brought her two sons, aged six and seven, to the rectory one afternoon. She insisted that the priest hear their confessions at once, and sobbed that she wanted to bring up her children "pure and decent." It seems that she had found her sons with a number of neighborhood pals of the same age running around the room with their trousers off. The mother was unaware that exploratory interest in their own and others' bodies is an innocent and widespread preoccupation of young children in both the preschool and grammar school years. Adults, and especially parents, are often much too quick to assume that their young children are seeking gratification which parallels adult stimulation. This is not true. When children demonstrate this normal curiosity it is more often the parents who need counselling than the children. The mother mentioned above, for example, needed the reassurance that her young sons were not irretrievably on the road to depravity.

Considerable evidence indicates that many boys toward the end of the prepuberty period and on into the early years of adolescence engage in at least occasional sex play of a homosexual nature. Again, while we do not condone such activity, we must be careful not to assume that this experimentation leads to the formation of a homosexual personality. In the vast majority of cases it does not. Boys at this age are often preoccupied with an absorbing curiosity about the size, shape, and function of their own and others' genitalia. Someone has described this period as that of "sloppy adolescence where sex is vague, curiosity compelling and exciting." Many boys seem to solve their curiosity among themselves in a singularly direct way, yet without any pathologically homosexual involvements.

Revelations of such experiences must be received with the greatest delicacy. It is here that adequate and sympathetic education can play a vital role in removing undue fear and guilt regarding sex. By directing the child's interests into healthy channels and by encouraging reverence and self-control in the youth's acceptance of his newly developing powers, the priest-counsellor can help resolve conflicts which might otherwise prove troublesome. He can avoid harsh and threatening confessional tactics; he can point out that such youthful experimentation is essentially an infantile phenomenon; he can help the boy take pride in his new manhood and encourage him to exercise, with God's grace, that self-mastery which must be part of the psychological equipment of every self-reliant adult.

Although somewhat more suspect, even occasional homosexual experiences in late adolescence or early adulthood need not mean that the individual who performs them is a homosexual. The satisfaction of a latent curiosity, the haphazard release of sexual tension, the complete absence of heterosexual outlets are all circumstances which do not necessarily lead to an inverted personality. Many of the findings of Kinsey are certainly open to question, but the remarkably large number of men who are reported to have had homosexual experiences before the age of thirty-five without any apparent need to continue such overt activity seems at least in part to support the theory which we have sketched above.

This chapter is concerned chiefly with a consideration of the *male* homosexual, since the large majority of cases the priest will meet will be of this sex. This is a curious circumstance, since there is solid evidence to show that the incidence of homosexuality is considerably higher in the female. Since public expression of affection between women—kissing, hugging, fondling, rooming together, etc.—is much more socially acceptable in our culture, latent forms of Lesbianism do not carry the same sort of stigma as similar relationships between males do. Also, the apparent slowness of many women to reach physical excitement suggests that many of these common interchanges are not stimulating enough to generate guilt or arouse misgivings.

When we come to consider the *de facto* homosexual, we are confronted with a bewildering variety of types, symptoms, and motivations. There is the bisexual who is capable of both homosexual and heterosexual stimulation. There is the latent homosexual who may go for years, and often for a lifetime, without a single overt experience; indeed, he may never be aware of the nature of his deviation. True, overt homosexuals have been divided by the experts into innumerable categories. Dr. George Henry and Dr. Albert Gross have, for example, distinguished three homosexual types: the fairy, the hoodlum, the orderly (including the "Madison Avenue" and "Ivy League" varieties).[2] In his classes, Dr. Marcel Frym, the famed criminologist, scorns such arbitrary division. He feels there are as many types as there are homosexuals, and that each case must be evaluated and treated as the problem of a unique personality. There are, in addition, homosexuals who are "active" and those who are "passive"; homosexuals who maintain an exclusive relationship for long periods of time; others who make more shallow and fleeting liaisons. Psychologists often notice overtones of sadism, masochism, voyeurism, fetishism, transvestism, exhibitionism, etc.

It would be pointless to attempt, in a page or two, to outline the clinical origins of homosexuality. Even among the experts, the opinions as to the cause and nature of this illness are intricate and diverse. Laboratory experiments continue to give evidence of some possible chemical or biological predisposition. The psychoanalytic school feels that at least a large part of the propensity is developed in the early years of childhood. While the family relationships are not always rigidly predictable, there is a good chance that the mother of a homosexual will be a dominant, inclusive, and aggressive female, and that the father will be submissive and unassertive by temperament. Homosexuality develops in the young child trapped in a complex pattern of love, fear, and resentment for an overpowering mother. Such a child usually loves and yet is repelled by a poor model of masculinity, the father. There are endless and subtle variations of this interaction, but one can see why one of the first steps in therapy is to free the patient from the cords of steel which bind him invisibly but powerfully to these parental influences.

These details demonstrate, without beginning to touch the psychological and environmental beginnings of this disorder, how diverse and complex a problem homosexuality is. When this conviction hits home the priest-counsellor is much less disposed to make quick judgments, propose facile solutions, or pronounce hasty condemnations. If the counsellor has a profound respect for the intricacies of human nature, he will be far more capable of holding his tongue in case of doubt, and bearing with Christlike patience the apparent failure of the moment.

COPING WITH THE PROBLEM

The average parish priest, when confronted in the confessional or in the parlor with a parishioner who admits to homosexuality, is baffled and often helpless. What can he do?

Many of us need to be better informed about psychological matters in general, and about this problem in particular. Part of the solution lies in more adequate seminary preparation. Fortunately, many of our theological students are getting excellent courses in pastoral psychology and counselling. Meantime, priests who are already caught up in the myriad and time-consuming activities of parochial life can attend clergy conferences and pastoral workshops. They can also keep abreast of some of the latest counselling information by a judicious reading of pertinent periodical articles and books. The bibliographical sources given at the end of this chapter are just a few of the current writings on this subject.

Secondly, the parish priest should make a special effort to acquaint himself with the community agencies in his locality, both public and private, which may be of help to him. (See chapter 9.) Psychiatric clinics, Catholic charity agencies, individual doctors and psychologists can be of tremendous help to the busy shepherd of souls. He should also take pains to discover any priests or clergy-men in his area who have had special training in psychological counselling. Finally, the regular parish priest must not overlook his own possibilities as a counsellor. By a careful cultivation of the virtue of prudence he will learn to be at least a good listener and, with some experience, will be able to apply his rich treasure of spiritual truths in an effective, consoling, and encouraging way.

In some large cities, certain agencies dedicate themselves especially to the treatment of homosexuality. Early in his appointment to a new parish, the priest should carefully investigate not only the agencies, but also the psychiatrists and psychologists in his area to whom he might with reasonable assurance refer specific mental and emotional problems. These individuals need not necessarily be Catholics; in fact, the most competent available professional may be a non-Catholic. It seems, however, that some theories regarding the origin and treatment of homosexual problems cannot but violate the moral teaching of the Church. Certain doctors and psychologists hold to the rigid determinism of human behavior: if a homosexual is "born that way," fate intends that he shall seek and enjoy perverse sexual gratification. Psychologists and psychiatrists of this school have only one aim, namely to help the deviate adjust without guilt to his overt homosexual experiences. They will often encourage the individual to seek companions of his own kind, and they attempt to explain away the gnawings of conscience which bedevil even the most confirmed profligates.

One possible way of checking a psychiatrist's or a psychologist's attitude toward this matter is to ask him if he can agree, at least in principle, to the following points:

1. Almighty God, in His plan of nature, intended that humankind be heterosexually oriented. The homosexual, regardless of the origin of his tendency, is afflicted with a disorder of nature.

2. The homosexual must make every effort to avoid those persons and places which will lead him to a deliberate participation in overt homosexual activity.

3. The ultimate, ideal goal (often unattainable) of therapy must be the heterosexual adjustment of the individual.

These are principles which the therapist of a Catholic patient must accept, at least in theory. Having stated them, we must point out some qualifications. While homosexuality is a distortion of nature, it is in some cases a distortion which, practically speaking, cannot be undone. We do not yet know whether the psychic processes of the true invert are organically determined, are fixed by the early environment, or develop from an interaction of both. Psychoanalysis is at present the only technique which claims to cure this aberration in the true sense of the word. Analysis is obviously time-consuming, very expensive, and still in the process of evaluating its own successes. It is certainly for the few. Thus, though there are hopes for new solutions in the future, we must face the inevitable fact that large numbers of today's inverts will have to live with their alien tendencies to the end of their lives.

UNDERSTANDING THE INVERT

The true invert (we are not speaking here of the bisexual) became so very early in his childhood. As an adult he faces life as one who is psychologically handicapped. It is a medical error and a moral injustice to call him depraved or perverted. Both these words imply a deliberate *turning away* from a healthy, normal heterosexual state to a homosexual one. The true invert has never had such a choice. He has not turned away from anything. Heterosexual affection has never been a reality for him. He has known only one attraction—an attraction to his own sex. He is no different from a child born crippled. We can hope and pray and work for a cure, but the medical challenge in this psychiatric area seems as great as that task which would, say, restore 20/20 vision to myopic eyes.

The positive and universal rule of the Catholic Church permitting directly voluntary sexual expression only in marriage applies to the homosexual as it does to everyone else. In that remarkable book, *The Invert* (which should be on every counsellor's shelf), the anonymous author suggests again and again a persistent parallel between the normal and the abnormal in this regard. "Among the normal are saints and profligates. Between those who have achieved sanctity and those who have chosen vice will be found the larger number, struggling sinners, whose faltering progress is marked by many a pitiful tumble. Among inverts there are saints and profligates, and between the extremes many who are struggling in a more or less successful attempt to follow the dictates of conscience and direction of authority."[3] The homosexual, then, can expect to practice self-control and continence with the same spiritual helps as the heterosexually oriented woman or man who is besieged with temptation.

There are differences, however. The invert often has a more difficult time avoiding stimulatory situations. The typical unmarried person has at least the capacity for normal sexual expression, and may actively and hopefully work towards wedlock within acceptable dating patterns. The confirmed homosexual can never entertain the prospect of a legitimate outlet for his drives. To suggest that he seek his recreation and relaxation in female company is unrealistic —such attempts will usually lead only to more anxiety, tension, and frustration. Yet he must live in a "man's world" which is often inescapably disturbing to him. He will find himself in contact with persons and situations that may constitute an occasion of sin for him. But alternative consequences—namely, complete withdrawal and isolation from accepted social circles—are so much more damaging that exposure to certain risks is justified.

Habitual fear-and-flight responses to normal social situations can create severe psychological and moral problems. This is important for the spiritual guide to know. The uninformed confessor has a tendency to demand that the invert avoid every contact which might possibly be a source of stimulation for him, e.g., swimming, sports, stag society, artistic circles, male friendships. In many cases such involvements help to drain off a more basic urge for physical contact. To stifle these outlets could very well precipitate the penitent into more frequent and more overt homosexual activity. In other words, the invert should be encouraged to participate in all the social activities which bring him satisfaction, unless he feels morally certain that a given person or place is an inevitable source of seduction.

It is important, too, to help the distressed and guilt-ridden penitent understand that there is a significant difference between acted-out, overt homosexual behavior and the compulsive, involuntary imaginings and desires which form so large a part of the fantasy life of the invert. He must be helped to see that in certain situations such fantasies are bound to become more persistent and vivid, and that as long as he does not consent to them or act on them he is blameless.

In rare instances an overt homosexual experience may be the only outlet which prevents a seriously disturbed individual from crumbling into a psychotic. Such compulsive behavior is almost certain to be largely free from responsibility. In such instances especially, it would be extremely unwise for the confessor to emphasize the heinousness of these actions. However, such a judgment should never be made without the expert opinion of a consulting psychiatrist. In most cases one might safely presume that the homosexual penitent will benefit from the kinds of spiritual advice that the confessor would give to those whose temptations are of a heterosexual nature. We will have more to say of this in the final section of this chapter.

Occasionally a priest will meet a homosexual problem through a referral from the courts. It is a tragic fact that in many states—probably most—legal procedure and penal custom is both harsh and unfair to the homosexual. Only a small proportion of offenders—usually the most pathetic and compulsive of the lot—are apprehended and imprisoned. Prison is not only ineffective, but more often than not contributes positively to the delinquency of the young deviate. Imprisonment is contaminating rather than rehabilitative. A revision of the laws in this regard should be of concern to the priest as the representative of all his people and a public figure, who, more than many, is capable of bringing about realistic civic opinion and legal changes for the common good. Highlighting the inadequacies of present penal codes in reference to the homosexual is the *Report of the Roman Catholic Advisory Committee on Prostitu-*

tion and Homosexual Offenses and the Existing Law published in the *Dublin Review* of Summer, 1956. Here are a few key sentences:

The existing law does not effectively distinguish between sin, which is a matter of private morals, and crime, which is an offense against the state, having antisocial consequences. Under the existing law criminal proceedings against adult male persons in respect of consensual homosexual acts in private (whether of the full offense of sodomy or of gross indecency) inevitably fall upon a small minority of offenders and often upon those least deserving of punishment. It is accordingly recommended that the criminal law should be amended in order to restrict penal sanctions for homosexual offenses as follows, namely, to prevent: (a) the corruption of youth, (b) offenses against public decency, (c) the exploitation of vice for the purpose of gain. It should be clearly stated that penal sanctions are not justified for the purpose of attempting to restrain sins against sexual morality committed in private by responsible adults. They should be discontinued because (a) they are ineffectual, (b) they are inequitable in their incidence, (c) they involve severities disproportionate to the offense committed, (d) they undoubtedly give scope for blackmail and other forms of corruption.[4]

Chief Magistrate John M. Murtagh of New York City concurs with the substance of this report and has incorporated it into his book on prostitution, *Cast the First Stone.*[5] He points very strongly at many present juridical and penal procedures which are most unfair, inadequate, and detrimental to the public as well as the private good.

THE PRIEST AS A COUNSELLOR

Foregoing observations have emphasized the danger and futility of the untrained clergyman's attempting psychological counselling. Without special study and experience, any probings into the whys and wherefores of this deeply rooted disorder can only lead to confusion and distress. In this area, the average priest must sternly repulse a natural tendency to investigate the bizarre and probe into the unconscious.

In particular, the homosexual should be protected from the guidance techniques of two types of priests. He should be kept away from the confessor who has no patience with human weakness and who speaks of homosexuality in cynical, often vulgar jargon. (Interestingly enough, such a priest will often be something of a "woman hater" as well, reflecting a crude, disdainful, unsympathetic attitude toward everything sexual.) The other type of cleric who should be dissuaded from counselling homosexuals is the "boyologist," the youth enthusiast who is obviously reaping intense and unusual emotional satisfaction from his avocation. Such dedicated and absorbed involvement is almost always quite innocent and praiseworthy. But such a counsellor's inability to remain detached, so necessary in such a delicate guidance relationship, puts too many emotional blocks in the way of an effective and objective airing of homosexual problems.

The phenomenon of emotional transference (at work in any one-to-one counselling relationship) can completely befuddle and mislead the well-meaning but inadequately informed counsellor and counselee. A tendency to probe for detailed and confidential material may be a particularly attractive device for the occasional priest who is, in perfectly good faith, sublimating certain latent homosexual characteristics of his own.

Although the average priest must shy away from protracted depth-therapy of any kind, he can still be tremendously effective as a supportive counsellor. As a matter of fact a priest is more often than not the most practical and effective referral source. At present there are not nearly enough professional agencies and experts to whom we can send the homosexuals who might come to us. It remains, then, for us to exercise, in the most informed, judicious, and Christlike manner, those techniques which can give at least a modicum of help and reassurance to the penitents who seek our aid.

What are some of the qualities which the effective counsellor can bring to this work? Of chief importance are the attitudes and feelings which the priest himself entertains in regard to the problems of his clients. Can we accept the homosexual as another person with a problem? Or are we filled with biases, revulsion and impatience in the face of such an aberration? "I have no absolution for the likes of you," thunders a priest to a homosexual penitent. This approach can do nothing but harm. If the priest is persuaded that the tendencies of the invert are of themselves evil, or that a fall from grace constitutes the unpardonable sin, then there is no lasting good to be gained, even in the sacramental relationship.

The counsellor of the homosexual must be personally and fervently convinced that, in the eyes of God, the homosexual is as capable of fruitful, chaste—yes, holy—living as the heterosexually oriented person. Such a counsellor must be deeply persuaded that the homosexual can, through grace, psychological help, and the sacramental guidance of his confessor, avoid obvious occasions of sin and refrain from voluntary overt activity.

One of the chief reasons the homosexual seems to find it difficult to sublimate his lower tendencies into healthy and acceptable behavior is because society as a whole has made him, at least in his own mind, an outcast and a derelict. The average homosexual, either through hostility or despair, feels himself abandoned by his fellow men. Society finds it much easier to tolerate the masturbator, the fornicator, or the adulterer. The homosexual often has no other consolation but the inadequate and fleeting solace of his own pathetic sexual practices.

The priest-counsellor can help the homosexual to regain a conviction of his own worth. By stirring up new hope in the real possibilities of a chaste life, the homosexual can also strengthen his faith in the bounty of God's grace and his own ability to co-operate with it, and can thereby stir up a new and deep supernatural charity prompting him to lead a useful, altruistic, and devoted life in the service of God and of his neighbors.

Wherever possible, the homosexual who is consistently involved in overt activity should be referred to psychological help. More often than not the co-operation of an understanding confessor is desired and appreciated by the therapist. In this connection, something should be said about the function of guilt and fear in the behavior of the homosexual, because the attitude and response of the priest can be a very helpful or a hindering factor in his treatment.

Regardless of whether the penitent is receiving therapy or not, the priest cannot go wrong in helping to minimize undue fear and guilt—part of the psychological make-up of most homosexuals. To stress the terrors of mortal sin and damnation, the foulness of the occasions of sin, and other such matters, is more than likely to increase the number of falls. The mere feeling of guilt helps to strengthen the obsessive-compulsive mechanism which is so much a part of the homosexual character. A constant preoccupation with the fact that one has done or desired something wrong generates excessive anxiety and the fear of retribution and punishment. Time and again we see that a purely negative fear—whether it be the religionist's fear of God or the atheist's fear of fate, is an insufficient deterrent to undesirable moral behavior. The confessor, therefore, should be careful not to instill more fear in an already frightened human being. The paranoic element, so common in the homosexual, tends to distort and exaggerate further these threats of punishment. Very often punishment is precisely what the homosexual is unconsciously seeking as a palliative for the dreadful desires and drives he fears within himself.

The priest must above all show the mercy of Christ to his troubled penitent. He must not be punishing or rejecting; he must not show amazement or disgust. He must assure the homosexual that neither he nor his emotional tendencies are evil in themselves. He must help him to accept the fact that something is wrong, that there is a blocking of heterosexual desires—a blocking for which the invert is not responsible. He must convince his discouraged penitent that God loves him as much as, and perhaps more than, the heterosexually orientated folk around him. He must persuade him that this inclination can be lived with in a life of tranquil self-control and sublimation most pleasing to God and most meritorious for him who practices it. When the homosexual slips and falls, the priest can face this failure with the same patience, tolerance and readiness to help which he brings to the masturbation and petting problems of his other penitents. A true representative of his compassionate Lord, the priest can commend the struggling homosexual to the grace of the Church in a seventy-times-seven-fold extension of Heaven's mercy.

PRACTICAL INFORMATION

The following are some specific suggestions which have been found useful by Catholic counsellors who deal with homosexual problems. These comments may be particularly helpful to those counsellors who are at least temporarily unable to find a professional referral for a homosexual client.

The untrained counsellor, for reasons stated earlier, should avoid long and frequent personal interviews with a true invert. He can be most effective as a kind and understanding confessor, though he might find that an occasional word of encouragement in the parlor is not out of place.

The priest-counsellor should be aware that discouragement and self-centeredness are usually characteristic of the confirmed homosexual. He needs great patience, and must be prepared for many disappointments inherent in the counselling relationship.

There is real danger in presuming that only homosexuals engage in homosexual activity. This is especially true when adolescent experimentation is in question. The priest can do much damage by implying outright or subtly that a youngster has all the earmarks of a deviate. Male adolescents often regard sex play among themselves as signs of masculinity and virility. To identify their behavior with the effeminate perversions which they fear and despise may wound them emotionally for life.

Teachers, school prefects, scout leaders, etc., can often distinguish between the sexual "horse play" fairly common among adolescents and the more significant relationship between two boys which involves a persistent, intimate, and exclusive interchange of *affection*. The latter is much more likely to suggest the development of a permanent homosexual pattern. (More often than not, the true invert is most powerfully attracted not to another homosexual but to a normal, fully masculine male. The fact that two young adolescents engage in a series of promiscuous experiences may mean that only one of them, the seducer, is a true homosexual.)

Occasionally, the priest may be influential in effecting some change in an incipient homosexual's environment. The evidence of a too-exclusive feminine upbringing; the presence of an overdominant mother and a too submissive father; the problem of over-stern parents; puritanical or stimulatory attitudes toward sex in the home; poor relationships between mother and father or parents and children—these are some situations which can occasionally be eased by the prudent and gentle suggestions of an interested counsellor. Occasionally too, the priest may help find legal help, a new job, new recreational interests, and even new living quarters for a young person with homosexual tendencies.

If it is certain that the male homosexual is a true invert, then the priest should dissuade him from attempting marriage. Counselling a bisexual is more complicated, but there is more chance of marriage successfully diverting his homosexual tendencies into heterosexual channels. Female inverts are able to perform the marital act and raise children without as many difficulties. There seems to be somewhat less danger of marriages involving bisexuals ending quite so disastrously as the marriages of true male inverts. In any case, the opinion of a qualified psychologist or psychiatrist should be obtained.

The confessor should avoid speculating about the degree of responsibility involved in the overt homosexual activity of his penitents. As Dr. Rudolph Allers has pointed out, we cannot know anything about the true nature of "allegedly irresponsible impulses unless we know all we can find out about the total personality."[6] If at all possible, we should avoid discussing culpability with the penitent. Certainly we should not tell him that he is not responsible. On the other hand, we cannot actually determine his guilt either. There are certain cases, for example, where the penitent must be treated as insane, even though he is completely lucid and in control of his will in all other aspects of his behavior. Father John F. Harvey, C.S.F.S., writing on "Homosexuality As a Pastoral Problem," suggests that this type of homosexual is analogous to the full-fledged alcoholic and should be similarly dealt with.[7]

In dealing with young people, spiritual advisors should be careful to avoid instilling an excessive sense of guilt about matters sexual, particularly those of a heterosexual nature. One must always remember that fear of the opposite sex, much more than an attraction to one's own, is the hallmark of the homosexual. Petting and dating practices of the bisexual must sometimes be viewed as attempts to risk and test a genuine heterosexual relationship. Ventures into normal warm and close dating experiences can be tremendously threatening and bewildering undertakings for the timid or inhibited neophyte.

The invert must seek in works of love and service an outlet for his zeal and energy. The priest can sometimes encourage such sublimation by providing opportunities for charitable works of mercy and personal sacrifice.

A sense of humor on the part of the counsellor and counselee can help tremendously. The author of *The Invert* suggests, for example, that we "take the passing amorous adventures of sentimental youth with a certain gaiety and lightness of touch to avoid sexual obsession."[8]

The priest can help his penitent focus his perspective so that his whole life is not clouded and colored by this one problem. The invert can be helped to develop the many positive talents he is sure to have, and be proud of them. In doing so, he can actually minimize the obsession with sexuality which can so poison the mind with guilt, fear, and helplessness that all other creative and compensating activity becomes stifled or sterile.

We have already indicated how reluctant an advisor should be to suggest that a homosexual abandon his normal social contacts. The counsellor should, for similar reasons, be slow to presume that certain occupations are likely to mean trouble. Teachers, social workers, athletic directors, scout leaders, etc., who have been involved in actual sexual activity with their charges should, of course, be dissuaded from continuing in such positions, and pastors must exercise prudent vigilance in screening applicants for these parish posts. On the other hand, such occupations can be desirable and healthy outlets for those who have no problems with overt seductive behavior. As long as the worker is honest with himself and his confessor, the dangers of remaining in any job where deviate tendencies are being effectively sublimated are largely imaginary. It is quite possible, too, for a penitent to be so emotionally constituted that he has difficulties only in his private, off-the-job hours which never involve his vocational contacts, tempting as they might appear.

Both counsellor and client must be deeply convinced that grace is an indispensable help to the dawning of adequate self-knowledge through which the cause of inner conflict is gradually revealed. The homosexual penitent must be fully convinced that chastity is a supernatural gift which requires a firm action of the will and a confirmed dedication to an ascetical ideal. Earnest, placid prayer for such healing grace should be the persistent recommendation of the clerical counsellor.

On the other hand, we must not fall into the error of pan-religionism. *Gratia perficit naturam* is never more apt than here. There is no magic quality to the genuine reformation of any life. Both the counsellor and the penitent must be resigned to a long period of patient struggle. We can safely say that where the invert honestly faces up to his problem, avoids the avoidable occasion of sin, has the determination to get well psychologically and spiritually, prays constantly for the grace of God, confesses and receives communion frequently, formulates a plan of ascetical striving in the world and co-operates closely with priest and psychiatrist—then he can validly hope for a fruitful, meritorious, and happy life.

NOTES

1. A. C. Kinsey, W. B. Pomeroy and C. E. Martin, *Sexual Behavior in the Human Male* (Philadelphia: Saunders, 1948).

2. "Social Factors in the Case Histories of 100 Underprivileged Homosexuals," *Mental Hygiene,* XXII (1938), pp. 591–611.

3. *The Invert and His Social Adjustment* (London: Baillière, Tindall & Cox, 1948).

4. "Homosexuality, Prostitution and the Law," *Dublin Review,* 471 (1956), pp. 57–65.

5. John M. Murtagh and Sara Harris, *Cast the First Stone* (New York: McGraw-Hill, 1957).

6. "Irresistible Impulses," *American Ecclesiastical Review*, 100 (1939), p. 219.

7. *Theological Studies*, XVL, No. 1 (1935), pp. 86–108.

8. *The Invert and His Social Adjustment*, p. 110.

6

ALCOHOLISM

The authors debated for some time before including the subject of alcoholism in our book. Originally we were confronted with this question: What can we say to the seminarian or parish priest about the nature and treatment of alcoholism in twenty-five or thirty pages? Will not our very efforts to synthesize give the impression that the problem is a simple one and the solution equally simple? In so many circles this is precisely the attitude one finds toward alcoholism. We did not wish to perpetuate this misconception by contributing an oversimplified treatment of our own.

On the other hand, in keeping with the image so many have of him as a universal resource person, the priest will sooner or later be called upon to counsel an alcoholic, or the family of an alcoholic. We hope the material which follows will be of some help in defining the nature of the affliction, even though we cannot possibly spell out its complex ramifications or indicate the multitudinous approaches by which it can be treated. We hope that this chapter, along with the other chapters in this book, will spur the reader to further study. This subject, especially, needs to be carefully understood before effective help can be given. We shall therefore deal with the nature of alcoholism in this chapter, and reserve until Part Two, chapter 12 a discussion of its moral implications.

It is estimated that in the United States five million persons suffer from alcoholism, and an additional twenty-five million non-alcoholics, family members of the afflicted, are directly affected. The problem, therefore, involves over one-seventh of our population. The very fact that there are so many sufferers is an indication that this problem is not understood by the general population. There is, in fact, a vast ignorance on the part of the public. As priests and community figures of influence, we should enlighten our people as to the true nature of this tragic blight with the same earnestness that we combat any block to natural and supernatural growth.

What is alcoholism? It is a *disease* which is characterized chiefly by the *uncontrollable* drinking of a victim whose life is in some way negatively affected by his illness. Regardless of appearances, the alcoholic is no longer able to choose whether to drink or not, the times when he gets drunk, or the amount of liquor he will consume. (Occasionally, the power of choice seems miraculously restored. There are periods when control seems to return. These are, in a sense, tragic interludes, because they reinforce the conviction of the drinker and those about him that he is able to continue to drink and to retain control over his drinking.)

The nature of the disease is still widely debated. These facts we do know: alcohol itself does not cause alcoholism. The alcoholic does not become so because of his deliberate abuse of drinking; nor does he suffer from a lack of "will power." The pressure of circumstances (ill health, unsatisfying work, a nagging wife, bad companions, etc.) also cannot be assigned as direct causes. All these shortcomings are observed in other people who do not solve their tensions with drink.

Several hypotheses are advanced by equally expert schools of research and speculation. One group feels that alcoholism is essentially a physiological phenomenon, caused by a chemical imbalance of the glands or an impairment of the nervous system. Another school believes that the underlying reasons for alcoholic symptoms lie in purely psychological or emotional causes. They believe the alcoholic seeks this particular device as a means of escaping and dulling the painful imperfections of his own personality, many of them rooted in early childhood. A third school feels that the answer lies somewhere between these two. They cite the almost overwhelming evidence of many reformed alcoholics who have obviously profited from psychological help of some sort, but are still not able to drink with impunity. The *psychosomatic* aspects of their theory seem to be supported by such evidence.

Several things *are* clear, however. True alcoholism must be considered a *medical,* not a moral problem. Secondly, with few exceptions (and there are always exceptions) an alcoholic cannot be cured so that he can drink socially—the odds against his continuing to drink and still achieve a happy life are far too great.

WHO IS AN ALCOHOLIC?

If an alcoholic is to be helped, or if he is to help himself, the first and paramount requirement is *knowledge*. For this reason, we will try to summarize in the next few pages some of the important characteristics of the illness and its treatment. Much of the material which follows has been condensed from a simple and splendid treatment of the problem called *The New Primer on Alcoholism* by Marty Mann.[1] Miss Mann is Executive Director of the National Council on Alcoholism, and her book cannot be recommended too highly. It is written in clear, easy-to-read, nontechnical language by an expert who has made this subject her life's work. We venture to suggest that the priest who proposes to work, even on a small scale, with alcoholics who seek his help *must* have a firm grasp of most of the material in this book.

Let us begin by describing very briefly the chief symptoms which usually mark the true alcoholic's progress from the early stages of his illness to the final and acute symptoms.

The Early Symptoms. The alcoholic is heard making promises and half-promises to give up drinking (he plans on this "soon" or "next month"). He lies about his drinking, especially to himself; he cannot believe that he is developing a problem. He finds himself gulping drinks, rather than sipping them. He drinks regularly before a party or before a business appointment. He feels the necessity of drinking at certain times: he *must* have a drink before lunch or at five each day; he *must* have a span of time allotted for drinking before dinner, regardless of inconvenience to others; he *must* have drinks on every special occasion—whether a theatre party, sports event, a wedding, funeral, holiday, etc. He *must* have a drink for that "tired feeling" or for "nerves"; he must drink to forget troubles for a while, to offset a depression. Behind some of these reasons for drinking lurk deep feelings of inferiority and inade- quacy, fear of isolation and of "not belonging." Only close family members may be alert enough to see the connection.

It is very important to remember that an *overwhelming majority* of the above listed symptoms must be present to indicate incipient alcoholism. It should further be noted that most alcoholics carry their liquor well and have a great capacity in the early stages. Hangovers are rare, and very few alcoholics get obviously sick—two characteristics more typical of the nonalcoholic. In this early stage, blackouts (hazy thinking to the point of unconsciousness) unnotice- able to others frequently occur, but alcoholics rarely pass out during this early stage. Most alcoholics are about ten years developing these beginning symptoms and are usually unaware that their drinking is in any way different from anyone else's.

Middle Symptoms. Promises to reform now come thick and fast, are made desperately and broken quickly. The drinker still believes that he has control, still believes in his promises, is panicky when he fails. Lying becomes an integral part of his life. He may have heard that loss of will power means "insanity," a truly frightening possibility. So he desperately refuses to admit he is sick, rationalizing to himself, lying to others. He still really thinks he can stop if he wishes.

He is gulping his drinks more frequently now, often from his own private supply. He must "get one under his belt" before he goes anywhere. The extra drinking times are pushed ahead, and he is now drinking before meals at a bar rather than at home. His eating is irregular; he is bored, "dog tired," nervous, worried, troubled and depressed without a drink. There are pick-me-ups at eleven in the morning and four in the afternoon; he is drinking alone and at the wrong times. Week-end bouts with Monday morning hangovers or "sick headaches" (in women) are more frequent. The occasional morning drink makes its appearance.

Periodic "on the wagon" intervals may continue to give the alcoholic a false confidence that reinforces his wavering trust in his own self-control. During these periods when he is not drinking there is a highly noticeable degree of irritability. At times of real drunkenness a kind of Jekyll and Hyde change of character displays itself. Control is fast disappearing—he must *feel* the effects of liquor, and he puts off eating so that the impact of his drinking will be more pronounced. Rarely, if ever, is he willing to talk about his drinking —he never admits he has been "just plain drunk" or that he suffers from hangovers.

The old feelings of inferiority are now hidden behind aggressiveness and arrogance, accompanied by a "grandiosity of thought and behavior." Feelings of isolation are now buried under a talkative and convivial façade. Alcohol is becoming food; hunger is less and less demanding. Hangovers lead to terrible symptoms, experienced for the first time in all their intensity—physical near-collapse; mental remorse; emotional self-disgust; terrifying self-doubt. Such attacks on the nerves and on the emotions are beyond description, and it is no wonder that the sufferer resorts to "a hair of the dog that bit him" at the earliest possible opportunity. Nausea, blackouts, and passouts become more and more frequent. It is perhaps during this middle stage that alcoholics are hardest to reach. Their fright, the fear of losing their grip plus a desperate unwillingness to admit that they are slipping, is the reason for this. This middle stretch often lasts for from two to five years before the late symptoms finally develop.

Late Symptoms. The unfortunate victim of compulsion now "drinks to live and lives to drink"—any time, any place, on any occasion. He lies as a matter of course. He rarely wants to eat (though he gorges like a wolf on the occasions when the "chuck-horrors" set in). His promises are limited to periodic and vehement vows—"I'll never touch the stuff again as long as I live"—resolutions almost impossible to attempt, because at this stage the individual could not on any account go on the wagon without a great deal of medical help. These promises to reform are a last "dimming symbol of hope to the alcoholic himself," a final pathetic attempt at self-assurance which invariably ends in failure. Drunken behavior inevitably occurs at the wrong time. Often the acute alcoholic will give an uncanny impression that he is sober—belied, however, by the peculiar sweetish-sour odor which an experienced observer immediately recognizes as the telltale evidence of almost perpetual drunkenness.

Heavy drinking bouts are frequent, lasting from a few days to a week or longer. Morning drinks have become a necessity. The dry periods have become infrequent indeed, usually because the nervous system and physical condition of the drunkard no longer permit him to function without drink. Irritability and highly tense emotional responses are the rule rather than the exception. Complete drunkenness is the alcoholic's condition most of the time, so that he is fired from or leaves his job, sometimes after an almost endless series of "one more" chances from sympathetic bosses.

At this stage the alcoholic procures drink by any means possible. The alcoholic husband steals from his wife's purse, the alcoholic wife from her husband's pockets. Moveable objects are sold or pawned. The fact that the alcoholic is often a fundamentally honest person becomes an added strain as he or she realizes what is happening. The attitude of the alcoholic toward his family becomes increasingly significant. He watches them struggle on their own, sinking into destitution, perhaps finally leaving him, all with *apparent* indifference (excepting tearful monologues to strangers in bars). If the alcoholic is a Catholic, he avoids the Church and the priest. If a Protestant, he has in many cases given up religion altogether and has become in his own view an atheist or agnostic.

The alcoholic has lost the sense of time. Life becomes more and more centered upon the bottle, and control has become a meaningless word. He lives in a sort of perpetual "numbness" which has deadened delicate feelings which once hurt. He no longer admits drinking or acknowledges his drunken behavior, except for very rare outbursts of horror, self-disgust, and a tragically real desire to "be like other people." Almost continuous, round-the-clock drinking forestalls ordinary hangovers. However, nightmares, extraordinary sicknesses, and extreme fatigue confirm his terrifying suspicion that the crisis is approaching. Extreme feelings of inferiority and inadequacy alternate with equally extreme swings to grandiosity. Isolation and evidences of "not belonging" (especially characteristic of alcoholic women) become very prominent. In the early stages of alcoholism the individual persisted in the delusion that his drinking was not different from anyone else's; now he cannot be convinced that he will ever be able to feel well and enjoy life without drinking. There is a pressing need to keep a certain amount of alcohol in the system at all times, and a craving for food is rare. There are terrors upon awakening, frequent nausea; blackouts and passouts occur at odd and unpredictable times. The alcoholic loathes himself, but must conceal his loathing. He has arrived at a point where he literally cannot function as a human being without the aid of drink.

This, then, is the somber saga of the drinking alcoholic. It can happen to anyone. Nothing is further from the truth than the common belief that only bums and degenerates are drunks. (Only from 8 to 12 percent of the nation's alcoholics are on Skid Row, and only 25 percent of these are true alcoholics. The rest are social misfits, professional beggars, etc.)

The five million alcoholics in the United States (one-sixth of them women) are scattered through every walk of life—in leading families, among the poor, in all the professions—irrespective of personality, position, religion, or intelligence.

"An alcoholic is someone whose drinking causes a *continuing* problem in *any* department of his life."[2] The word "continuing" in this definition means compulsive; it means that the drinker lacks control over his drinking. "Any department of his life" means just that. Drinking may first affect the *inner life* of the alcoholic, causing him to suffer nagging doubts which rob him of his peace of mind. It can touch his *home life* in such a way that the family is the first to notice the growing problem. His *social life* may be affected when friendships cool and finally are rudely terminated. The *physical life* of the alcoholic is eventually affected—drink seems to be more and more a constitutional need, with the alcoholic becoming increasingly incapable of going anywhere or accomplishing anything without it. Hangovers and the inability or unwillingness to eat are also obvious impairments of physical well-being. Finally, the business acumen, financial affairs, and professional life of the alcoholic are bound to suffer. The first signs of alcoholism may appear in any one or several of these ways. Helplessness in the face of such deterioration is a sign of alcoholism.

If drinking is causing a continuing problem in any department of a normal or social drinker's life, he will either cut down or cut out the drinking. That is the logical or normal solution to the problem, and for a normal drinker it would present no great difficulty even though he may intensely dislike or resent having to do it. But if the drinker is an alcoholic, he might equally well realize that that is the solution; he may even say so and be convinced that he is going to do it; but he won't do it because he won't be able to do it. In this lies his alcoholism; and his continued drinking, for whatever reasons he might give, proves it, since it thus continues causing a problem.[3]

There are other, more complicated, illnesses associated in some way with alcohol which cannot be called alcoholism per se. The *situational drinker* because of unusual outside pressures finds himself involved with frequent or infrequent bouts of drinking but is able, sometimes with professional help and other times on his own, to return to normal, controlled drinking without detriment. The *mentally ill person* sometimes seems to be an alcoholic, but drink for him is just a minor aspect of a much larger problem. This is especially true of the *psychopathic personality* (see Appendix I), whose entire emotional equipment is awry and who is almost bereft of any sense of right and wrong. All these cases need expert psychiatric help. It is senseless to think that an amateur can meddle with such complicated mental disorders.

In addition to drinkers who are obviously mentally ill, there are other types of drinkers who are not alcoholics. Over sixty-five million Americans drink who can in no sense be called alcoholics. The vast majority of these drink without being a problem to themselves or to people around them. Occasional, frequent, or regular drinkers imbibe alcohol for medical reasons, in keeping with family custom or tradition, to reduce physical discomfort or anxiety, to add flavor to their meals, as an important aid in social relations, or to afford satis- faction and relaxation in their recreational life. These drinkers achieve through alcohol such effects as mild animation or gaiety, conversational ease, and feelings of physical and psychological well- being.

Certain borderline drinkers can dull feelings of inferiority, frustra- tion, and personal failure in occasional heavy drinking, even to the point of intoxication. None of them, however, are alcoholics. The *social drinker* can get mellow, tight, or quite high, but can go for weeks or months without drinking. The *occasional drunk,* found especially among the young, can be quite frequently intoxicated and yet not be considered an alcoholic. A certain type of teen-ager who feels browbeaten by his parents, ill-at-ease in dating situations, and generally frustrated in his bid for independence, will often go on periodic binges with his friends. This "masculine" acting-out compensates for the smouldering resentment or deep feeling of inadequacy he has not learned to express in other ways. Such drink- ing may or may not lead to alcoholism. The *heavy drinker* is particu- larly deceptive. He may have several cocktails before lunch, four or five drinks before dinner, and continue to drink on through the night. Drink is obviously important to his life, and he exhibits some of the symptoms mentioned in connection with the alcoholic. But all these drinkers differ from the alcoholic in two respects. 1. There is a decided absence of *progression,* which is inevitable in the alcoholic. These "nonalcoholic" drinkers remain their basic selves for ten, fifteen, or twenty years without significant change. 2. Their drinking need in no way seriously cripple any important aspect of their lives, because—most important—the element of *choice* re- mains. Even though they are heavy drinkers, they are still able to control their drinking if and when they wish. Personal vanity, a new job, poor health—any number of things can pressure them to bring their drinking to a halt or persuade them to cut down drastically. We do not suggest, incidentally, that because such drinkers are not alcoholics their state is a healthy one. In many cases, drinking does affect their physical health—often more noticeably than that of the alcoholic. Drinking can also impair one's career and interfere with the efficiency of one's work. But such drinking is still not alcoholism.

Anyone who has any doubts about whether he might or might not be an alcoholic should make every effort to find out. Marty Mann suggests one fairly simple and effective test which the puzzled drinker can use:

For the next six months *at least* decide that you will stick to a certain number of drinks a day, that number to be not less than one and not more than three. If you are not a daily drinker, then the test should be the stated number of drinks, from one to three, on those days when you do drink. Some heavy drinkers confine their drinking to weekends, but still worry about the amount they consume then. Whatever number you choose must not be exceeded under any circumstances whatever, and this includes weddings, births, funerals, occasions of sudden death and disaster, unexpected or long-awaited inheritance, promotion, or other happy events, reunions or meetings with old friends or customers, or just sheer boredom. There must also be no special occasions on which you feel justified in adding to your quota of the stated number of drinks, such as a severe emotional upset, or the appointment to close the biggest deal of your career, or the audition you have been waiting for all of your life, or the meeting with someone who is crucial to your future and of whom you are terrified. Absolutely no exceptions, or the test has been failed.

Try your control against your drinking. If you are not an alcoholic, you are bound to win. Many people do this for the assurance it gives them that they are safe to continue enjoying a drink when they want one. Don't make the mistake of testing yourself by "going on the wagon." That is no test, because even the most advanced alcoholic can do that for quite a considerable time. The test, to have any real validity, must be of controlled drinking, since alcoholism is identified by drinking which has gone out of control.

This is a simple test which has been used hundreds of times. . . . Even an extremely heavy drinker should have no trouble passing it, whereas an alcoholic, if able to complete it at all, can do so only under such heavy pressure that his life would be more miserable than he thinks it would be if he stopped drinking altogether. The chances are 100 to 1,

however, against a true alcoholic's being either willing or able to undertake the test.[4]

Having read the foregoing summary of the traditional symptoms
and the traditional tests, the uninformed reader might suppose that
it is an easy thing to determine who is and who is not an alcoholic.
Be assured that this is not so. The distinction between the alcoholic
and the heavy drinker is often an especially difficult one to make.
Nevertheless, an informed and an observant person can often tell the
difference.

[Alcoholism] is noticeable, for instance, if someone almost always
continues to drunkenness when drinking. It is even noticeable if one
drinker in the crowd consistently finishes his drink well ahead of the
others, gradually drawing ahead in consumption. It is noticeable if
a drinker is continually "going on the wagon" for short periods, or constantly talking about "going on the wagon" at a future date which never
seems to arrive. It is noticeable if a drinker displays marked Jekyll and
Hyde characteristics while drinking, such as a normally quiet and reserved person who becomes loud, argumentative, belligerent or violent,
only when drinking . . . or the converse, where a usually alert and intelligent person becomes morose and silent or appears to be in a walking
coma. In short, drinking behavior provides the most obvious signs to an
informed onlooker who does not live with the alcoholic.[5]

WHAT MAKES AN ALCOHOLIC?

Why do some people become alcoholics while others do not? The
answer to this question could take up the bulk of this chapter's space,
and indeed, might fill many a volume. The experts feel that in addition to some sort of biological intolerance to alcohol, the alcoholic
suffers from a personality disorder most likely rooted in early
childhood experiences.

Denis McGenty, former Director of Professional Education for
the National Council of Alcoholism in New York City, writes:

Recent careful researches reveal two important points; that early in
life, especially during preadolescence, oftentimes parent-child relation-

ships created the seed-bed for alcoholism; that recurrent family relationships tend to trigger and retrigger the need to drink compulsively. One study, not unlike others in the same field, shows that at least 91% of the 109 male alcoholics analyzed had a history of parental rejection, over-protection, or loss before the age of 15. This would seem to indicate that pathological parental attitudes and parental loss are important in the resort to alcoholism in a majority of alcoholics. Children are dependent on parents not only for physical needs, but even more importantly, for emotional security. Through uncritical identification with strong, loving, affectionate parents, they acquire a healthy self-image and anticipation of acceptance and belonging necessary for basic security and adequacy in the extra-familial world that makes alcoholism unnecessary.

You will find four characteristics common to alcoholics: (1) egocentricity, a person extremely self-centered; (2) inability to face external pressures (in sociology, called low tolerance for tension); (3) overdependence; and (4) paradoxically, a sense of omnipotence. It is my opinion, after over 10 years of close observation and after examining innumerable case histories and holding interviews, that to the alcoholic, as he views it from the inside, all four of these traits are compensation mechanisms for a deep, underlying sense of inadequacy.

Let us trace what happens in an alcoholic, and view life as he does from the *inside*. First of all, in most cases, he has had some abnormal parent-child relationship. This marks him with a deep, persistent sense of being rejected so that ever after he is painfully insecure. This insecurity affects his behavior. He becomes egocentric, with everything revolving about himself. To protect his frail ego against what he considers outside threats, he develops a belligerent exterior as a defense mechanism.

To illustrate this attitude in another illustration, suppose a person with sore toes is in a crowd. His whole attention is focused on protecting the sore toe from being stepped on. To do this he may elbow and push others rudely, things he probably would not do if it were not for the sore toe. The insecurity developed early in life makes him dependent upon others repeatedly as he confronts the realities of life. This increases his initial sense of worthlessness. He feels rejected. He expects to be rejected. He feels he should be rejected. A "selective" sensitivity seeks out rejection where it occurs, anticipates and interprets rejection where none is offered. It makes him distrust, even blinds him to, evidence of acceptance. Like an infant, he tries desperately, time and again, to walk alone and erect. But his lack of self-confidence, his low level of self-regard, his painful sense of inadequacy trip him up repeatedly into the dependency he has loudly renounced.

His one hope of escape is a never-never land of omnipotence, where insecurity will be no more, and where no one will reject. There will be, at long last, acceptance. There will be love. The alcoholic does not know this is happening to him. He knows only the pain—constant psychic pain—and desperate loneliness. One day, by chance, he discovers alcohol, which in our modern culture and society is generally accepted. It is a magic elixir, not of intoxication, but to him one of elation. Instantly, tension is relaxed. Gone suddenly is nagging insecurity.

Elation brings an immediate sense of grandiosity, of omnipotence. No more dependence. The mouse becomes a giant, a demi-god striding the universe. It is my firm conviction that, to the alcoholic, alcoholism is the solution to his problem *before* it is the cause. Not only conscience, but his unconscious psychic pain as well, is soluble in alcohol. From the inside out, his drinking makes sense. It is a defense against subterranean pain.[6]

Raymond G. McCarthy of the Yale Center of Alcoholic Studies writes in a similar vein:

From the time you were an infant, your parents and relatives showed you in many ways how they felt about you. Their affection and love were freely given. These two valuable items played an important part in your life. Because you felt they loved you, you were able to return their affection. You developed warm feelings for other people, too.

Unfortunately, not all children get the right measure and balance of praise, attention, and affection. Some do not get enough. Some get an overdose. Some get love and criticism in mixed-up doses. When any of these things happen, though it may be no fault of their parents, children may get the feeling, "I'm not nice," or "I'm not as handsome, pretty, or clever as the other kids."

These feelings may not have any basis in fact. But if a child *feels* this way, if he feels *insecure* about his own relations to himself and to others, he may carry these feelings over into adult life. He may be severely handicapped when he needs to make decisions and to assume the responsibilities of a job, or of caring for a home and children.

The immature person finds the chemical effects of alcohol on the nervous system particularly appealing. Usually, the greater the immaturity, the greater the appeal.

I'm not a worthwhile person. No one thinks of me. These are the feelings of the insecure person. And he finds them intolerable to live with. He feels he can't go on day after day thinking he's no good. So he unconsciously looks for some way of escaping these feelings. He may daydream excessively, imagining himself a general dripping with gold braid, or a great statesman solving all the problems of the world. Or maybe he's just himself, but loved and admired by everyone. This is one way in which he may escape from problems. He may find other means of escape. He might become a tyrant who bullies his family or the people who work for him. Or he might spend all his time in the movies.

He might take refuge in excessive drinking. He may discover that he can push his insecure feelings away off into some never-never land if he drinks enough. Alcohol, the sedative, blurs anxieties. In fact, it can make him feel he's admired, heroic, feared—anything he'd like to be. But like any other means of escape, drinking is unsatisfactory because it prevents him from doing anything constructive about his problems. And what's more, it creates new and serious problems.

What about the person who can't make decisions or shoulder responsibilities? If he drinks enough, he can imagine himself a kind of human dynamo, able to solve any problem at the drop of a hat. Or he can just blur all problems in an alcoholic mist where no decisions face him and no responsibilities exist.

Most important for the alcoholic, he can use alcoholism as a magic carpet that carries him back to childhood and infancy when he was cared for and no decisions or responsibilities bothered him. After a few drinks, he may get loud and argumentative, even coarse in speech. You can recognize the small boy boasting that he can lick the world. As he drinks more, he gets into a stupor. He needs to be undressed, put in a safe place to sleep—like a child tucked in by Mother. Finally he passes out—back to helpless infancy. When he comes to, he drinks again till the liquor gives out. He's the infant who is fed, and sleeps, awakes to pangs of hunger, cries, is fed again, and drops off to sleep again. An alcoholic at this stage needs psychiatric help, professional treatment for his personality problems.

Alcohol is just one of many possible roads of escape. The same person might have worried so constantly about illness or the fear of it—in other words become a hypochondriac—that he couldn't think about real problems. Or he might have escaped into a routine job, free from all competition and responsibility. Or he might have tried to forget everything by constant reading of romances, mysteries, thrillers. Again, finding escape means ignoring the real problems and their solutions.

Alcohol can help reserved or shy people by eating away all the walls of reserve they have built up between themselves and others. An ill-at-ease party-goer may find it easier to talk, joke, and get along with others when he's had a few drinks. But the person who feels completely out in the cold when he's with other people may use the alcohol as the *only* means of feeling close to them. It may work temporarily, but not in the long run, for alcohol or any other chemical cannot build lasting, warm attachments between people.

. . . The individual who consistently drinks to cover up or escape from his problems is running the risk of becoming an alcoholic. By relieving his tensions through drinking, he is overlooking opportunities to solve his problems in a more satisfying and permanent way.[7]

What can be done about the alcoholic? How can he be helped? Unfortunately, the alcoholic is often subjected to the very worst kinds of approaches in an environment which is itself so often the cause of part of his problem—his home and family. Because of ignorance, family members often speak and act in ways which are bound to increase the guilt and hostility of the alcoholic. Alcoholics call this approach the "home treatment." It begins with the mistaken conviction shared by both the alcoholic and his family that all he needs is a strengthening of his *will power*. The arguments begin in tones of sweet reasonableness. "Friendly discussions" repeated over and over again become repetitious and nagging interferences, which will often be used by the alcoholic as an excuse to drink, and will produce no results except impatient promises made largely to silence the argumentative party.

Then come emotional appeals. "If you love me, why do you drink?" "How can you do this to your children?" Such highly charged appeals, often linked to morality "lectures" of various kinds, create additional shame and guilt in the alcoholic, thus increasing his need for drink. Often wheedling, coaxing, and promises ("If you'll stop drinking, I'll do such and such") produce temporary success, but end in even more severe failure. Next, the more direct approach is tried. The family seems to forget to reorder liquor; bottles are hidden, locked up, or poured down the sink. This merely encourages the alcoholic to procure his own supply. Make no mistake about it, the alcoholic will always get liquor when he wants it, and the more devious his family becomes, the more devious will be his approach to drinking.

The final indignity comes when money is withheld from him, and friends of the family are asked to help. He is publicly embarrassed by verbal references to his problem. Obvious attempts to provide him with nonalcoholic beverages at public gatherings when others are drinking alcohol can be especially painful experiences. Marty Mann quotes one alcoholic, a filling-station attendant with five children: "I knew something was wrong and it worried me, but my wife went on at me so that I had to defend myself. I really loved her and the kids, and I knew I wasn't bad, but what she said made me sound that way, and she nagged about it till I thought I'd go nuts. I had to drink to get away from it. Then when she began hiding my liquor and counting out pennies to me from my own paycheck, I really got sore. I know now she was trying to help me, but it sure didn't look like it to me then—it just made me worse."[8]

HELPING THE ALCOHOLIC

What, then, is the answer? How can we help the alcoholic to rehabilitate himself? To begin with, there must be a clear understanding on the part of the alcoholic—and equally on the part of those near to him—that his problem is a *disease,* and that it will not be solved by appeals to morality or through the exercise of will power. All concerned *must be convinced* that this disease can be arrested. They must see that the social and mental climate in which the alcoholic lives is all-important to his recovery. There are two key periods, especially, when the alcoholic needs all the understanding and kindness that can be given him, namely that time when alcoholism is first beginning to show, and then when he is making initial efforts to recover.

The alcoholic, above all, needs *knowledge.* He must be informed as to the precise nature of his difficulty. Enlightenment will lead to the conviction that he is suffering from a disease as real and as crippling as cancer, tuberculosis, or any other serious ailment. He must come to realize that the one thing he *cannot* do is drink, but that in every other respect he can hope to achieve a happy and fruitful life.

The alcoholic needs the sympathetic understanding of people who are important to him. He must not be ridiculed by others who consider the ability to consume alcohol a sign of virility and strength. Nor must he be regarded with skepticism—"Once a drunk, always a drunk" is a slogan all too readily accepted by an uninformed populace.

Finally, the alcoholic must have help. Supporting hands from the outside must buoy him up; experienced and understanding people must help him to regain his self-confidence and his self-esteem. He must find hope; he must be led to achieve success.

It is important at the outset that the alcoholic, or a member of his family, contact one of the many *Alcoholism Information and Consultation Centers* found in the principal cities and counties of the United States. These centers give free service to alcoholics, their families, friends and employers. They initiate treatment and are responsible for the beginning of recovery. They do educational work as well, to help change community attitudes toward alcoholism. *Alcoholics Anonymous* is listed in every phone book and will provide expert and immediate help to anyone who sincerely wishes to do something about his drinking problem. This organization has been the single most effective gateway through which the alcoholic has found rehabilitation. At this moment there are 200,000 alcoholics living happy and useful lives who have learned through Alcoholics Anonymous that they do not need to drink. The *Alanon Family Group*, an adjunct of Alcoholics Anonymous, is an organization which helps family members of alcoholics who do not have the problem themselves to understand their role in the rehabilitation of their loved ones. Frequently, *medical help* is most desirable, and at times absolutely necessary. *Psychiatric help, counselling,* and *group therapy* have proved most effective in the period following the acute stage during which the patient makes the initial attempt to reorganize his life through self-understanding.

What are the steps of treatment? In the acute phase, alcoholism must be seen primarily as a medical problem. A competent physician should be called at any crisis. With the help of the new tranquillizing drugs, and perhaps a few days of hospitalization, the patient is withdrawn from his overdose of liquor. This is often a dangerous time, and the physical illness of the alcoholic should not be minimized by family members or any other persons to whom he comes for help. The first objective during the acute phase is to get alcohol out of the patient's system as soon as possible and make him feel well without it.

It is often during such a crisis that his motivation to do something about the problem can be capitalized on. The hangover period is a particularly good time to make a new start. Frequently, a doctor has more influence than anyone else at this stage. He can help his patient to see that his illness must be approached like any other illness; a diagnosis must be made, remedies prescribed, and a systematic plan for good health devised. Occasionally, the doctor may wish to administer Antabuse, a drug which prevents the individual from drinking—so long as he takes the medicine. It is a kind of "chemical fence" which, of itself, does not arrest alcoholism, but which can, in conjunction with psychotherapy or other kinds of help, support the good intentions of the alcoholic to refrain from future drinking. It is during this acute phase that some individual in whom the alcoholic has confidence can persuade him to try Alcoholics Anonymous or the help of a good counsellor.

Once the alcoholic has been "dried out" after a severe drinking bout, the chronic phase of his illness remains. He must now face his compulsion to drink, and the lack of control he has over his drinking. *No treatment exists which can restore the alcoholic's control so that he may drink normally.* He must understand this with all the conviction of his being. A reorientation of his whole self and of his whole life is the task he must now face. This reconstruction can often take place with the help of religion when spiritual conviction is strong and provides the sort of inner motivation which will help re-examine goals and reorganize behavior. In many cases, however, religious concepts are distorted and misunderstood by the alcoholic. In such cases, other things must come first.

In many cases rehabilitation can best be approached through a medical diagnosis. This keeps the focus of the patient on the *disease* aspects of his problem. "A thorough diagnosis, with a physical, psychiatric, and social 'work-up' is followed by a recommendation of the particular course to be followed. It will probably include physical care such as vitamin shots, and at least a few interviews with the psychiatrist, long-term counselling with one particular member of the team: a social worker, or perhaps a psychologist. It may also include early introduction into group therapy, with this soon becoming the only clinic therapy the patient requires. In most cases, the clinic staff urges the alcoholic to attend AA meetings as soon as he is willing to do so, while still continuing therapy at the clinic."[9]

Psychiatric help is especially important for those who, because of business or other reasons, are reluctant to seek the more open resources of Alcoholics Anonymous. Psychiatric help is, of course, a long-term process. All too frequently, we hear people say of the alcoholic, "Oh, yes, he tried psychiatry, and it didn't do him one bit of good." In so many cases, psychotherapy was not given a chance. Often, the individual had merely one or two diagnostic interviews with the psychiatrist, which in no sense can be called therapy. Psychotherapy is essentially a talking-out process by which the individual comes to understand himself and his behavior more clearly. This takes time.

Psychoanalysts are somewhat reluctant to accept alcoholic patients unless they have been sober for a considerable time. Free association, an essential part of this treatment, cannot work effectively in a mind clouded by intoxication. Furthermore, the deep-probing process of analysis can be extremely unpleasant for the patient. As a result the suffering alcoholic is liable to resort to more drink to deaden his distress. Psychoanalysis, therefore, is used only in extreme cases where the roots of the problem are deeply buried in the unconscious.

Group therapy can be most effective. Under the passive direction of a trained therapist, a group of alcoholics exchange information and feelings about their problem and, in the process, help each other to see the underlying causes of their difficulty.*

A special further word must here be said about the organization known as Alcoholics Anonymous, the single most effective tool which alcoholics have used to help themselves. Alcoholics Anonymous is a "loosely knit, voluntary fellowship of alcoholics (and of alcoholics only) gathered together for the sole purpose of helping themselves and each other to get sober and to stay sober."[10] It has no official connection with any other organization. It espouses no causes, and does not proselytize in any way. Members wait until the alcoholic himself asks for help. Once such a plea has been made "AA members willingly perform all the functions so often asked of them in vain on behalf of an unwilling alcoholic: playing detective, doctor, nurse, policeman, and constant companion; giving understanding and sympathetic help at all hours of the day or night; helping out with family problems; sometimes even taking the alcoholic in to live with him."[11]

The first and vital step must be the willingness of the alcoholic to seek help. Once he has made his first contact with AA, he finds that he dares to hope. He sees with his own eyes that others have recovered. He mixes with alcoholics who are not drinking and who are apparently *enjoying* their sobriety. Gradually he begins to understand the nature of his problem. He comes to think of alcoholism as an obsession of the mind coupled with a kind of "allergy" of the body. Most likely, he will have a sponsor, a member of AA who will be his friend, answer his questions, help him to understand himself, and, if necessary, get medical aid for him. He will learn to live on the

* The alcoholic and members of his family should be cautioned to make a careful investigation before they use the facilities of a hospital, sanitarium, or convalescent home for alcoholics. There are many excellent institutions of this kind, but there are others that are indifferent or just plain "racket joints." None of these institutions provide cures for alcoholism. They sometimes afford the patient and the doctor a certain type of environment conducive to the early rehabilitative measures which must be taken. In the vast majority of cases, however, the road back is a slow and time-consuming process, a large part of which must be carried out in the day-to-day environment in which the person lives.

"twenty-four-hour plan," making promises to no one, but simply trying to live for twenty-four hours without a drink, one day at a time. Then his sponsor will take him to an open meeting where he will hear other alcoholics describe their own experiences with drink and rehabilitation. He will be given telephone numbers of other alcoholics who will invite him to their homes, to meals and social gatherings. He will be attending closed meetings, barred to all but alcoholics. The attendance at such a meeting marks a milestone, namely, his open admission that he is an alcoholic.

Gradually he comes to see the meaning of the twelve steps,* the foundation of the Alcoholics Anonymous program. Very often the spiritual aspects of the twelve steps are developed last in the alcoholic's process of rehabilitation. The religious character of so large a part of the Alcoholics Anonymous program is an in-

* The suggested steps are as follows: 2-13-65

1. We admitted that we were powerless over alcohol—that our lives had become unmanageable.

2. Came to believe that a Power greater than ourselves could restore us to sanity.

3. Made a decision to turn our will and our lives over to the care of God *as we understood Him.*

4. Made a searching and fearless moral inventory of ourselves.

5. Admitted to God, to ourselves, and to another human being the exact nature of our wrongs.

6. Were entirely ready to have God remove all these defects of character.

7. Humbly asked Him to remove our shortcomings.

8. Made a list of all persons we had harmed and became willing to make amends to them all.

9. Made direct amends to such people wherever possible, except when to do so would injure them or others.

10. Continued to take personal inventory, and when we were wrong, promptly admitted it.

11. Sought through prayer and meditation to improve our conscious contact with God *as we understood Him,* praying only for knowledge of His will for us and the power to carry that out.

12. Having had a spiritual awakening as a result of these steps, we tried to carry this message to alcoholics and to practice these principles in all our affairs.[12]

triguing phenomenon. And yet, knowing what we do of distorted childhood attitudes towards authority figures, this emphasis makes sense. "Where he knows God at all, the alcoholic selects only certain attributes of God on which he dwells to the exclusion of their opposites. Based on his parent-conditioned insecurity, low self-regard, and intense guilt feelings, he sees God as all-powerful, all-knowing, all-just. Since His justice is supreme, therefore He will punish evil, reject the unworthy, and therefore reject him. This unconscious neurotic selectivity completely excludes an awareness of the opposite attributes of God as all-loving, all-merciful, all-forgiving, imminently helpful. Is it because a balanced understanding of God is restored through this program of personal conversion or 'spiritual awakening' that Alcoholics Anonymous is so effective in the recovery of alcoholics? One authority, Dr. H. M. Tiebout, believes the force of religion in an atmosphere of hope and encouragement in the AA program produces a profound change in the typically egocentric, alcoholic personality, dominated by defiant individuality and drives for omnipotence. The negative characteristics of aggression, hostility, and isolation are replaced by peace and calm and a lessening of inner tension."[13]

This spiritual rehabilitation must, however, take place in an Alcoholics Anonymous setting, or one very similar to it. We cannot be certain just how the psychology of this procedure works. But we can venture an opinion. The basic spirit of the AA fraternity is one of love. Even the visitor immediately senses the electric compassion and mutual acceptance which forms so large a part of the AA atmosphere. The members enjoy each other, entertain each other, listen sympathetically and with understanding to each other. They support each other; in short, they love each other. The absence of convinced love and acceptance is one of the chief characteristics of the alcoholic personality. Now, for the first time in his life the alcoholic is able to grasp something of what it means to be loved and accepted. For the first time, perhaps, he is able to imagine that God, too, can be a God of charity and mercy. He begins to ap‑ preciate these attributes of God because he is experiencing them at work in His children. Very likely the alcoholic has never been able to think of God in this way because he has never been able to think of his fellow man in terms of friendship, charity, and genuine kindness. The words of St. John were never more true: "If a man love not his brother whom he sees, how can he love God whom he sees not?" (1 John, 4:20). Thus the alcoholic, bereft of love as a child and as an adult, feels himself loved and accepted by the brethren around him, and learns to return such love. Through this process he finds his way to the Author of all love, God Himself, and this new relationship provides him with the additional stimulus to plan and hope anew and to fulfill his resolution to avoid the drink he knows he cannot take.

Finally, Alcoholics Anonymous not only provides individual help, insight and support, it also creates a whole new social milieu in which the alcoholic can move without self-consciousness. In AA he can find the most satisfying kinds of social gratification in the company of all sorts of personalities, professions, and avocations sharing one common characteristic—a conviction that drink is not for them. The unique character of this organization is the reason, perhaps, for the conservative estimate that considerably more than fifty percent of those who have tried AA have recovered—an incredibly high record, considering that alcoholism was regarded until very recently as a hopeless affliction.

THE PRIEST AND THE ALCOHOLIC

What is the role of the priest in the counselling of the alcoholic? It is not unusual for an alcoholic, or the wife, husband, children, or employer of an alcoholic, to seek advice from a priest. Generally speaking, it is wise to counsel the family member who comes, rather than to interfere at once with the alcoholic who has not asked for help himself. Confession, however, often provides an excellent opportunity to confront the penitent alcoholic with some motivation to change. The confessional is often the only place where the alcoholic admits to himself and his God that he has a problem; at these times it is up to the priest to take the initiative in such a way that he does not discourage the alcoholic from returning. Often the suggestion that he come to the parlor for a more leisurely discussion of his difficulty is a first step to further help.

The priest should not attempt to counsel an alcoholic unless he feels reasonably secure in his understanding of the problem. His first duty, therefore, is to inform himself as early as he can about the causes and remedies of alcoholism. He should be in contact with the local Alcoholics Anonymous organization, and, if possible, he should attend a number of their meetings. He will learn more about alcoholics and alcoholism at AA or at an Alanon family group meeting than anywhere else.

Once the priest has properly informed himself, he must work toward building deep and genuine attitudes about alcoholism and the alcoholic. The priest himself must become strongly convinced that alcoholism is to be approached and treated as a disease. It is precisely because he is a priest that such convictions must be carefully cultivated, for his chief role in the counselling of the alcoholic is to minimize the guilt and shame associated with the problem. The greatest harm the priest can do is to lose the concept of alcoholism as a disease and to tell the alcoholic that his trouble is merely a matter of will power, or a fall from grace.*

The priest can show the alcoholic that he need be no more ashamed of his illness than other individuals who have cancer, tuberculosis, or diabetes. The priest can suggest that the alcoholic should feel guilty only when he is unwilling to do something about his illness. The priest, at all costs, should avoid lecturing and preaching, which are "exactly equivalent to rubbing coarse salt into a gaping wound. They are truly unbearable, and violent reactions simply must result. The alcoholic will do and promise anything at all to stop such suffering, but usually the quickest way he knows to stop it is to seek oblivion in drunkenness."[14] A holier-than-thou

* The traditional phrase, "You are an alcoholic," often sounds like an accusation. A more helpful phrase might be, "You *have* alcoholism," suggesting that the person has not sought this condition, but is its victim. Such a phrase often establishes a more promising climate between the priest and the alcoholic.

attitude on the part of the priest will merely confirm in the mind of the alcoholic the conviction that the priest, along with everybody else, does not understand him and therefore will not be able to help him.

Finally, the priest, along with other authority figures, should be careful not to threaten the alcoholic. It can be fatal to suggest that, if drinking continues, the alcoholic will suffer terrible physical anguish and great moral damage. There is a kind of self-punishing drive within many alcoholics which warnings and threats merely propel to fulfillment. The attempt to frighten an alcoholic into sobriety has often precipitated suicidal, compulsive drinking, symbolizing an unconscious desire to "end it all."

Father Joseph Mangan, S.J., touches the heart of the priest-penitent relationship with these words:

> The priest should look on the alcoholic as a physically, mentally and spiritually sick man. He comes to us to be helped in his spiritual sickness. We must be willing to spend time with him. While with him, we must be careful not to persuade, not to push, not to nag, not to plead, not to pity, but to give understanding. We must make it clear to him, not so much by words as by the way we treat him, that he is welcome and that we are interested in him. We must point out the purpose of his life. For him we cannot overemphasize the mercy of God. The alcoholic is struggling with a sense of worthlessness, rejection, lonesomeness, shame, and confusion. A deep realization of the mercy of God can be of tremendous help in counteracting these depressing thoughts.
>
> The priest can help remove the alcoholic's objective sense of guilt, relieve him of his sense of guilt, and help him prepare to make amends for the past failures. But in the final analysis, the measure of our personal success with him will be proportionate to the sympathy, understanding, kindness, and love that we put into our work.
>
> The priest should consider himself a part of a coöperative team working to help the alcoholic understand himself and achieve sobriety. The immediate therapeutic goal of every member of the team is the same: to help this individual not to take the *first* drink—ever! The priest who understands a little about alcoholism and a lot about the need of the alcoholic for sympathetic help can offer important assistance in the achievement of this goal.[15]

Priests ask many questions about what they should and should not say and do in dealing with an alcoholic. We will attempt to outline brief answers to these questions. The beginner, however, should be cautioned not to undertake extensive counselling of alcoholics without much more reading and contact with Alcoholics Anonymous personnel.

To begin with, both priest and alcoholic must be prepared to spend *time* in reaching worthwhile solutions. Each alcoholic's problem must be defined a bit differently. Progress is not possible until there is considerable understanding of the problem on the part of both the priest and the alcoholic. In the beginning, the priest should have just a few specific goals. He must, of course, do all in his power to persuade the alcoholic that he suffers from a *disease*. He must stress with optimism and conviction the very real possibility that this disease is arrestable, that this sick man can become well. He must minimize, as much as he is able, the excessive guilt and shame which the alcoholic has undoubtedly long associated with his problem. He must try as early as possible to introduce the alcoholic to a local Alcoholics Anonymous organization or its equivalent.

What should the priest avoid? Especially at the beginning, the priest should not debate the defenses which the alcoholic presents to the world. These explanations may sound like lies to the priest, but to the alcoholic they are rationalizations which have assumed some validity in his own confused mind. These rationalizations, resentments, and feelings of self-pity should be accepted with good grace. The only responsibility which can be made a matter of morality is the effort which the alcoholic is making to get the kind of help which the priest suggests is available to him. In other words, the alcoholic should gradually become aware of his responsibility to get proper treatment for himself.

The priest who is working with an alcoholic should concern himself with one thing at a time. Consequently, he should avoid extended discussion of other religious and moral responsibilities. "Easy does it" is one of the unofficial slogans of Alcoholics Anonymous. The patient's inability to deal with his drinking should, for the moment, be his chief and even exclusive concern. Many alcoholics have other problems. Sexual difficulties especially are often intensified when the alcoholic is not drinking. The alcoholic often drinks because he is convinced that sex is his real problem and he is unable to cope with it. In many cases, this is not so. Minimizing the sexual difficulties, refusing to deal with them in any detail, will often help to convince the alcoholic that his first problem is drink. When a priest declines to probe into sexual difficulties and avoids moralizing and insisting on responsibility, the alcoholic will gain more confidence to deal with his primary problem, and the first step toward self-understanding will be made.

The priest should also carefully avoid stressing religious obligations, for the time being. Occasionally an alcoholic stays away from drink by applying himself in almost superhuman fashion to the duties and pious observances of his faith, clinging to the sacraments with an almost desperate dependency and without any real insight into the compulsion he is fighting. This religious formalization is precisely the kind of blind commitment which the alcoholic eventually rejects. It produces a sort of rigid and fanatic sobriety which most priests have seen in some non-drinkers and which often ends with an emotional breakdown or a return to the bottle. The priest should urge the alcoholic to wait until he is ready before he returns to the regular practice of his faith. Some alcoholics should be dissuaded from confessing right away. "When you are really ready to go to confession, you will know" is a phrase which often relieves the confused penitent and opens another door towards self-determination.

While the priest should always show great kindness, patience, and forbearance with the alcoholic, he must also keep in mind the limitations of his role. The priest-counsellor can be used and "taken in" by the alcoholic. The alcoholic is a born "con man," and it is important for the priest to understand the ways in which he can rationalize and manipulate. Consequently, the priest should avoid becoming entangled in the network of personal problems in which the alcoholic can involve him. It is the priest's role to give assistance toward sobriety, not to become an intercessor with a wife or an employer or involved with the endless new problems which develop with each drinking spree. The alcoholic, precisely because he is ill, often becomes a master at involving others in his day-to-day affairs. The priest can find himself a sort of errand boy, expected to listen for hours to repetitious material, and asked to arrange countless details in the constantly developing and changing life problems of his client.

By and large, it is not wise to deal with the alcoholic while he is drunk. He should not be berated or condemned, but encouraged to come back when he is sober. It is difficult, sometimes, to decide how long the priest should continue to see an alcoholic when no progress is being made. If the alcoholic is making no effort to join Alcoholics Anonymous, and seeks no help in other professional areas, the priest may hinder him by "carrying him along" in useless, though sympathetic, discussion. There are times when the priest may have to say, "Unless you get the kind of help you need, I believe that continuing our present discussions is unfair to you and to me." This will occasionally bring to a head the decision to seek help from Alcoholics Anonymous or from a similar referral source.

Suggestions of the priest, like those of the doctor, can often exert a tremendous influence. He must, therefore, be careful to make the right suggestions. If an alcoholic comes to him during an acute attack, he may have to make preliminary medical arrangements for hospitalization. If possible, he should encourage the family to do this themselves. The priest must remember that he is not a doctor, and should never recommend specific medication of any kind. Furthermore, he should be careful not to encourage psychiatric treatment too soon. So many alcoholics are propelled into psychiatric treatment for which they are not ready, find it unsuccessful, and end up more discouraged because it fails.

After a good period of sobriety, psychiatric help is often worthwhile. Psychotherapy teaches the patient how to cope with stresses whose origins are in the past. The Alcoholics Anonymous program avoids delving into the origins of tensions and problems; the AA, rather, helps to develop here and now the positive drives and capacities within the individual. Once the alcoholic, as an AA member, has made some progress in approaching current life stresses without panic he can solidify his gains by achieving further insight through psychotherapy.

A word or two should be said about the wife of an alcoholic. More often than not, she has emotional difficulties of her own. Such marriages do not just "happen." In some subtle way, each partner is catering to certain needs of the other, regardless of the pain and hostility which seem to be a part of the marriage. So often, the dependent alcoholic personality marries a wife who needs to have someone dependent upon her. (Her problem is not that she drinks, but that she needs to marry a drunk!) A characteristic of the cure is the development of maturity and independence on the part of the alcoholic. When both husband and wife are immature to begin with, and the alcoholic "grows up" and learns to live without drinking, he often leaves his wife behind. At the end of such a long history of dependency, the wife often finds herself lost and aimless. She no longer has a dependent husband to care for, to complain about, to reinforce her "martyr's complex." She too must be helped to accept the change and grow herself.

It is unwise for the priest to attempt to show the husband or wife of an alcoholic the shortcomings and emotional difficulties which they may suffer from. The priest can, however, encourage the family to develop certain kinds of behavior and attitudes which will assist the rehabilitation of the weak member. The priest can encourage the wife to leave helpful literature around the house describing the true nature of alcoholism. Sometimes he can persuade the wife to seek counselling herself in an effort to understand her husband better. (Sometimes the husband gets "jealous" because his wife is in therapy, and will go and seek it himself.) The priest can tell family members not to fight the alcoholic, not to question and accuse, or make alcoholism a battleground. So often the husband *needs* to be dominated by his wife, *needs* to have the liquor poured down the drain in order to justify his drinking. When these incentives to rebel are removed, the need for drinking is sometimes lessened.

The priest can also encourage the wife and family members to manifest consistent attitudes towards the alcoholic. Threats, recriminations, wheedling, and tears are to no avail if they are not followed through. It is better for the family not to make threats, but merely to act when necessary. It is far better to say nothing beforehand about "taking the children to a motel or to a relative for the night," but to go ahead and do it when the alcoholic is impossible to live with. If all efforts for improvement fail over a six-month period, it is often beneficial to try a non-legal separation for a while. When the alcoholic is face to face with himself and without the supporting attentions and vacillating sympathy of his loved ones, he is often spurred to seek the help he needs.

The priest can persuade the wife and family not to cover up for the alcoholic. The sooner he faces the reality of his situation, whether it is through the loss of his job or the absence of his family, the more liable he is to face the future realistically. Furthermore, the priest can help the family of the alcoholic see that there is no reason to feel ashamed or degraded. If the concept of alcoholism-as-a-disease is constantly stressed, the problem loses its onus. The priest must help the family members to expect that progress will be slow. Alcoholism, like any other serious illness, is not arrested instantly. There will be relapses, and it is precisely during the times when he is trying and failing that the alcoholic needs all the love and understanding that those dear to him can give.

It should be noted here that the words "alcoholic husband" in the preceding pages can often stand for "alcoholic wife" as well. The alcoholic woman often drinks in considerably different fashion from the man. Women alcoholics are very rarely convivial or social drinkers; almost from the first, they drink alone. For this reason it is possible for an alcoholic wife to get away with her drinking for a much longer time without her husband's realizing its extent. Public opinion seems especially hard on the woman alcoholic: "If there is one thing I can't stand, it is to see a *woman* really *drunk*." "The husband of an alcoholic woman must always remember, however, that because of this double standard, this near-universal public opinion, the guilt and fear and shame of an alcoholic wife are tenfold those of an alcoholic husband. So his approach must be even more delicate and reassuring; the stress on the disease nature of alcoholism even stronger; and his sympathetic understanding, his affectionate desire only to be of help, and the steadfastness of his love despite the unpleasant ravages of her disease made ten times more clear."[16]

Finally, the priest can often help the children of an alcoholic to understand that their parent suffers from a serious illness. They are quite capable of understanding this, often at a much earlier age than many people realize (even at three or four years old). The loving sympathy of an understanding child is often the reason why a parent will ultimately seek the help that will lead to recovery.

The priest who counsels the alcoholic, then, must be a man of precise knowledge and infinite patience. He must see his role chiefly as an instructor and confidant who by the communication of facts and the dissipation of myths confronts the alcoholic with the true nature of his condition and gives him hope. It should not be the priest's task to probe deeply into the causes of the alcoholic's problem. He can, however, render significant service by introducing the alcoholic to those social and professional circles which can help him live with his problem in the here and now. The priest can minimize guilt and shame which block true insight; he can help the alcoholic live with the rise and fall of resentment and self-pity so characteristic of his condition; he can console and instruct the family of the alcoholic in an effort to create a sympathetic and tolerant atmosphere so necessary to his rehabilitation; in short, the kind and knowing priest can be a steadfast friend, a reassuring dispenser of mercy, an encouraging prophet of success for the struggling alcoholic who is walking the stony road toward self-knowledge and self-direction.

NOTES

1. New York: Rinehart, 1958.
2. Ibid., p. 66.
3. Ibid., pp. 69–70.
4. Ibid., pp. 82–83.
5. Ibid., p. 95.
6. "How to Understand an Alcoholic," *Information Magazine,* LXXII, No. 12 (1958), pp. 37–38.
7. *Facts about Alcohol* (Chicago: Science Research Associates, 1951), pp. 37–39.

8. Op. cit., p. 108.

9. Ibid., p. 146.

10. Ibid., p. 166.

11. Ibid., p. 168.

12. Ibid., p. 176.

13. McGenty, op. cit., p. 39.

14. Mann, op. cit., p. 204.

15. "Helping the Alcoholic," *The Catholic Mind*, LVI, No. 1136 (1958), pp. 149–150.

7

SCRUPULOSITY

Scrupulosity—the persistent, gnawing, unreasonable conviction that one has offended God or is about to do so—is no respecter of persons. The rich and the poor, the virtuous and weak, the young and the old, the intelligent and dull—all are potential victims. The scrupulous Catholic is a pathetic sufferer, often vexing to his confessor and a problem to himself.

Striking psychological insights of the last two or three decades have had a profound influence upon the current pastoral approach to scrupulosity. Traditional views as to the causes, nature, and treatment of scruples have been closely examined and in many instances found wanting. The new and somewhat revolutionary character of the latest views explains why some priests are still unfamiliar with the revised techniques. Because of these changing tactics, the peripatetic scrupulous penitent is often bewildered by the varied and often contradictory directives he receives from the numerous confessors he is aimlessly consulting.

There is little question in the light of modern psychological findings that many of the traditional concepts about scrupulosity are inadequate. This does not mean, however, that current scholarship has provided all the answers. Far from it. There are at least several schools of experts who explain similar phenomena in quite different ways. We do not propose to delve deeply into the controversies. We will try to explain, instead, why some of the old concepts and methods are not effective, and to highlight those new causative factors and counselling methods which seem accepted by all, or nearly all, who have studied them.

THE NATURE OF SCRUPULOSITY

One thing is certain: scruples are not simple, nor are they easily dispelled. Though the symptoms of two individuals may seem similar, the contributing causes are often quite diverse. There do seem to be some general categories, however, into which scrupulous penitents may be loosely classified.

To begin with, let us recall a distinction which spiritual writers have been making for centuries: a *delicate* conscience is *not* a scrupulous conscience. A delicate conscience is sensitive, without being anxious, to anything which might offend God, no matter how small. A scrupulous person has a persistent and unreasonable fear that he has sinned or is about to sin at every turn. Such a conscience exaggerates sin, or sees sin where there is no sin. A delicate conscience confesses personal failings simply, calmly, directly; the scrupulous conscience confesses in a confused, meandering, doubtful and repetitious sort of way. The delicate conscience is immediately relieved and at peace after absolution; the scrupulous conscience finds in frequent and compulsive confession only temporary relief, or none at all. The delicate conscience evokes a healthy and proportionate sorrow for human failings but remains unanxious and untroubled in its hopeful relationship to Almighty God; the scrupulous conscience is persistently uneasy, fearful, distrusting not only self but the confessor, and even Almighty God. The delicate conscience belongs to a soul striving for sanctity; the scrupulous conscience has nothing to do with spiritual development, but is rather an emotional illness which can be a block to higher spiritual development.

Other distinctions are worth noting. Often *ignorance* can be mistaken for scrupulosity. An individual may be concerned about the observance of a supposed, but actually nonexistent, Church regulation which he in all sincerity believes is binding. Once he is properly instructed as to the true nature of the precept, he ceases to worry and the "scruple" disappears.

Again, certain cultural or national *customs* or local interpretations of moral or religious behavior may, in another setting, take on the appearances of scrupulosity to the uninformed observer. Young people coming to the United States fresh from Ireland or Spain may seem to have some scrupulous attitudes toward American dating and company-keeping. However, boy-girl relationships in Spain and Ireland are taken a good deal more seriously as a general rule, and for this reason immigrants used to a sterner discipline feel a good deal more concern about these matters. This point of view cannot be called true scrupulosity.

There are mental mechanisms which bear some of the earmarks of the problem we are discussing, yet certainly do not fall into the category of true scrupulosity. There seem to be *key times* and events in most people's lives which can raise temporary anxiety and exaggerated fears. One might call these constitutional or vocational tension spots. Often the early adolescent who becomes aware of his newly developing sexual powers will go through a period of intensified anxiety. Vital decisions may bring on a sudden case of scruples. Thus a deacon before ordination, a nun about to take her final vows, a groom just before his marriage, a patient deciding on a dangerous operation, may all have a momentary and sometimes panicky concern about the wisdom of their choice. (Such events may, of course, trigger off an attack in the *truly* scrupulous person too.)

Other critical periods of life, in addition to adolescent, religious, or vocational crises, can bring on seizures of scrupulosity. The unpredictable conflicts during the menopause; a revived and vivid memory of past sins in old people; the disconcerting worries which prolonged illness or pain may produce in otherwise cheerful and placid people; overwhelming self-blame at the death of a loved one—these are examples of acute anxieties which sometimes spontaneously occur, last only for a time, then gradually melt away in the lives of many. They cannot be classed with the deeper and more persistent distress of the truly scrupulous person.

There are also certain minor patterns of anxiety observable at some time or other in most of us. The reader, for example, may find himself unduly concerned about certain of his failings and weaknesses rather than others, with no apparent objective reason for his sensitivity. One prime example of such a "blind spot" is the almost compulsive necessity which drives so many lay Catholics to make a point of confessing that they "missed Mass" even though they were so ill that they were certainly excused. (*"I feel better* when I tell it, Father."*) Although such compulsive confessing has some of the earmarks of true scrupulosity, yet most confessors and penitents see the clear distinction between a slightly superstitious soothing of hidden anxieties and genuine pathological scrupulosity.

What, then, are the characteristics of severe scrupulosity properly so called? First, we must distinguish some basic variations.

Some individuals are consistently apprehensive that they are about to commit sin even though they rarely, if ever, fall grievously. Such people either focus their attention on one particular phobia, or are victims of a sort of "free-floating" anxiety. The latter see sin lurking around every corner. They feel perpetually involved with potentially sinful persons, places, and situations. They constantly confront themselves with supposed moral decisions which they are unable to solve with calm assurance. Says Father Noël Mailloux:

> Thus, for example, an adolescent enters the school only at the ringing of the bell for fear of hearing "dirty jokes" in the schoolyard; he is afraid of going to communion . . . because a tiny piece of food from the evening snack might have remained between his teeth he had forgotten to brush before bedtime. The young lady hesitates to wear some nice, although perfectly modest dress, because she might appear too attractive and arouse sensual desires in men; she is also upset by the idea of leaving town on the week-end with her husband because her neighbor friend might be unable to get a baby sitter and would find it impossible to attend Mass on Sunday morning. An older man is scared to accept his promotion to a well-paid supervisor's position, because he would be then responsible for checking all the sales bills and might do some injustice to clients through occasional error.[1]

There are other scrupulous sufferers who feel that they are actually and constantly sinning, that almost everything they do has a sinful quality about it. Such persons seem to be saturated with guilt. They are quick to label indifferent actions as sinful, prone to see venial sins as mortal sins. They worry about past confessed sins which their memories are forever dredging up. They are fearful that the description of the circumstances and characteristics of their sinning has not been accurately communicated to the priest and that therefore their confessions are invalid. They receive no solace from absolution, but carry away a gnawing suspicion that they have not really received forgiveness. They are certain that the confessor "doesn't understand" if he attempts to minimize their guilt by pooh-poohing their fear that they will forget to tell everything or their need to repeat the same sins over and over again. This type of scrupulous person perpetually mistrusts himself and cannot be re-assured by anyone; he clings obstinately to but one conviction—the reality of his own sinfulness. The self-punishing needs of this type make confession a wearisome ordeal for the confessor and a tortuous ritual for the penitent.

The two afore-mentioned classes of scrupulosity are the more prevalent types. There are, however, other subtle and complicated varieties which are more difficult to understand and much harder to cure. There is the suspicious type who comes ostensibly for advice, but who eventually turns on the priest, often with considerable hostility, with the charge that he has misunderstood and misinterpreted the whole case, has violated confidences and given fresh reasons for keeping on guard. Such people are often the product of inconsistent moral and spiritual home-upbringing; their emotions shuffle between stern demands of conscience and deep hostilities toward authority figures, whether these be parents, priest, teacher, the Church, or even God Himself.

A somewhat more common scrupulous type is the individual who is engaged in objective sinful behavior on the one hand, but develops tremendous anxiety about other moral trifles. Thus a father may be quite unconcerned about spending the meagre family finances for alcohol but be disproportionately worried about his habits of profanity. A woman may be a vicious shrew or a danger-

ous character assassin who will at the same time never miss daily
Mass, and is unduly disturbed by distractions in her prayers.

These latter cases are particularly difficult to deal with, because
of the frequent impossibility of discovering the causes and nature
of the aberration. There can, for example, be influences at work
which are at one and the same time characteristic of the lax conscience, the erroneous conscience, and the classically scrupulous
conscience. To unravel all these biases and embark on a program of
re-education can be a complex and often frustrating undertaking.

THE SOURCES OF SCRUPULOSITY

Let us now examine some of the factors which seem to contribute
to the development of the scrupulous personality. Many ascetical
theologians have blamed misleading and distorted spiritual books
and over-rigorous religious instruction as contributing factors to
the development of scrupulosity in the growing child. It is difficult
to assess the degree of influence which exposure to such teachings
might have. While much harm has certainly been done, it is obvious
that many other individuals exposed to such inhibiting influences
have still developed normal and adjusted spiritual lives.

Some writers on the subject have noticed that the scrupulous
person often suffers from a rundown physical condition or a
debilitated nervous system. Others have pointed out that scrupulosity is often accompanied by fanatical introspection; it is a malady
frequently suffered by those who are alone too much, or who are
unable to lead healthy social lives. There are evidences, however,
which indicate that physical and nervous impairments, as well as
introspective, withdrawn characteristics are *results* rather than
causes of the scrupulous personality.

Finally, scrupulosity has been attributed by some spiritual
writers to the influence of the devil. While we can by no means rule
out diabolic interference in a soul's bid for sanctity, we must be careful not to jump too quickly to the conclusion that it is in many, or
even most, cases the devil who must be dealt with. The sound theo-

logical principle that supernatural causes must not be applied to a phenomenon which natural causes can explain is very apropos here. (More than one confessor has discovered to his dismay that the supposedly reassuring comment to the scrupulous person: "Pay no attention to these doubts; it is only the devil tempting you" only produces an additional worry. The poor soul is now convinced that he is possessed!)

How, then, do we explain the development of the scrupulous personality? Let us begin by stressing the hypothetical nature of much of what follows. The great majority of clerical and lay psychologists today agree that the problem of scrupulosity is not nearly as simple or as rational a phenomenon as earlier theorists seemed to indicate. Today's experts, however, are by no means agreed on every aspect of the problem. Father Noël Mailloux, the Dominican psychologist quoted earlier in this chapter, has made the following comments which seem pertinent to this discussion:

. . . the phenomenon of scrupulosity has a much wider scope and requires a much more elaborate interpretation than is generally supposed in contemporary studies. . . . It is only when we have more precise information . . . which has not yet been systematically submitted to empirical investigation that a decisive step will be made to a full understanding of scrupulosity as a symptom *sui generis,* not merely affecting but actually involving the moral and religious life of the individual. Of this we must be keenly aware as theologians and as spiritual directors. If we intend to adequately fulfill our responsibility towards those who, quite involuntarily, are meeting almost insuperable obstacles on the way toward salvation, we will not hesitate to start gathering observational data until the most intolerable secret sufferings of the human conscience are thoroughly understood and effective means have been found to relieve them.[2]

Having stressed the tentative nature of our speculation, let us now sketch those characteristics of the problem which are more or less agreed upon by the experts in the field.

Scrupulosity, in essence, is not an intellectual but an emotional problem. (Most confessors have had personal knowledge of the futility of attempting to talk through the worry of a scrupulous penitent on the basis of logic and reason.) The roots of scrupulosity are buried in the emotional wastelands of unreasonable anxiety and fear. We have seen in earlier chapters that hidden anxieties and engulfing fears do not usually emerge suddenly and inexplicably into adult consciousness. Rather, these emotional threads can be followed, subtle and devious as they might be, back into the individual's past until we arrive at their source in the child's earliest experiences.

More often than not, therefore, many elements of scrupulosity can be explained by examining early childhood development. The theory goes something like this. The two most basic human drives, love and aggression, make early demands within the young infant. These drives have not only a psychic significance, but seem, almost from the first, to have certain physical determinants. As the child grows, these drives become more and more demanding, more and more complex. Imperceptibly, the child becomes aware of the approval or disapproval which his parents show towards his manifestation and management of these drives. Little by little, he incorporates parental attitudes regarding emotional and moral behavior into his own attitudes. Dr. Vincent P. Mahoney has phrased this process succinctly:

As the child develops, he uses his parents' personality to build his own. This process is called identification. It implies both the addition of something to the personality, and a change in behavior as a result of the addition. His adaptation progresses as a result of both his learning through experience, and his use of parental controls. When he refrains from doing something, even though the parents are not present, he has internalized their permissions and prohibitions, so that they are now part of him. A child controls activities he knows will displease the parents because he fears loss of their love and punishment. The part of the personality formed by the parental internalization is called the superego. It is different from that part of the personality called the ego, which perceives, remembers, thinks, and executes in the child. In the young child, the ego is weak and unsure of itself, so that an extra control is needed in the personality. Because of the long period of both physical and psychological dependence of the child on the parent, and the constant incorporation of their attitudes, the superego exerts a strong influence on us as long as we live.

. . . (the young child) doesn't know what he wants clearly, but he feels both love and hate for his parents. . . . He becomes disturbed and frightened by these . . . desires. By now, he has developed a way of handling such anxiety. Instead of loving and hating the parents, who he believes would oppose such wishes, he becomes like his parents in the repudiation of such wishes, and thus further additions are made to the superego. This whole process never becomes conscious, but is reflected in the behavior, verbal communication, and dreams of the child. The severity of the child's superego is derived in part from the parental prohibitions, but also, and more important, from the strength of the child's drives. The stronger the drives of the child, the stronger the superego needed to control them. It is the reaction between the child's drives and the internalized parental controls that determines the force of this part of the personality.

The superego at this stage has two important characteristics. One is the talon law concept of justice, and the second is the lack of discrimination between the wish and the need. The child fears he will get hurt just as much as he wants to hurt in this eye-for-an-eye type of retribution. It is important to realize that this concept persists unconsciously into adult life in the superego. Due to the lack of discrimination, the superego threatens punishment for the wish, nearly as severely as for the need. A child between four and five distinguishes between fact and fantasy much less clearly than he does in later life. This magical attitude is perpetuated by the unconscious operation of the superego in later life.

During latency (the grammar school years), the superego functions in repressing the drives. Beginning with the age of six and seven, the conscience is developing. It has its origin in internalization of parental control, but it deals with conscious activity. Conscience, unlike the superego, is not made up of fear, but of regret for having done something wrong. Conscience is realistic and does not deal with fantasy as does the superego. Conscience is forgiving, the superego is not.

Two different types of guilt are experienced in relation to conscience and the superego. First, there is the conscious sense of guilt, related to the conscience, with the acknowledgment of having done wrong, the regret for loss of love, anxiety, confession, penance, restitution, and relief of anxiety. Second, there is the unconscious sense of guilt, related to the superego, which is more an unconscious need for expiation and self-punishment. This need for punishment is developed as a result of the addition of excessive hostile feeling in the building of the superego. Now part of the individual is punishing himself. One of my patients with a severe unconscious sense of guilt said, "It's like something inside you tying your hands and hitting you." Thus, a continued need to confess, to do penance, exists, but following this there is no relief, only repetition of the process. It would be very helpful to say that there was a clear-cut distinction between conscious guilt related to conscience, and the unconscious guilt related to the superego. However, like most processes in mental life, there are no sharp lines, only gradations.*

With the onset of adolescence the drives are physiologically stimulated by puberty. The resulting excitation is felt by the ego, but much of the control of the drive is done by both the conscience and the superego. With the concepts of the drives, the formation of the superego, the development of anxiety as a result of superego activity, the differentiation between conscience and superego, and conscious and unconscious guilt, meaning is given to the thinking of the scrupulous patient. We begin to understand why he needs to be labeled a sinner, why he is so repetitious in his constant feeling of sinning, why his sins have to do so much with fantasy.

To summarize, the cause of scrupulosity lies in the interaction between the forces within the patient and the environment. The following factors contribute: (1) congenitally strong aggressive and sexual drives; (2) the character of the parental superego and the degree of hostility it possesses; (3) the reaction of both of these forces in the formation of the child's superego; (4) misinformation or misinterpretation of information during latency or adolescence; (5) overstimulation of the adolescent in a sexual or an aggressive way; (6) the presence of physiological changes with resultant increase in drives seen in adolescence, involutional stage (e.g., menopause in women), and sometimes, senility; (7) a change in life status with consequent stimulation or denial of these drives (such as engagements, marriage, or entrance into the religious life).

When an individual with a severe punitive superego experiences anxiety as a result of sexual or aggressive stimulation, he may develop scrupulosity.[3]

The reader should not be distressed if portions of the above are not entirely clear to him. It is an unusually brief and accurate description of one professional view of scrupulosity. One concept it does demonstrate very clearly is the process by which the anxieties and fears of the scrupulous person become a part of his unconscious emotional life rather than a part of his conscious rational functioning. Somewhere deep in the infantile past of the scrupulous adult, one can trace the beginnings of problem attitudes toward love and

* See Father Gustave Weigel's comments on interplay of conscience and superego, p. 53.

sex, aggression and hostility. Often one will find the powerful influences of an over-protective, over-perfectionistic, too-demanding, or sternly rigid parent. Often too, one will see the development of insecurity, confusion, and mixed feelings about these basic emotions because of the inconsistent attitudes and expectations of parental or authority figures.

In his discussion of the nature of scrupulosity, Dr. Mahoney explains some of the mental mechanisms by which scrupulous people manage their anxieties. Many, for example, regress to an earlier level of personality development. Their emotional responses become like those of a young child. There is often a constant interplay of feelings of love and hate, directed to family figures, teachers, priests and confessors, and even God Himself. There is also the childish device of "magical thinking." The scrupulous person is able to associate the most horrendous crime and guilt with objectively indifferent or innocent acts.

Another characteristic of a scrupulous person is rooted in the reaction formation. (See chapter 1, p. 25.) The scrupulous person is so frightened and threatened by the demands of his basic drives and urges that he overcompensates in an opposite direction, going out of his way to protect himself and to counteract his instinctual impulses by fleeing, denying, or fighting the true desire.

Because the scrupulous person is troubled by a sort of perpetual guilt complex about these basic passions and urges which he cannot manage to live with, he is subtly propelled to "expiate" or "make reparation for" these instincts he sees as evil and harmful. For this reason, the scrupulous person feels a constant need to confess, engages in detailed and repetitious recitations of his "sins" in an effort to undo the harmful wishes he feels he carries within himself.

Displacement (see chapter 1, p. 26) is also at work in the scrupulous personality. The individual transfers his feelings of love, hate, and fear for his parents—and similar feelings which he feels his parents have for him—to Almighty God Himself. It does not help him to know intellectually that God is a loving and merciful Father; his earlier experiences with his parents make it impossible for him to see the Supreme Authority Figure as anything but threatening and punishing.

Finally, we can see why stubbornness and a certain degree of perverse satisfaction are often a part of the scrupulous personality. This frustrated and fearful sufferer has cut himself off from love and affection. To balance this lack, he deviously perseveres in his stubborn stand in such a way that he provokes people around him, including the confessor or spiritual director, to impatience and "unfair" responses of various kinds. Thus the scrupulous person gains a sort of interior superiority and consolation based on the feeling that he is being unfairly treated. Occasionally, too, he will force a kind of affection, or at least acceptance, from those individuals who may feel sorry because they have manifested impatience or irritation. Finally, there is often a masochistic (self-punishing) quality to the scrupulous individual's concentration on his suffering. Since he has often denied himself legitimate affection or permissible sexual satisfactions, he compensates for his frustrations by distorting his pain to this weird kind of "pleasure."

MISCONCEPTIONS REGARDING SCRUPULOSITY

Before we outline some of the possible ways in which the confessor might help rid a penitent of scrupulosity, let us point out some traditional theories related to the nature and cure of the problem which seem to need refinement and/or correction in the light of the above explanation.

In 1932 Father Daniel A. Lord, S.J., in collaboration with Father Francis J. O'Boyle, S.J., wrote a pamphlet called *Are You Scrupulous?*[4] This little treatise summarized in popular fashion the best and most expert thinking of spiritual and psychological writers at that time on this subject. The majority of priests who have not had access to more recent and more technical religio-psychological material still accept and use the theories and therapies outlined by Father Lord. We do no irreverence to the distinguished authors of this pamphlet by using some of their quotations as a means of highlighting new approaches. In fact, those sacerdotal readers who may feel a bit uneasy because they are still committed to the traditional techniques will find themselves in the reassuringly good company of two scholars who were in the forefront of the latest research in both the religious and profane sciences. We cannot overemphasize the fact that the critique which follows is the result of very recent scholarship, and in many aspects still highly hypothetical in nature.

Scrupulous people must realize that they have no conscience in their own regard. [They must] clearly recognize that fact and substitute a correct conscience for their false one . . . which conscience they are to get from a confessor.[5]

This statement would seem to express the prevalent implication that scrupulosity is an impairment of the conscience itself. Even though many of the theologians would not accept this literally, it is an impression which is particularly misleading to those who are searching for causes. Conscience is, after all, an intellectual, rational exercise. Conscience is not an entity in itself; it is a description of the intellect making valid judgments about right and wrong. In most cases, the intellect of the scrupulous person is in no way impaired; he is usually quite able to judge the moral actions of others and to give them correct advice, though he may be helpless in evaluating the simplest of his own activities. The impairment lies in the emotions, not the intellect. Feelings of anxiety and fear (quite clearly recognized by the authors of *Are You Scrupulous?*) block the implementation of healthy judgments by the intellect. The scrupulous person *feels* guilty, *feels* unforgiven, *feels* unsure about his decisions.

Since, in the past, the conscience itself was thought to be impaired or totally cancelled out, it made good sense to suggest that the decisions be taken over by somebody else's conscience. The scrupulous person was seen as a ship without a rudder or compass,[6] or an aviator whose instrument board has failed him. The great solution becomes *obedience*. The scrupulous person must fly blind.

He must listen to the voice that comes to him out of the air, the voice of his confessor. Though he flies through fog, so long as he obeys that voice and follows those directions, he is absolutely sure of making a safe landing. . . . The priest is God's representative in this regard. The voice of the priest is for him the voice of God. When the priest prescribes, God approves, and the penitent has no further responsibility in this matter.[7]

As soon as we understand that scrupulosity is not a matter of faulty judgment, but of faulty emotions, we can see the inadequacy of this approach. The chief difficulty of the scrupulous person is precisely his over-dependence, his need to have others make decisions for him. This approach of "obedience, obedience, and more obedience" plays right into his emotional infantilism. What he needs more than anything else is somehow, in some way, to learn to stand on his own two feet and make decisions for himself. He must come to see and to understand how *his emotions* interfere with his judgment. Through such insight he will cease to be intimidated by them.

Here and there, strict blind obedience seems to work. But more often than not, the penitent is not content. Sooner or later, he will be found throwing up a barrage of ifs and buts; he will protest that the confessor cannot possibly know the particulars of his case; the deep anxieties and fears will remain, and often psychosomatic symptoms will develop. Sooner or later the great majority of scrupulous penitents who are forced by a confessor to a "blind obedience" relationship leave such a priest and start again the weary search for a confessor who "might understand."

Another general misconception is that all scrupulosity is the same, that one scrupulous persons is just like every other:

. . . Scrupulous people are unconsciously and blamelessly a little conceited. Each one thinks his case is so terribly different from any other case. . . . If there is anything in the world that is stereotyped, it is scruples. A few minutes of explanation tell me all I need know about the most complicated case. When I, or any other experienced priest, say to a scrupulous person "I understand now; you have made it perfectly clear," that person can be absolutely sure that I do understand and that nothing he could add could make his story any clearer.[8]

The conviction that scrupulosity is a simple problem with universal symptoms which can be treated by a simple and universal counselling formula is no longer held. Says Father Noël Mailloux:

. . . Scrupulosity may present extremely variegated patterns, emerging from totally different dynamic backgrounds. . . . Clinical observation has revealed that such more or less generalized disturbance is liable to present significant and differentiated patterns, according to the nature of the particular conflict in which it is rooted, as well as to the individual motive which was at the origin of the latter and continues its whole development.[9]

The old conviction that one case of scruples was just about like another is perhaps one of the reasons why the scrupulous penitent becomes discouraged at the readiness of some confessors to assign specific causes and remedies after hearing only a brief recital of the problem. In other words, the lament of the penitent, "He cannot possibly understand my case," is not an entirely neurotic suspicion. Symptoms may be the same, but the fact that the roots of the difficulty are developed deep in the past and linked to very specific, delicate and complicated human relationships means in reality that the problem of each scrupulous penitent is unique and must be approached as such.

"Blind obedience alone can cure you, and it will certainly do so."[10] "God will not allow the priest, who is taking His place in soothing the anguish of the troubled soul, to make mistakes."[11] There are two possible implications to these statements, both of which are unlikely in the light of modern scholarship. The first is the assumption that fear can be dispelled and resolute self-direction can be developed by the frequent, complete, and blind carrying-out of a confessor's directions. The second is that a priest, by the very nature of his office, is qualified to preside over the therapy of emotional disorders. True, an unquestioning, frequent repetition of threatening behavior was, in days past, considered to be the effective remedy for scruples. Says Father Weigel:

Even writers in our day still follow Janet and his theory of neurasthenia, whereby . . . scrupulous persons are persons deficient in psychic energy, which must be built up. The way it is built up is by exercise, for the psychic energy was considered to be like a muscle which can become flabby if not used. . . . Perhaps the most dangerous element in the older books on scruples was the treatment prescribed. All insisted that the scrupulous person was to follow blindly the counsels of the spiritual director. This tactic was justified practically as well as theoretically. Practical justification was that only in this way could the scrupulous person live. If left to his own devices, he would abstain from action because he was always concentrating on the over-rigorous precept relevant to the action. The result would be collapse. Theoretical justification was that the will had to be strengthened like a flabby muscle. This would only happen if the person decided for action. Repeated decision would render the will strong and so it would overcome its neurasthenia.

This oversimplified technique has caused much suffering and very little good. The reason for its inadequacy was the lack of reflection on the total phenomenology of scrupulosity.[12]

Occasionally, confessors and penitents labor under the misapprehension that scrupulosity is a sign of spiritual and moral excellence. "Scrupulosity should be not a source of unhappiness but a kind of guarantee that they are in God's grace. They would not be so anxious to stay in God's grace if they were not safe in their love of God."[13] [Scruples can] "contribute to increase the purity of our intentions by detaching us from spiritual comforts and by telling us to cling solely to God for whom our love increases the more He puts us to the test."[14] To these opinions, Father Weigel makes the following comment:

Scrupulosity rooted in childhood authority fears derives not from conscience but rather from the superego, the punitive device and inhibitory influence of the cruel father image. This kind of scrupulosity neither supposes a strong attachment to morality nor does it deny it. It is a mistake to consider scrupulosity as a sign of virtuous striving. It is just psychic disease affecting the intellect's capacity for moral judgment, ranging from inevitable neurotic disorder in all men to extreme psychosis.

As long as the patient is led to believe his scrupulosity is really a credit to him, he will cherish and nurture it. If he is made aware that he is suffering from a mental disease, he will be better able to rid himself of it. Spiritual directors should therefore treat scrupulosity as a disease and make it clear to the subject that it is not the sign of holiness but rather of *moral sickness*.[15]

We have tried in the foregoing pages to outline the best thinking on the causes and nature of scrupulosity. We have tried to show that the problem is anything but simple; that because the roots lie deep in the unconscious emotional past, an appeal to logic and reason will, in the majority of cases, prove largely ineffective. We have suggested that blind obedience to the confessor's directives is in the long run unavailing because such counsel reinforces the inability or the unwillingness of the individual to make judgments for himself, and leads him further and further away from resolute and convinced decisions of his own. Now we will attempt to describe some of the ways the scrupulous penitent can be helped by the confessor.

Because of the truly hypothetical nature of so many facets of scrupulosity, we encourage the confessor to continue to use whatever techniques work for him, whether they are included in the theoretical treatises or not. Often the individual personalities of both penitent and priest collaborate so that understanding and improvement come in ways not mentioned by the books. We suggest just one word of caution: the confessor should be careful to test the validity of his methods in every way possible. A great many priests have met scrupulous penitents in the confessional, and have often given such penitents much advice. However, there are comparatively few priests who have followed through a counselling process with a scrupulous person to the point where they are able to say they cured him. The very fact that most scrupulous individuals seem to "float" from one confessor to another, rarely remaining with a single confessor for a protracted period of time, is a further indication that not too many priests can be confident of permanent cures. In any case, the complex nature of the affliction should make us wary of any obvious, "fool-proof" formula.

COUNSELLING THE SCRUPULOUS

What are some of the general principles which the confessor should keep in mind when confronted with a case of scrupulosity? To begin with, the severity of the affliction is an important factor. Where the confessor feels that he has before him a very sick person, suffering from an obviously advanced obsessive-compulsive malady, his only recourse is to refer him, if possible, to a good psychiatrist. In therapy, the priest's aid will often be needed and appreciated, especially when he helps reinforce the concept that the penitent's problem is an emotional and not a moral one. For the severely scrupulous person, professional help of the medical man is the only safe and certain answer. It may sometimes need a preliminary diagnosis by a psychiatrist to determine whether referral is called for.

There are times, of course, when psychiatric help is not available or feasible. In such cases, where the individual is obviously very sick and has very few inner resources, the priest can try the supportive kind of help which the more traditional methods have advocated. The very sick person is not able to understand the deeper reasons for his problem, and it would be too threatening if the priest encouraged much introspection. The priest can, in simple language, assure the penitent that he has no moral problem, that he is pleasing in the sight of God. He can give him permission, and even encourage him, to receive the sacraments if the penitent obviously wishes to do so. He can show understanding and give sympathy in any way that seems effective.

The usual case of scrupulosity is an incipient, or mildly advanced, specimen of a potentially more severe illness. Here the priest's help can often be very effective if he keeps in mind the following suggestions.*

In each case the priest must decide whether he is able and the penitent is willing to continue in a counselling relationship over a considerable period of time: regular forty-five minute periods for several months or more perhaps. The priest must ask himself, "Am I really convinced that this person is suffering from a mental illness?" This must be an inner conviction on the part of the confessor, or the penitent will sense the priest's vacillation. (Sometimes a priest will hint at "pride" or "willful obstinacy," which is enough to send the person scurrying away.) Counselling, in most cases,

---

* See Dr. Vincent B. Mahoney's "Scrupulosity From a Psychoanalytic Point of View"[16] for a more complete discussion of ways to counsel scrupulous penitents.

should be done outside the confessional. This not only makes communication easier, but emphasizes the fact that the problem is not a moral one but an emotional one. If possible, the priest counselling the scrupulous person should not be hearing his confession. (There will, of course, be obvious exceptions to this statement.) The penitent must not see the priest in his traditional, authoritative role as a judge and dispenser of advice, but should rather see him as a therapist who is to preside over the growth of self-reliance in his client. Finally, the priest must have some knowledge of psychology —of the role of the unconscious, the superego, and the mental mechanisms in the development of the scrupulous personality.

In the course of the first few interviews, the priest will probably do little else but listen. Permitting the penitent to unburden himself, as completely and in as much detail as possible, of all the fears, worries, anxieties, distortions, frustrations, etc., which he is experiencing will, if nothing else, help to build up the kind of open relationship between counsellor and counselee which is indispensable to a cure. The fact that the priest is quite content to listen, merely injecting a question here or there to indicate that he is following and trying to understand, can be enormously reassuring to the stricken soul. The priest should not attempt to abate the penitent's symptoms, nor try to show him the unreasonableness of his thinking and behavior. This will only make the patient cling more tightly to his pattern of automatic response. Nor should the priest tell the patient that because he is sick he is incapable of doing wrong. This will often frighten the penitent, who is already disproportionately afraid of his primitive drives and does not want to hear, at a moment when his whole energies are attempting to repress these urges, that he might satisfy them with impunity.

In these early sessions, the priest should also be particularly attentive to the kinds of material the patient is verbalizing. Is it primarily sexual or aggressive in character? Does it have an active or passive quality? What is the patient's emotional reaction as he is relating the material? Does it have an element of perversion, homosexuality? Is there a great deal of fear of dirt, contamination? irrational anxiety over the obligations of fast days and Fridays?

Does it have to do with fears of looking, feeling, touching?[17] Such details may have considerable meaning when, later on, they are examined in the light of early, infantile experiences and attitudes.

Sooner or later, particular facts and experiences of the past will assume important proportions. What was his early relationship to parents, brothers and sisters? How did he learn to control his aggressive and sexual drives? How did he feel about the way he was disciplined as a child, and what were the emotional reactions of the parent, teacher, or other authority figures who administered this discipline? What was his concept of religion as a child and adolescent? How did he feel towards his religious teachers?

The critical point in this counselling process comes in those sessions which attempt to relate past experiences and attitudes with present fears and anxieties. The patient gradually comes to see a parallel between the threats of the present and the subtle indoctrinations of the past. Shocked and violent reactions of parental figures to his childhood displays of temper or irreverence make it difficult for him as an adult to accept strong feelings within himself, much less act them out in any way. He sees how early taboos against dirt, sex, disobedience, and so forth, have determined the kinds of response to similar situations in his present life.

Very often the kinds of price tags which parents attach to the bestowal of affection can have tremendous influence on the psychological development of the individual. There are some perfectionistic parents who, for reasons of their own, are unable to give unstintingly and wholeheartedly the kind of demonstrative love which their children need so desperately. No matter what grades the report card might show, the child is exhorted to "do better"; chores can always be improved upon; the behavior of the child is always something short of what it should be. The child who is bombarded day after day, month after month, year after year, with such perfectionistic displays of dissatisfaction often becomes involved in an almost desperate plea for acceptance.

Such children no longer content themselves with what ordinary mortals would consider good performance. They are never satisfied with a piece of work they do, but feel always that it could have been done better. They have been disappointed so often in their bid for honest praise (which comes to symbolize love for them) that they are really convinced they are inferior and, at the core, inadequate.

Such disappointing childhood experiences with over-demanding authority figures are imperceptibly but resolutely transferred to the whole moral sphere. Occasionally, the overemphasis on negative aspects of religious education will intensify this concern for perfectionistic kinds of achievement. These attitudes often extend to many areas of their lives. So convinced are they, on the deep psychological level, of their inferiority and unworthiness that they think others see them as they see themselves. Scrupulous people often have difficulty in relating openly and warmly with others because they feel that others sense their "glaring" shortcomings and failings. It is but a short step to the application of this mode of thinking (or rather, feeling) to their relationship with God and the moral life.

One can well imagine the bewildering combination of emotions which such a person feels for his parents. Resentment, frustration, fear, as well as love, work together to create that muddled, painful, indecisive relationship characteristic of the insecure and scrupulous personality. These feelings are easily transferred from parents to other authority symbols—in particular, priests, the Church and its laws, and God Himself. Such a person sees God as another parental figure. His view of God is of a commanding, demanding figure who will never be really pleased with anything His child might do. The individual becomes more and more concerned about the inadequacy of his spiritual and moral life; he feels that Almighty God is saying to him, "Do better! This is shoddy! You are going to 'goof' again! What else can I expect but more mistakes and failures?" The scrupulous penitent, like the insecure child, is making a perpetual bid for a pat on the head, an affectionate "Well done" from his earthly father and later on from his heavenly Father. But it never comes for him.

This is but one example of many kinds of parallels between the present and the past which with time, patience, and encouragement the patient can be helped to see. As he gains more insight into these links of the adult present with the childhood past, he is able to face the experiences of everyday life in a more placid, hopeful, and tolerant way. He understands how yesterday's disappointments and taboos have become today's fears and bugaboos. The final stage of the counselling process will involve the realistic evaluation and adaptation of the penitent's practical day-to-day, here-and-now living. This is something that he must work out for himself; it is not something which he can be told to do. Thus the cure of scrupulosity involves a recognition of one's emotional distortions, some knowledge of how the early experiences of childhood have contributed to the unconscious feelings of the present, and the gradual development of self-knowledge and confident decisions through inner-directed motivation and choice. While it is a slow process it can be a genuinely rewarding one for both priest and penitent.

OCCASIONAL COUNSELLING

There are a good many times when the average priest will have only a "one shot" opportunity to help the scrupulous person. Even in his own parish a priest may have the suspicion that no matter what he says the penitent will not return to him a second time. Penitents from outside the parish will be making a casual or calculated visit which is not likely to be repeated. In particular, the missionary, the occasional confessor, retreat master, or "relief" confessor will be temporary and fleeting figures in the lives of those whose confessions they will hear once, or perhaps twice at the most. Scrupulous penitents will often seek out the confessor who is "passing through," not only to preserve their anonymity, but in the possible hope that some new insight might be gained. Often a dynamic speaker can entice the scrupulous person to his confessional through fear or encouragement (depending on the emotions he appeals to in his sermons). What can the confessor say to the scrupulous person in these single contacts with him?

It is usually helpful, at the outset, to ask the scrupulous person if he has a regular confessor with whom he feels he is making some progress. If there seems to be a genuinely positive reply, then the confessor need not delve into the matter at all, but merely encourage the individual to continue in his permanent confessional relationship. In most cases, however, the scrupulous person will be floundering and unhappy. In some way or other, then, leaving a considerable degree of choice and flexibility to the confessor, the following procedure should be observed.

More often than not, the scrupulous penitent will want to relate a fairly long and involved chronicle of failings to a new confessor, or will ask to make a general confession. The confessor is usually inclined to discourage such wearisome litanies and to forbid the scrupulous person to make a general confession. We have some reason to think that these restrictions are enforced by the confessor as much for his *own* peace of mind as for the penitent's. To give patient attention to a long-winded personal account of petty sins and tiresome details is surely one of the most pointless and exasperating prospects a confessor can face. It is hardly likely, however, that such a recitation can cause any psychological harm to the patient (though it may generate considerable emotional anguish in the confessor!). On the contrary, an occasional verbal "catharsis," which a complete account of one's inner distress provides, can bring a healthy though temporary measure of relief to the tension and anxiety of the typically scrupulous person.

There is no harm, therefore, in allowing the penitent to have his say, whatever it might be: short or long, naive or knowledgeable, coherent or confused. "Tell me whatever you like" is a good reply to the request: "May I make a general confession?" Be sure to give the penitent the impression that there is plenty of time, even though there may be long lines outside the confessional. (You will find that, generally speaking, it takes no longer to sit and listen until the scrupulous person has quite completed his story than it does to battle with him in an effort to force him to say only what *you* want him to say.) As the penitent struggles with the various details he is attempting to relate, there may be considerable pauses as he rummages for material. Keep silent during these pauses. Remember, it is more than likely that the penitent is expecting the confessor to interrupt him at any moment. This has been the story of most of his confessions. It will be an unusual experience to find a confessor who shows no impatience but on the contrary remains completely silent while the penitent attempts to explain himself. When the penitent has finally come to the end of his saga, the confessor might even ask, "Is there anything else now?" in an effort to demonstrate his concern, showing in this way that he is making a real effort to understand.

Once the confessor has heard the penitent out, he should do his best to give some evidence of his genuine sympathy for the sufferer. "This is really a painful trouble, isn't it?" or "You have been living with this cross for some time, haven't you?" or "It is difficult to make others understand how bewildered you are, and how much you suffer, isn't it?" The confessor who has tried this approach cannot fail to be impressed with the kind of surprised gratitude which such compassion evokes from the scrupulous penitent. Understanding and compassion—these are two enormously consoling responses which the scrupulous rarely hear.

The next step should attempt to explain the difference between truly moral and purely emotional guilt. Try words something like these: "This will not cure your anxiety, but it may be a slight consolation to know that many, many good people suffer the pain of scrupulosity. This worry that you have about your present sins, your past life, or the state of your soul in general, is a worry which often comes at certain times of life and under certain pressures. We may not know the real causes of your distress, but of one thing we can be certain—these fears belong to your feelings, and not to your spiritual life. Sin and healthy guilt belong to the thinking part of you; this scrupulous kind of worry belongs to the feeling part of you. I am sure there must be times when your real self tells you that God is not displeased, knowing that you try to live up to His law. But that does not change your feelings—they keep on gnawing and bothering you. And so while your mind says, 'I'm trying to do my best,' your feelings are saying, 'I am a terrible sinner and deserve punishment.'

"We may never know why our feelings play tricks like this, but it is important for you to know that your guilty feelings do not mean that you are always sinning or that God is displeased with you. People who are not particularly religious, but have similar emotional tensions, often worry that their bodies have diseases of various kinds. These people are called hypochondriacs. You might know some of them—they usually have a medicine chest full of pills and bottles, and they are always anxious about their health even though they are not really sick. They *feel* that they are sick, or they are afraid that they are about to become sick. The scrupulous person is a sort of *spiritual hypochondriac*. He has not really sinned, but he *feels* his soul is sick. He thinks he is suffering from frightful spiritual illnesses. When the physical hypochondriac gets very panicky he thinks he is going to die. When the spiritual hypochondriac is terribly anxious, he thinks that his soul is dead, that he is in mortal sin, and that God will damn him to hell.

"These feelings, although they do not mirror reality, are still very frightening and painful. It is very hard to explain this torture to others who do not suffer in the same way. It is, however, very important to understand with your mind, even though your feelings will not always go along, that this is an emotional and *not* a moral problem. Only then can something eventually be done about it.

"There are lots of little ways by which you can prove that your scruples are a matter of feeling and not a matter of honest and willful sinning. You will notice that the ordinary person, once he has gone to confession and received absolution, leaves the Church contented and at peace with himself. He does not worry whether he has told the priest everything, whether he really has sufficient contrition, whether he was trying to hide things from the priest. He tells his story, is absolved, and leaves a free and happy man. This does not happen for you. After confession there may be a little easing up of tension, a momentary impression that the burden is lifted, but sooner or later the dark cloud of fear overshadows your peace of mind, and the old gnawing doubts begin again.

"Take this confession you made just now as a good example. You have had an opportunity to say everything that could possibly be on your mind; no one has stopped you or cut you short; you have done your best to tell me everything, and I have done my best to listen. Yet I can almost certainly predict, as I think you can, that sooner or later—a half hour, hour, day, or week from now—you will not be satisfied with this general confession. You will worry again about the past, you will be uneasy and dissatisfied. These are *emotions*, not sins, at work, and it will help you to remember this as soon as you begin to feel the old doubts coming back. You must say to yourself, 'Here I go again, back to the old worries!' and if you are able to laugh a little, and to say with real conviction, *'So what?'* you will perhaps be able to live with them a little more comfortably.

"And of course this is what you must do, learn to live with these unpleasant doubts and worries. They will not disappear overnight. They will come and go, sometimes very persistently, at other times very faintly. The fact that they are never quite the same is another proof that they belong to your emotional and not your moral life. You will notice, for example, that the severity of your scruples will often depend upon the mood that you are in and the troubles you are having. When you have had a particularly bad day at the office, when you have found yourself having a really violent argument with someone dear to you, when a task you had hoped would go well did not turn out right, when you have experienced some major disappointment—when at such times you are blue and down-in-the-dumps—your doubts and fears and scruples will very likely be quite powerful. On the other hand, when life is sunny, cheerful, and rewarding; when things are going right and you are enjoying your friends, looking forward to pleasant things to do; when you are relaxed and content with life and the world around you, then the scruples are not nearly so demanding and intruding and painful. Haven't you noticed this?"

Observe some of the characteristics of this approach. The emphasis is on the *emotional* nature of their illness, which from the very beginning takes the matter out of the realm of sin, morality, and responsible guilt. Secondly, this approach does not impose upon the penitent *a burden of blind conformity* to specific directives determined by the confessor.

In one way or another, the priest should also try to help the penitent see that his main difficulty is an unreasonable dependency upon the judgment of others. His goal must be the development of free choice and autonomous judgment. He should be encouraged to seek the help of an understanding counsellor, invited to return, or urged to seek, by trial and error, a permanent confessor who can, over a period of time, help him to work through his difficulty. Usually the penitent will be relieved to hear that someone else also feels that the problem cannot be quickly and simply solved. He should never be told that his difficulty is hopeless, or that he must resign himself to inevitable suffering. He should be assured that he will not always have to feel this pain, that the picture can change, that his conflicts need not continue forever.

On the other hand, the penitent must be prepared for varying degrees of conflict and frustration. He often asks, "May I do this or that?" "Shall I go to communion?" "May I act on this choice?" In all such indecisions, the confessor should, from the outset, reply with the general answer, "Whatever *you* wish." This answer should be followed by an explanation. The scrupulous penitent should be helped to see that, for the present, some of the choices he makes will have to be painful, no matter what they are. For example, the priest can point out to the penitent who is afraid to go to communion even though he wants to go: "You will have to decide which will make you more uneasy—to go or to stay away. Either decision will give you some pain, even though I tell you that sin is in no way involved and that you cannot possibly do any moral harm by receiving. If you receive you will worry that you are not worthy; and if you don't receive you will be uneasy and unhappy too. I cannot solve this dilemma for you. As you work through such conflicts with an understanding counsellor it will become easier to make these choices. But in the meantime you can only ask yourself, 'Which decision will be easiest to live with? Which will give me the *least* pain?' Whatever one you choose will be morally good though emotionally somewhat unsatisfying." In this fashion the penitent begins to make choices on his own. Even though the choice is painful, he makes it himself, with direction but without a *directive* from the confessor.

At times the re-education of the penitent must progress very slowly. There is a certain type of scrupulous person who becomes panicky when first attempts to establish self-directed choices begin. In such cases the priest may find it necessary to give some authoritative answers and directions to a penitent who is used to them. But authority, except in severe obsessive-compulsive cases, should be used sparingly, with a view to the eventual development of inner-direction and self-reliance.

Finally, the priest should avoid overstressing the weak aspects of the scrupulous personality. He can overdo his insistence on "sickness." In fact it is generally better not to use the word but to speak positively from the start about the need for re-education and self-understanding. *Hopefulness* is an important ingredient of the cure. The priest can discover the stronger qualities of the individual's personality and encourage expansion of them. Priest and penitent should search out compensatory talents and capacities whose fulfillment can bring positive satisfactions, ease tensions, and build confidence.

The emergence of an autonomous personality from the shambles of doubt and dependency is one of the truly gratifying experiences over which the sensitive priest is privileged to preside. Armed with patience and compassion, he can approach the challenge with confidence.

NOTES

1. N. Mailloux, O.P., "The Problem of Scrupulosity in Pastoral Work," *The Proceedings of the Institute for the Clergy on Problems of Pastoral Psychology* (New York: Fordham University Press, 1956), pp. 55–6.

2. Ibid., pp. 61–62.

3. "Scrupulosity from a Psychoanalytic Point of View," *Bulletin of the Guild of Catholic Psychiatrists,* V, No. 2 (1957) pp. 12–14.

4. St. Louis: The Queen's Work Press, 1932.

5. Ibid., p. 21.

6. Cf. Tanquerey, *The Spiritual Life* (Tournai: Desclée, 1930), p. 447.

7. Lord and O'Boyle, op. cit., p. 22.

8. Ibid., p. 23.

9. Op. cit., pp. 54–55.

10. Tanquerey, op. cit., p. 448.

11. Lord and O'Boyle, op. cit., p. 22.

12. "A Note on the Phenomenology of Scruples," *The Proceedings of the Institute for the Clergy on Problems of Pastoral Psychology*, p. 70.

13. Lord and O'Boyle, op. cit., p. 13.

14. Tanquerey, op. cit., p. 446.

15. Op. cit., pp. 71, 72.

16. See note 3.

17. Ibid., pp. 17–18.

8

MENTAL ILLNESS AND
MENTAL HEALTH

It is surely no longer necessary to defend the important roles psychology and psychiatry are playing in the growth and treatment of the total Christian personality. There remain in Catholic circles, however, islands of suspicion and misunderstanding. For this reason, we have thought it helpful to deal at length with these points elsewhere in the book. (Cf. "Catholicism and Psychiatry," Part Two, chapter 13.)

> . . . be assured that the Church follows your research and your medical practice with a warm interest and her best wishes. You labor on a terrain that is very difficult. But your activity is capable of achieving precious results for medicine, for the knowledge of the soul in general, for the religious dispositions of men and for their development.[1]

These are the words of Pope Pius XII, quoted from one of three addresses he made to scholars in psychological and allied fields. As in other papal references to sciences which touch intimately the volitional and rational aspects of man's nature, this allocution carefully distinguishes a number of moral considerations, includes words of encouragement and praise.

RELIGION AND PSYCHOLOGY

It is not our purpose to present a treatise on religion and mental health. Others have written adequately and eloquently on the subject. It is important, however, for the parish priest to have a clear understanding of those human involvements which are essentially religious, and those others which are primarily psychological in nature. Dr. Karl Stern, the eminent Catholic psychiatrist, has indicated two possible pitfalls:

> On the one hand, we may fall into the error of psychologism. . . . The hypothetical therapist—we are assuming him to be a person for whom the supernatural does not exist—would reduce all of his patient's anxiety to the level of purely psychological mechanics. All of the patient's searching and restlessness would be understood entirely on the natural plane and reduced to infantile ambivalence or a fixation on the mother or guilt toward the father or some other basic psychological issue. The anxiety would be completely dissolved, even down to the precious residuum of creativeness.
>
> Christian therapists, on the other hand, must beware of precisely the opposite fallacy. When a patient comes to us with what he calls spiritual problems, we may be tempted to treat these problems as though the carnal substrate did not exist, as though therapy was something like a battle of disembodied spirits. This fallacy is related to what Maritain has called "angelism". . . . The patient who brings spiritual difficulties to a Christian therapist (just because the therapist is a Christian) is frequently using these "problems" as intellectual defenses to camouflage other difficulties that are of a natural order.[2]

The psychologist and the religionist have much to learn from each other. We have a mission to infuse Catholic concepts of morality and the nature of man into certain areas of psychiatric thinking and practice. On the other hand, we priests who deal daily with the most intimate and complex human concerns must become far more sensitive than we have been to the influence of those forces which are largely or wholly psychological in nature. The words of Karl Stern are, again, strong and significant:

> Clergymen of all faiths have dealt with psychiatry in sermons and lectures, books and pamphlets. Too often, they say something like this: "If there were only more faith in the world, people would not be nearly as neurotic as they are."
>
> This is an oversimplification. I can show you a number of happy atheists who have never known a sleepless night; and many good, even saintly, people who are haunted by terrible states of anxiety and melan-

cholia. That formula not only does not work, but is also morally wrong. There is a touch of the pharisee in it. When a man says "People are neurotic because they lack faith," he implies "Thank God, I am not like one of those. I have faith."

Remember, psychiatric illness in many cases involves more suffering than any physical illness. From many of the books and talks of clergymen on psychiatry the lay person gets the impression that the psychiatric patient must choose between the psychiatrist's office and the confessional, or the psychiatric textbook and the Gospel. It is erroneous to give such impressions. . . . Nobody would ever think that an abcess of the gall bladder could be treated by "pulling oneself together." But many religious people use towards our neurotic patients a kind of spiritual "pull yourself together" approach. In this way, things of the natural order are treated as if they were of the spiritual and moral order.

When a clergyman makes the statement that we would need fewer psychiatrists if there were more faith in the world he has succumbed to a fallacy quite similar to the "pull yourself together" treatment. By this attitude, religion becomes a sort of mental bandage which must not be missing in any well-equipped psychiatric first-aid kit. I mean only to say that the clear distinction between natural and supernatural means of help which we make in cases of broken legs must also be made in cases of emotional disturbances. The reason why preaching does not help a lady with an anxiety neurosis is that the neurosis deprives her of her freedom of spiritual choice.[3]

Mental illness is a very *medical* problem. Without going into the historical details, it might be valuable to point out how reluctant humankind has been from the very beginning to accept this simple fact. So many great academic disciplines have claimed priority of jurisdiction over this aspect of man's emotional life. From pre-Christian times, the philosopher has declared that a man is mentally ill because "his thinking is awry." The law, by means of courts and penal institutions, professes to cure certain mental disorders by legislating to correct perverse human behavior. We have already mentioned the inclination of some theologians and clergymen to assail the mentally ill person as one whose spiritual values and moral judgments need radical revision. Finally, some practitioners of organic medicine have been, and in some cases continue to be, unsympathetic to the psychotherapist who plies his art in the intangible and rarefied laboratory of human emotion.

Even today the pseudo-experts persist in presenting their remedies for mental illness. The philosopher continues to exhort such sufferers to "think positively, and use will power to snap themselves out of it." Some religionists say, "Forget psychiatry, and pray more." The courts profess to cure such mental disorders as juvenile delinquency, alcoholism, and sexual depravity by punishing and imprisoning. A wing of the medical profession, subtly denying the sensitive and spiritual character of human personality, hopes one day to cure *all* emotional derangements with drugs, brain surgery, electro-shock and other purely mechanical devices.

WHAT IS MENTAL HEALTH?

All these disciplines have, of course, an important and legitimate contribution to make to the healthy disposition of the total personality. The effectiveness of their contributions, however, depends to a great extent upon the emotional health of the recipient, which only dynamic psychology and psychiatry can explain and achieve. If a man's basic emotions are twisted, seething, or out of control, he cannot think straight, he cannot pray right, his behavior may be socially unacceptable, and many of his bodily organs may writhe, as it were, in painful tension.

Psychic disorders have always been a part of human history, but "mental health" seems to be in a special way a problem of our times. This may be due to the unbelievable giant-steps which science and technology have taken in the last few generations. Modern marvels of transportation and communication have suddenly thrust extremely divergent peoples and their emotions into shoulder-to-shoulder contact. Traditions clash, ambitions meet head on; old ways protest mightily in giving way to new.

Uprooted and indifferent family life, the working mother, unstable employment, the uncertainties of military service, the fearful spectre of the fission bomb have robbed many of that needful ingredient of the happy life: a sense of security. Today's young adults, the last war's bumper crop of babies, are reaping the results of a

178 Counselling the Catholic

childhood of unpredictable and often mobile living. In addition, old-fashioned moral concepts have often become hopelessly tangled with new-fashioned "isms" and "ologies." The amoral ethics of the libertine and the agnostic collide with the poisonous and still potent ethics of the Jansenist and the Puritan. The unsettling anxieties, fears and insecurities engendered by such clashes have made a battleground of men's minds.

What is mental illness and mental health? This is often difficult to answer. There is no line that neatly divides the mentally healthy from the unhealthy. All of us fit somewhere along a continuum which ranges from the obviously disturbed individual who has withdrawn totally into a fantasy world of his own to the vast majority of us who occasionally find ourselves puzzled or frustrated or not managing our emotions quite as capably as we would like. No one characteristic can be taken by itself as evidence of mental health, nor the lack of any one as evidence of mental illness. And nobody has all the traits of good mental health all the time. The environment and social climate of the age often have a significant influence upon the quality of the population's mental health. Teen-age hotbloods like Daniel Boone and Davy Crockett, who were able to vent their energies and tensions by shooting Indians and opening the West, might very well have found themselves frustrated juvenile delinquents in the asphalt jungles of today's urban communities.

The National Association for Mental Health has listed some characteristics of people with good mental health:

1. *They feel comfortable about themselves.* They are not bowled over by their own emotions—by their fears, anger, love, jealousy, guilt or worries. They can take life's disappointments in their stride. They have a tolerant, easy-going attitude towards themselves as well as others; they can laugh at themselves. They can neither underestimate nor overestimate their abilities. They can accept their own shortcomings. They have self-respect. They feel able to deal with most situations which come their way. They get satisfaction from the simple, everyday pleasures.

2. *They feel right about other people.* They are able to give love and to consider the interests of others. They have personal relationships that are satisfying and lasting. They expect to like and trust others, and take it for granted that others will like and trust them. They respect the

many differences they find in people. They do not push people around, nor do they allow themselves to be pushed around. They can feel they are part of the group. They feel a sense of responsibility to their neighbors and fellow men.

3. *They are able to meet the demands of life.* They do something about their problems as they arise. They accept their responsibilities. They shape their environment wherever possible; they adjust to it whenever necessary. They plan ahead but do not fear the future. They meet adequately the common crises of normal human living. They welcome new experiences and new ideas. They make use of their natural capacities. They set realistic goals for themselves. They are able to think for themselves and make their own decisions. They put their best efforts into what they do, and get satisfaction out of doing it.[4]

The newly ordained priest who is sensitive to the emotional overtones he hears in the parlor and the confessional will often ask, "Am I imagining it, or are there a great many emotionally disturbed people in our congregation?" He is not imagining it. One in every ten Americans (sixteen million of them) is suffering from a mental or emotional disorder. One out of every ten children born each year will need treatment in a mental hospital at least once during his lifetime. One family in every five has a relative who is at this moment in a mental institution. Over half the hospital beds in the United States are occupied by mental patients. And for every hospitalized patient there is another seriously sick individual walking the streets who should be institutionalized. You have most likely met some of them.[5]

Many authorities feel that mental illness or other personality disturbances are unusually significant factors in criminal behavior, delinquency, suicide, alcoholism, narcotic addiction, and, very often, in cases of divorce. About 1,750,000 serious crimes are committed a year. About 30,000 people are addicted to narcotics. About 5,000,000 people are problem drinkers. About 17,000 people commit suicide each year. About 500,000 cases come before the juvenile courts each year. For every four marriages there is one divorce.

It might be appropriate to point out here that fear and ignorance have forced the general populace, from the earliest days of history, to deal with mentally ill citizens in the most shameful and inhuman fashion. Psychotics were beaten by the early Greeks; the Inquisitions—Anglo-Saxon as well as Spanish—burned many of them as witches; modern society has more often than not condemned its mental patients to overcrowded, inadequately staffed, poorly supported institutions for the living dead. It seems a clear duty of the clergy to help stir up concern and support for the nation's number one health problem. Fortunately, we seem to be entering a more enlightened era. The philosophy of "out of sight, out of mind," is no longer propelling the general public to avoid, at any cost, a personal involvement with the problems of the mentally ill. The very fact that emotional diseases are becoming so prevalent, touching as they do one out of every five families, has forced the old attitudes to change.

THE PRIEST AND THE PATIENT

Father James E. Royce, S.J., estimates that in addition to the 12 percent of the population suffering from severe mental disorders of one kind or another, "30 to 40 percent of the remainder, though they will never be actual mental cases, will have unwholesome emotional habits preventing them from reaching a reasonable maximum of efficiency and happiness."[6] The average priest can do very little for parishioners who suffer from serious mental illnesses; his chief contribution here will be made in his role as a referral agent. However, in the prevention and alleviation of those far more numerous minor emotional difficulties of a large portion of the population, the priest can make a significant contribution.

In the cause of prevention, he can encourage healthy family life education in our parishes. He can check on the stability and adequacy of his parochial school teachers. He can stress the positive, hopeful content of the Catholic faith and avoid the negative, crippling, Jansenist-tinged distortions still far too prevalent in some aspects of Catholic life. Finally, Father Royce's estimate of the large influence that emotional confusion and upheaval have in the lives of so many Americans should encourage the priest to mistrust the surface, black-and-white, first impressions he may have of some parishioners and look more closely for possible psychological difficulties which contribute to their odd or undesirable behavior.

We have tried, in a special chapter (see chapter 2), to indicate ways in which the priest can help an individual who has minor emotional difficulties to arrive at healthy solutions to his everyday problems. In addition, need a parish priest concern himself about serious mental illness? There is no evidence to support a commonly held view that if a person is a Catholic he is less likely to suffer severe mental disorders. There are, in fact, indications that Catholics who have been inadequately instructed or hold distorted notions of Catholic teaching are more liable to certain types of mental illness than the general populace. In brief, the parish priest must expect to find serious mental illness among his parishioners.

The ability of the priest to make a preliminary, elementary diagnosis can be of enormous value. While, ideally speaking, a medical specialist alone is competent to make a judgment on the nature and severity of mental illness, many patients and their families will confide their problem, at the outset at least, only to a priest. The priest, depending on his training or lack of it, can respond in any number of ways. There are extremists on both ends of the continuum—some priests see almost every mental disturbance as a problem of "poor thinking or poor living," and will prescribe the use of will power, prayer, and the sacraments as the chief remedies. Others go overboard in seeing psychiatry as the answer to every difficulty, and will refer a parishioner to psychiatric agencies on almost any occasion, even when the difficulties can be more adequately dealt with in other ways.

THE PRIEST AS DIAGNOSTICIAN

Following the directives of Dr. J. Lawrence Evans to general practitioners, the priest should, before deciding on psychiatric referral, "evaluate three aspects of the patient's emotional symptom: namely, its intensity, its duration, and its appropriateness. Take as an example the patient who is anxious. If his anxiety is associated with some situation or threat from the outside and is proportionate in degree and duration to this threat, the parishioner probably does not require psychiatric care. As a rule, this kind of anxiety disappears as soon as the threat is removed. If, however, anxiety is out of proportion to the threatening situation or arises in the absence of any objective danger, expert psychiatric evaluation and treatment is usually necessary."[7]

The priest is often the only neighborhood figure—aside from immediate family members—who has enough information about the patient to make a judgment about the degree of behavior change. He is traditionally involved in the critical events of life—birth, marriage, sickness, and bereavement. Thus, with even minimum training, the priest is often in a position to decide the ability of the person to withstand new pressures or sudden changes. The priest must decide whether in a passing crisis he can give the troubled parishioner the support and reassurance which will help him to survive the experience with confidence and fortitude.

What are signs of serious mental illness? Reverend Thomas W. Klink, in the *Clergyman's Guide to Recognizing Serious Mental Illness*,[8] gives us an expert's opinion: "There are occasions when the inner stress, confusion, detachment, agitation, feelings of isolation, deep depression or helplessness felt by the person are sufficient to impair his day-to-day functioning. It is almost as if meeting everyday problems is too much for him. He finds communicating with family and friends extremely difficult, functioning on his job a heavy burden, and he tends to deny the reality of situations around him. When the person is so overwhelmed and pained by the demands of everyday living that he begins to live in a world of his own, then he has a serious mental illness."

Specific signs of severe mental disorder in an individual, as outlined by the Reverend Klink, are as follows:

1. He shows big changes in his behavior. He may, for example, change from a serious, pleasant member of the community to a quarrelsome, antagonistic or unusually happy personality type.

2. He has strange periods of confusion or loss of memory.

3. He thinks people are plotting against him or has grandiose ideas about himself.

4. He talks to himself and hears voices.

5. He thinks people are watching him or talking about him.

6. He sees visions or smells strange odors or has peculiar tastes.

7. He complains of bodily changes that are not possible. Thus he may think that his face is disfigured or that he is suffering from a rare, fatal illness.

8. He suffers from the need to perform several repetitive acts many times over, is always plagued by foreboding thoughts. A compulsive hand-washer who has a morbid fear of germs, or the individual who is persistently plagued by sexual or morbid thoughts, falls into this category.

9. He shows marked depressed behavior. Such a person often feels utterly worthless and alone. He may be able to tell of his worthlessness in terms of his inability to control his angry or destructive thoughts toward those whom he loves. He may actually give up hope and think of suicide. The fact that such a person is able to talk of suicide is definitely no assurance that he will not make an attempt to do so. Rev. Klink cautions us that "when a clergyman encounters a person whose severe depression has come to 'lift' without treatment, the clergyman should recall that this period of early recovery is one of the times of greatest danger for suicide."

10. He behaves in a way that is dangerous to others, deciding to hurt another person who he feels is persecuting him.*

The priest who is convinced that a parishioner suffers from a severe mental illness can approach the problem in a number of ways. He may be dealing with a type of person, for example, who has been exhibiting certain of the above telltale symptoms for many years. Such a person may be able, despite his eccentricities, to function reasonably well and to remain adjusted to his present life situation. It would be rash to disturb this equilibrium; such a person

* Summarized from a more extended treatment in the afore-mentioned pamphlet.

should be referred to psychiatric help only when a radical change in the accustomed pattern takes place, indicating that the individual is so overwhelmed by the imbalance within himself that he is no longer able to function adequately.

In other cases, where referral is an obvious need, the priest can work with the patient himself, with his personal physician, and with the family of the patient.

The priest who deals directly with the person who needs psychiatric help can facilitate the referral process tremendously. He can help both the patient and his family to understand that to apply for psychiatric help is not a disgrace or a tragedy. Many persons still feel that those who seek such help are feeble-minded or "crazy." A priest can help to explain that emotional disorders are common, and that they are best treated by specialists, just as other specific organic diseases are treated by experts in, say, heart, lung, or stomach ailments.

The patient and his relatives are often inclined to accept these reassurances about many aspects of psychiatric treatment from a priest even though they would be unsympathetic or even unbelieving if they came from other sources. The priest, for example, can soothe the very real fears of most laymen who are under serious misapprehensions as to the cost of successful psychiatric treatment. Statistics show that it costs less to remove the symptoms of emotional discomfort than it does to go to the hospital to have an appendix removed or a fractured leg looked after.[9]

Many patients and members of their families are skeptical about the value of "just talking" to a psychiatrist. The priest can, at the outset, explain that the specialist in emotional disorders discovers the nature of the illness and treats it by having the patient talk about himself, just as a general practitioner uses a stethoscope or X-ray machine to diagnose organic problems.

Generally speaking, the priest is well advised to use the patient's family doctor as a first referral source. However, it is important to keep in mind the regrettable fact that some general practitioners are still reluctant to acknowledge the prerogatives of the psychiatrist in many areas of emotional illness. Some "old-fashioned" doctors—many Catholics among them—often prefer to try pills, medicines, and large doses of direct reassurance. This approach to mental illness often relieves the symptom at the moment, but it never gets at the real cause. In many cases the difficulties recur months, or even years later, and often with increased severity. It is without question a difficult decision to make, but if the priest is convinced of the necessity of a psychiatric diagnosis, he must occasionally circumvent the purely supportive management of the patient by a general practitioner, and take the initiative in urging a psychiatric diagnosis.

SCHOOLS OF PSYCHIATRIC THOUGHT

Occasionally, the priest himself will need to make a direct psychiatric referral. Here again, it is helpful to understand some of the divergent approaches to the treatment of mental illness within the psychiatric profession itself. One can distinguish roughly three major groups of psychiatric practitioners, but it should be kept in mind that this division is not at all definite. There is frequent overlapping. All psychiatrists are physicians duly recognized and approved. Preferably they are either diplomates of the American Board of Neuropsychiatry or eligible to take this examination.

1. The *organicists* are strict followers of the medical tradition of the nineteenth century which contends that every clinically observable fact must be related to a discernible disease process in the body. The more extreme organicists believe that the reason for our not having found a physical cause of such diseases as neuroses and schizophrenia lies in our still imperfect methods of

observation.* They think the day will come when all mental and emotional diseases will be reducible to physical and observable impairments of the body itself. Obviously, the more neurologically-oriented among the psychiatrists tend to be organicists.

The organic psychiatrists are practical, hardheaded and excellent clinicians, often extremely successful when it comes to diagnosis and treatment of actual anatomical or physiological disturbances of the nervous system. In their desire to be scientific they tend to overlook the fact that most people are not exclusively motivated by rational considerations; that symbols, dreams, unproven convictions, even superstition, may exert as powerful an influence on the behavior of a person as a virus or a germ, causing as much, if not more, actual pain and suffering. Organic psychiatrists tend to be precise in their diagnoses, but often quite pessimistic about the possibility of a behavior change in their patients.

2. The second group of psychiatrists in this country is that of the *psychobiologists*. They are psychologically-oriented psychiatrists. They are the most pragmatic and least dogmatized of all, for they do not expound any particular school, nor are they loath to use developments in the realm of psychology. They look upon their patients as psychobiological units; that is, they study the mind and the body as interacting parts of a single whole. The psychobiologists draw from the dynamic school of psychiatry for many of their concepts used in psychotherapy. They are also prone to use glandular injections, sedatives, drugs such as insulin, and electric-shock treatment.

3. The third school of specialists in American psychiatry, steadily gaining in numbers and influence, is that of the *dynamic psychiatrists*. They occupy a position at the opposite pole from the organic psychiatrists. They concentrate on the psychological origins of mental illness without, however, neglecting the possibility of phys-

---

* The brevity of our treatment may make it seem as though the authors are unduly harsh in their estimate. In fairness to the organicists, it must be pointed out that a great debate still rages on most of these points, and we would not wish to seem to have prejudged the outcome of that debate.

ical causation. They are highly trained, with a heavy emphasis upon psychoanalytic theory and techniques. They find the causes for mental and emotional disturbances in the developmental past of the individual. They believe that if the patient is helped to uncover and re-evaluate memories and feelings he has pushed back from the earliest days of childhood, and to relate these to the present, he can gain an intellectual and emotional insight into his personality development which can lead to behavioral and emotional changes. This procedure in treatment very often provides the cure.

It should be obvious from the first chapter of this book that the authors are sympathetic to the dynamic school of psychology. The reader is, of course, quite free to disagree. The authors feel that the dynamic concepts of human personality are far closer to Catholic philosophical and theological tenets than are the tenets of the organicists or psychobiologists. The dynamic approach to personality is wary of the tendency of the other schools of psychiatry to identify man's personality with materialistic chemical and biological forces. The dynamists believe in the inherent capacity of man to use insight and reason as aids to self-knowledge. They believe that analytic therapy not only helps a troubled personality to sort out his jumbled emotions but also, through an ever increasing insight into his unconscious motives and behavior, enables him to liberate the will from compulsive behavior, thereby encouraging ever freer and more responsible activity.

There are various psychoanalytic schools, with wide disagreements among themselves, all of which, however, base some of their theories and techniques on the work of Sigmund Freud. All have at least this in common: they attribute to man's unconscious a large, active, and dynamic role in his behavior, both normal and abnormal. These schools use a method of analysis to get at the unconscious, and by means of this analysis try to heal the sick mind, especially in the less severe mental disorders known as neuroses. Catholic authorities in the field are in substantial agreement that some of Freud's views on religion, on morality, and on the nature of man are at variance with the teachings of the Church. Most of these authorities, however, are agreed that these theoretical differences need not affect the usefulness of psychoanalysis as a therapeutic method, and that a Catholic can accept the latter without subscribing to Freud's philosophical and religious viewpoints. Contrary to popular impression, such therapy need not make use of immoral means to cure a patient. It is too early to be sure how many patients or what types of mental illness can best be cured by psychoanalysis. In any case, a Catholic patient may undertake such treatment with full confidence if it is administered by an analyst whose principles and practices are known not to offend Catholic morality.

It is important to note that the psychoanalytic approach to mental illness is a fast-growing and significant influence upon psychiatry today. The great majority of medical schools are training their students in this theory and technique. Catholic psychiatrists, both lay and clerical, are in the forefront of this research. Karl Stern and Gregory Zilboorg, Father John Devlin, S.J., and Father Jerome Hayden, O.S.B., in the United States, Father Noël Mailloux, O.P., of Canada, Father Louis Berniert, S.J., of Paris, Father Joseph Nuttin of Louvain are examples of Catholic scholars in the forefront of psychoanalytic research and practice. Publications such as *Cahiers Laennec* and *Etudes Carmelitaines, Séries Collection de Psychologie Religieuse* indicate the extent to which dynamic psychology has influenced the moral and spiritual writings of two distinguished academic groups in Europe.[10]

Psychiatrists who have had very little dynamic training, and who have not been analyzed themselves, are inclined to use shock treatment, glandular injections or drugs as their chief therapies. The psychoanalyst will also use medicine and electro-shock where indicated, but relies principally on fairly frequent, long "talking-through" interviews which gradually get to the heart of the patient's emotional difficulty. Physical treatment, such as electric shock or tranquillizers, even when administered without protracted counselling or psychotherapy, often has spectacular results; the "cure," however, if not followed up with protracted psychotherapy (talking through a problem), is often only temporary and fleeting, especially if the patient is fearful or skeptical about the treatment. The relapse of such patients is often more severe than the original illness.

This is not to say that the importance of biochemical and mechanical treatment is to be minimized or belittled. Psychotherapy and analysis, from a practical point of view, are still for the few. Then, too, certain mental illnesses are not successfully treated by the "talking-out" method. The general shortage of adequately trained doctors makes it imperative that the great majority of mental patients be given immediate symptomatic relief rather than deep, long-term therapy.

Electro-shock, insulin-shock, and in particular, the tranquillizing drugs are often remarkably effective, and in many instances spectacularly reduce the suffering of severely or violently ill patients. The analytic schools feel that these remedies strike at the symptoms of the disease rather than at the root cause. The psychoanalysts, however, would be the first to pay tribute to the wonder drugs, which they often prescribe as hold-over doses for their own patients, and which they know to be invaluable medications for patients for whom symptom relief is the chief concern.

Psychiatric techniques can be used by specialists who are not medical doctors. Under the supervision of a qualified psychiatrist, such co-therapists as psychologists, psychiatric social workers, and lay analysts can conduct successful therapy with many types of disturbed patients.

When a priest makes a psychiatric referral he should have two major concerns. One, is the therapist ready to respect Catholic religious and moral convictions? Two, is the therapist well-trained and competent? Too often the psychiatrist is chosen just because he is a Catholic. This detail alone will assure neither the cure of the patient nor the preservation of his Faith. Both of these desirable goals are more likely to be attained if the psychiatrist is competent in his field. The well-trained psychiatrist, be he Catholic or non-Catholic, will not attack or undermine the moral and religious convictions of his patient but will be quite capable of working through emotional conflicts within his patient's religious framework. The competence of a therapist is indicated by the fact that he is unwilling to enter into a purely theological discussion in therapy, but will rather advise the patient to seek such information from a priest.

Such a therapist, furthermore, will be quite willing to collaborate with the priest in matters which have moral or religious overtones, even though the difficulty is essentially a psychological one. We will have more to say of this collaboration in the closing paragraphs of this chapter. Finally, the clergyman can make certain that the therapists he recommends are members of reputable psychological associations. Such membership can be easily verified by getting in contact with the local County Medical Society, Welfare Council, or Mental Health Association. The priest should be careful to avoid the numerous quacks and pseudo-therapists, who are to be found especially in the urban centers of most communities.

We have seen how important it is that the priest refer psychiatric cases to the proper medical help. The priest is *not* a therapist. The best general rule he can observe is "when in doubt, refer." On the other hand, we have tried to highlight the vast mental health problems of our people today and the shortage of adequately trained personnel to deal with them. The sensitive priest, in making judicious referrals, can also help make sure that the precious and limited time of competent therapists is used to maximum advantage.

There are certain types of mental cases which should not be referred to professional help, at least not at the outset. There are many old people who are quite adequately (and often heroically) cared for by their families. There are certain types of temporary mental illness, such as are experienced by obsessively scrupulous or chronically uneasy people who can struggle through a depression or panic of short duration and emerge unscathed if time and patience on the part of a kindly counsellor is made available to them. There are the neighborhood "odd ones" who have managed with their eccentricities for years, have not sought medical help, and seem to feel no need for it. Until there is some spectacular change in their behavior, or until they come and ask for further help, there is often no need to disturb their equilibrium, bizarre as some of their behavior may seem to us.

Then, there are certain patients who do seem to need help but who are obviously not financially able to afford good professional therapy. Much depends upon the clinical facilities in the locality;

it would only complicate the illness if the patient began therapy and then found he was unable to pay for it. Finally, there are certain individuals who are financially sound, but who are not psychologically prepared to approach therapy positively. The patient who undergoes psychotherapy must have a certain amount of motivation. He must want to do something about his problem; he must want to get well. If this motivation is lacking, the priest should be hesitant in making an immediate psychiatric referral unless the patient is either violent, suicidal, or so very ill that he is not able to judge his own condition at the moment. If, for example, a disturbed husband sees his entire problem centered in his spouse, therapy might do very little for him. As long as he is convinced that his wife is the one who needs the treatment, little progress can be made. (A device which sometimes works is to persuade the supposedly "well" partner —who is really sick—to initiate therapy to learn to understand his or her spouse's "difficulties.")

THE UNIQUE ROLE OF THE PRIEST

The priest can, however, make a unique contribution in his dealings with a patient whose motivation is poor, in or out of therapy. The priest can do things which a psychiatrist cannot. He can point out a man's moral duty to try to save a salvageable marriage. He can help the patient realize the personal investment he has in his own problem. He can stir up a sense of responsibility in the patient which will motivate him to seek therapy, and to approach his role in the therapeutic process in an honest, earnest sort of way. In still other cases, when a mental difficulty involves a moral problem, the priest is again in a much better position to stress the obligation of the penitent to seek therapy. In such a situation, the priest might say, "I don't know whether you can control this sort of behavior or not, but you owe it to Almighty God and yourself to take it up seriously with a professional person."

There are times when tolerant reassurance is the last thing the priest should give the patient. To reassure and soothe a disturbed parishioner by underplaying the seriousness of his symptoms may only prolong the time it will take him to get into therapy. The priest must beware of the tendency to "try to handle this himself." He must seriously question the use of such phrases as "Don't worry," or "This will work itself out." This procedure is especially dangerous when the reassurance is in reality enabling psychosomatic symptoms to continue to affect his physical condition, so that as time goes on certain aspects of the emotional illness may have a permanently damaging organic effect. (See Appendix I.)

The priest who takes it upon himself to establish a dependency relationship with an emotionally disturbed person must always keep this question in mind: "What will happen if for some reason or another I will no longer be available to this individual? When our relationship is broken, will he be worse off because I will not be there to help and reassure and support him?" Admittedly, it is a decision of some delicacy; there is no easy solution.

It is always a good rule to be absolutely honest with a patient; if he seems really sick, tell him what you think. If you are not sure how sick he is, encourage him to find out from a capable diagnostician. Surely there are few priests, even those who have read a psychiatric textbook or two, who feel competent to venture interpretation and diagnosis, or, worse yet, to attempt to analyze the person's problem.

Once a parishioner is actually in therapy, the priest can often facilitate the recovery. The priest can make sure at the outset that the ill person is referred to a qualified therapist. We have already suggested the criteria whereby a psychiatrist acceptable to Catholics can be judged. The same principles would hold for psychologists or psychiatric social workers who might be assigned to the patient. The psychologist should certainly be a member of the American Psychological Association (clinical division). He should have his "boards," a diploma from the American Board of Examiners, and be certified by the State as a psychologist. Further, he should provide some guarantee that he has had adequate psychiatric supervision. A social worker should have a minimum of a master's degree in psychiatric social work, with five or six years of practice in a supervised team setting. He should be a member of the National Association of Social Workers.

Unless he feels it absolutely essential, the priest should not interfere in the therapy process of the patient. He must be careful not to accept at face value the description the patient might give him of what goes on in therapy. Resistance of the patient to a fruitful probing into his personal problems, especially in early treatment, will often encourage him to pit priest and therapist against each other. The priest must not be a partner to this sort of "out" for the patient. The patient, for example, will come hurrying to the priest early in therapy and accuse the psychiatrist of having encouraged or condoned some sort of immoral activity; or the patient may accuse the psychiatrist of "explaining away" matters of faith or morals in a manner contrary to the teachings of the Church. If the priest has serious misgivings about the therapeutic principles of the psychiatrist, he can ask the patient's permission to talk to the psychiatrist about them. In most cases the priest will discover that the patient has misconstrued the psychiatrist's words (or silences) to fit his own anxieties, prejudices, and unwillingness to face his deeper problems.

The patient, because he is Catholic, has an added opportunity to play into his need to balk at the probings of the therapeutic process. If often happens that difficulties essentially psychological in nature have a kind of surface relationship to religious and moral matters. The Catholic patient can avoid looking at his problems squarely, or fail to make an effort to change, by protesting that such insight or reformation would be in effect an affront to his Faith and its practices. Thus, an overconscientious mother will feel that the psychiatrist is attacking her religion if he suggests that she might discontinue her attendance at daily Mass and, instead, concentrate more on her duties to her husband and children at home. It is obvious how, in cases such as this, the priest can make a significant contribution in clarifying for the Catholic patient the essential and the peripheral beliefs and practices of our religion.

Occasionally a patient who has been some time in therapy and is making progress finds himself *actually* at odds with some of the philosophical, religious, or moral convictions of the therapist. Even in such cases, the priest should be slow to advise a break-off of therapy, unless it is obvious that the Faith of the patient is in danger. He should first of all challenge the need of the patient to accept all the analyst's views in place of his own. The inability of the patient to stand on his own two feet and proclaim his own religious and moral beliefs confidently is one indication that therapy has not yet made the necessary contribution to the patient's own inner strength and self-reliance. The patient's ability to stand up and maintain a healthy autonomy in the religious area, as well as every other, is one significant sign of therapeutic progress.

It is important for the priest to know that in the mind of an emotionally disturbed person he may represent many things. A symbol of authority; a fearful, avenging judge; giver of all love; beneficent dispenser of all good things—these are some of the stereotypes of the priest which occur immediately to many healthy, well-adjusted Catholics. How much more, then, does the priest unwittingly represent many things to the mind of the disturbed parishioner? The priest must remember, for example, that when a patient rebels and rails at the priest, often in violent and abusive fashion, the priest can offer himself as a most convenient "target" for the individual's emotions. If he can be understanding, listen quietly and sympathetically instead of fighting back and scolding, he may gradually make it less necessary for the patient to act out his confused needs and hostilities in this manner.

It is important that the priest learn not to be overwhelmed by the patient's symptoms, mannerisms, and behavior. Even if he finds himself quite shocked and upset inside, the priest who can remain calm and encouraging, at least on the surface, will be performing a valuable service. The individual who feels himself worthless, evil, and unredeemable may see rejection by the priest as the last straw. If, on the other hand, the Church (and her representatives) is able to accept and understand, extending the consolations of faith to the stricken and confused soul, then hope, at least, remains his solace. The accepting or rejecting attitude which the patient feels the

Church has towards him may mean the difference between suicidal despair and a fumbling resolution to try again.

On the other hand, sympathy can be overdone. It is possible to give too much kindness, especially to a patient suffering from severe depressions. Unqualified acceptance, the "arm around the shoulders" approach, could very well increase the individual's sense of guilt and plunge him further into depression. "Father thinks I'm a good person when I know I'm really horrible."

It is a great talent to be able to sense the times when the individual needs supportive help, and the other times when he needs to go it alone. There are occasions in the confessional, for example, when most priests seem too "queasy" about stressing the individual's positive resources and helping him draw limits to his undesirable behavior. In some instances, oversensitive priests are even too cautious and fearful about the harm they might do in being firm. We should not concentrate too much on the unhealthy element in any emotionally disturbed person. In fact, the patient will often resent a constant focus upon the sick aspects of his personality. The priest can highlight the healthy, hopeful part of human nature, and help, through encouragement and re-education, to build defenses and positive behavior wherever possible. A collaboration between priest and psychiatrist is often very helpful in this area. In his attempt to be firm and encouraging, the priest may well ask the psychiatrist: "How much direction or firmness can the patient take? What kinds of behavior can I insist the patient should attempt?"

One of the best offices the priest can perform is to help the patient understand the nature of mental illness. This is an especially vital need in the case of a deeply spiritual person. It is often very difficult not only for the patient, but for the family of the patient, to understand what the sacraments and the devotional life can and cannot contribute to the mental and emotional health of the individual. They must be helped to see, for example, that spiritual solutions cannot be substituted for medical help. In some cases the priest must explain why the psychiatrist does not want a patient to persist for the time being in the kind of devotional life to which he has accustomed himself. The psychiatrist may discourage frequent confession and communion; he may even suggest that the patient avoid Sunday Mass for a time. Such temporary measures may be quite necessary if the emotional problem of the individual is somehow mixed up with a distorted symbolism of religion and the sacramental life. This is very difficult for a religious person to understand, and the priest must reinforce the therapeutic suggestions with all the authority at his disposal, pointing out to the patient that only after the neurotic elements of the spiritual life have been eliminated can the individual appreciate the positive significance of his Faith and enter into it wholeheartedly and beneficially.

At certain times, the priest will meet seriously disturbed parishioners who obviously need immediate commitment to a mental institution. He should be very reluctant to take the initiative of commitment upon himself. This should be the responsibility of the personal physician or of the family of the ill person. The priest can help in every way he can to ease the process; he should, however, play the role of a neutral who is there to help if he is asked. In any event, he should keep in touch with the ill parishioner, visit him, write to him, send him parish bulletins, and assure him of his concern and his prayers.

Very often the priest can perform the frequently neglected task of working with the family of a mentally ill person. Fathers and mothers, husbands or wives, are often completely puzzled, shocked, and distraught about the mental collapse of someone dear to them. Often they feel they are to blame. The priest can explain that the end of the world has not come; he can take more time, often, than the psychiatrist to explain in detail what mental illness is, and the ways in which treatment can play a healing role in recovery. The priest can explain away the onus and the shame of mental illness in a family; he can prepare the family to receive the convalescing patient back among his own, or prepare them for new crises or set-backs. In this role, the priest becomes in truth a "comforter of the afflicted" who can bring the most consoling kind of help at the time when it is needed most.

The priest often makes a superior liaison between the psychiatrist and the family of the patient. He can communicate the misgivings and bewilderment of family members, and sometimes of the patient himself, to the doctor. In turn, he can explain to the family what the doctor is trying to do. Above all, he can clarify the characteristics of mental illness to the relatives of the sick person, relieving anxiety through understanding. If the patient is living at home, the priest can help the family create that kind of congenial and accepting atmosphere which the doctor prescribes. If the patient is under extreme tension, or involved in certain bizarre activities, the priest can help the family see that these actions must not be judged at face value, but must rather be tolerated or overlooked for the time being.

Where the patient is a child, adolescent, or young adult, the priest may help change undesirable parental attitudes which contribute to the youngster's problem. Following careful consultation with the doctor, the priest can help parents see that they are making unreasonable demands of their children or that their idea of discipline is too inflexible. In other instances the opposite may be the case—more firmness and consistency in parent-child relationships need to be developed.

All too frequently, the institutionalized patient who improves and is returned to his home suffers a serious relapse. Frequently the seeds of the original conflicts and tensions are still present in the family circle to which the convalescent patient returns. If there is no significant change in the environment, the patient struggles under a tremendous handicap in his efforts to make a new life for himself in the same threatening surroundings. Here again the parish priest may help both family and patient to work out the necessary adjustments by making sure the patient feels that he is wanted back and is accepted by the other members of his family; often the social stigma of mental illness demands that the family give extra reassurances.

The priest is often in a position to implement the suggestions of the psychiatrist in a supervisory way. Any number of practical attitudes can be gently and effectively encouraged by the priest. He can help the family invite a withdrawn old person, for example, to participate in household chores and family activities without making him feel that he is interfering or intruding. Conversely, the priest may help the family of a depressed, "too-precise" housewife by suggesting that they persuade her to loosen up a little in her compulsive need to keep the living quarters one-hundred-percent perfect. So often certain neurotic types need the encouragement of loved ones around them to relax their self-imposed, onerous routines without feeling guilty about doing so.

Puzzled and troubled family members who are worried because a loved one has ceased to go regularly to the sacraments, or no longer prays, can be reassured by the priest's explaining that such apparent laxity has deep psychological undercurrents and should be minimized or ignored by those around the ill person. The sudden inability of a heretofore devout patient to obtain consolation from his religion is often the reason for deep bewilderment and panic. The priest can give wholehearted assurance that such feelings and frustrations are a part of the illness which must be patiently and peacefully borne until such time as emotional balance returns.

This chapter has described a few, and only a few, ways in which the priest and the psychiatrist can work together for the benefit of a suffering soul. The Church has proved herself "all things to all men" by showing an age-old concern for the whole man. She has used every natural aid—music, art, literature, scholarship, ritual—to spur the devotional life of her children. For this reason, the Pope and the Bishops throughout the world have blessed the new and healing sciences of psychology and psychiatry. The Catholic priest, in his efforts to foster the *mens sana* which is every man's goal, can know that he is also laying good foundations for the *via gratiae* which is every man's privilege.

NOTES

1. Pope Pius XII, Address to the Fifth International Congress of Psychotherapy and Clinical Psychology, April 13, 1953. *The Catholic Mind*, LI, No. 1087 (1953), 428–435.

Cf. also, Pope Pius XII, Address to the Thirteenth Congress of the International Association of Applied Psychology, April 10, 1950.

Pope Pius XII, Address to the First International Congress of Histopathology of the Nervous System, *The Catholic Mind*, LI, No. 1085 (1953), 315–318.

2. "Spiritual Aspects of Psychotherapy" in *Faith, Reason and Modern Psychiatry*, ed. Francis Braceland (New York, Kenedy, 1955), pp. 132–133.

3. "Psychiatry and Faith," *Catholic Digest*, November 1955, pp. 86–87.

4. *Mental Health is, 1, 2, 3* (New York: National Association for Mental Health).

5. *Facts about Mental Illness* (New York: National Association for Mental Health).

6. *Personality and Mental Health* (Milwaukee: Bruce, 1955), pp. 3–4.

7. "How to Make a Psychiatric Referral," *State of Mind*, II, No. 4 (1957), p. 8.

8. New York: National Association for Mental Health, pp. 6–10.

9. Evans, op. cit., p. 4.

10. See *Conflict and Light*, ed. Bruno de Jésus-Marie, O.C.D. (New York: Sheed and Ward, 1953), p. 5.

9

USING COMMUNITY RESOURCES

There is almost no limit to the kinds of problems which an average parishioner might bring to his priest. It is surely a tribute, but can also be a handicap, to be considered as a sort of universal expert on all manner of human concerns. The priest is often consulted on legal problems, medical diagnoses, juvenile delinquency, marriage problems, housing mix-ups, geriatric difficulties, alcoholism, child guidance, education, vocational perplexities, and a host of other widely different and highly complicated subjects. The most gifted pastor cannot be sufficiently skilled and knowledgeable in all these diverse human affairs. The prudent and conscientious clergyman, therefore, makes every effort to use organizations and individuals in his locality who can supply professional and specialized kinds of help. A newly appointed pastor or curate should undertake very early in his assignment a survey of possible referral sources within his community and its environs. It is astounding how much time, effort, and heartache the priest can spare himself by knowing at first hand and in specific detail the numbers and types of organizations trained and ready to help him meet many of his parishioners' vexing problems.*

We might divide community agencies available to the parish priest into several categories. They vary, of course, depending on the state, county, city, or district. There are, to begin with, great

* In what follows we are describing the various agencies at their ideal best. It is obvious, however, that in the concrete order the agencies sometimes fall below the level of ideal performance, as do we all, alas.

public, government-operated and supported agencies, such as welfare departments. And there are the ubiquitous private charitable institutions like the diocesan Catholic charities. Both public and private agencies of this sort usually have local district offices in various sections of large cities, as well as a central office.

In addition to these large, inter-disciplinary organizations, the priest often finds that neighborhood associations of various kinds will help him in specific, group-orientated guidance needs. The local Elks or Kiwanis clubs might, for example, be glad to sponsor youth activities for problem children in the parish. Some of the ladies' social organizations might volunteer to help care for handicapped or convalescent parishioners. Finally, the priest can call upon individual professional people in his parish, who often can contribute valuable aid on an occasional, informal basis.

Many cities and rural districts have a community council, a voluntary city-wide association of organizations which co-ordinate, in a program of joint planning, the welfare and health of the territory represented. Such an organization, often called the Council of Social Agencies, usually publishes a booklet listing the co-operating agencies available to the public. The Community Chest occasionally sponsors such a project. In very small communities, where no such concerted planning has taken place, the priest should write to the state or county department of welfare and obtain a list of welfare facilities in the outlying districts.

It is difficult to overstress the necessity of the priest taking an active interest in community affairs, especially in those organizations servicing the community. There is, generally speaking, a sad lack of Catholic influence within many of these secular agencies. This is usually not the fault of the agencies; in most cases no priest can be found who is interested enough to serve on their boards. True, such jobs are often boring and sometimes time-consuming —but the mutual benefits such collaboration can produce are limitless.

Service organizations which minister to the following specific needs are found in most fairly large communities. The priest, depending upon the special problems of his parishioners, will use some a good deal more than others. We include a rather detailed list here to indicate the great variety of services available to the priest.

Adoption. The priest should always refer parents who wish to adopt children, or who wish to place their children for adoption, to official professional agencies for this purpose. There is a tragic laxity involved in arranging private adoptions without official investigation. Priests should not be a partner to anything resembling a "baby black market."

The Aged. There are public and private agencies which cater specially to the senior citizens of the community. The priest will want to know the available homes for the aged, and their respective boarding fees. Certain organizations will also help the pastor to plan activities specifically oriented to the educational, social, and recreational needs of the older members of the parish. Golden Age clubs usually prefer to find their home under church sponsorship rather than under the auspices of a community center. Pastors can offer their facilities to such clubs, and even benefit from them.

Alcoholism. It is important to know the local AA office and members, and any sanitaria which are specially equipped to give medical aid to the alcoholic. There may also be specific doctors and priests in the vicinity who seem to have a special talent for treating the alcoholic. (See chapter 6.)

Armed Forces. There is usually a local recruiting officer who can help teen-agers in the parish with their vocational problems. It is also important to know the various facilities available to veterans and their families, especially in medical and counselling areas.

Camps. Needy or disturbed children, as well as the average youngster, can usually benefit tremendously by several weeks or months in a local summer camp. The priest can often work out a subsidized financial arrangement with the director which will make it possible for some of his young parishioners to benefit from this experience at a very minimum cost.

Child Guidance. This is a most important area of service. The priest is often in a good position to spot embryonic difficulties in a child which might easily develop into a serious adult problem. Professional testing services and early guidance or psychotherapy can spare a human being a lifetime of unhappiness and suffering. There are usually several agencies in the community to which a priest can refer disturbed, mentally retarded, or emotionally distraught children. The public school often has a testing service open to all the children in the district. Both public and private agencies have special departments devoted to the counselling of the child and adolescent.

Child Placement. This is not an adoption agency but an organization which finds foster homes for children whose parents are unable or unwilling to care for them. Most pastors will find that ninety percent of children placed away from their own homes are in foster care rather than adoptive care. He might give greater attention to these children in his parish groups and in his parochial school— the latter particularly, by making school space available to such youngsters deprived of their own parents and frequently suffering from the effects of a disrupted home life. The pastor might also see to it that good Catholic foster homes are found in his own parish in order to preserve the Catholicity of children who are set adrift both emotionally and spiritually from their own parents.

Day Care. Working mothers or unusually busy parents will want to know about the nursery schools and day-care centers which will not only supervise their children for several hours during the day, but will provide an environment which can contribute to the valuable emotional and social development of the young child.

Delinquency Problems. A number of specific agencies such as the Probation Department, Youth Board, the Police Athletic League, Big Brothers, and various community centers are set up to give time and attention to the restless adolescent who threatens to become a serious problem.

Employment Agencies. These are operated by the state, Catholic Charities, or private industries.

Family Counselling. Here is one of the most significant needs in any parish. More and more emphasis is being placed throughout the nation on organizations which focus on the family as a whole, rather than on the isolated problems of individual members.

Homeless Men and Women. Many cities have one or more settlement houses, services agencies, or religious centers which provide temporary food and shelter and occasionally employment for the transient, down-and-out, unverifiable mendicant. The priest, as well as the parish Vincent de Paul Society, can save hours of investigation, and frequently irritation, by having the phone number and address of such centers. Streetcar or subway fare is all that need be risked in making such a referral.

Housing. An acquaintanceship with local superintendents of apartment houses, and some knowledge of the regulations controlling public housing projects, can be of great help to the newly arrived or evicted parish member.

Legal Aid. Indigent parishioners who need a lawyer are served by this agency.

Library. The public library will not only help the parish priest find those books and pamphlets which will be of help to his parishioners in many different areas, but will, in many cases, purchase items for its shelves which the priest suggests will be valuable reading for the Catholics of the neighborhood.

Mental Health. More and more communities are being serviced by a variety of guidance, counselling, psychological, psychiatric, and medical facilities which treat the mentally disturbed. We have devoted an entire chapter (chapter 8) to the role of the priest in this particular aspect of his ministry.

National Groups. In certain parishes which have a concentration of a specific nationality (e.g., Puerto Rican, Italian, German, Irish) there will be influential local organizations through which the priest can work.

Remedial Reading. A specific worry of many children today is their inability to read well. More and more agencies give special attention to this need. Speech handicaps are also often dealt with in such centers.

Schools. The parish priest should have close contact, not only with his own parochial school, but also with the programs of the public schools in his neighborhood. There are often individuals with special training in these schools whom he can call upon.

Adult Education Programs may offer a wide variety of interesting courses to the grownups in the parish. Co-operation between public and private schools can often be most fruitful. The lack of positive communication and interchange between parochial and public schools is one of the most glaring shortcomings of good parish public relations today.

Unmarried Mothers. Most cities and religious bodies have excellent institutions which give expert care and kindly counsel to these girls.

Vocational Counselling. Today over three thousand occupations are open to the high school graduate. Vocational counselling and testing has become one of the most important guidance services to which the priest can refer young parishioners who are planning their vocational futures.

Welfare and Health. Under this general classification come many services which deal with specific financial and health problems. Financial help is extended by state, city, and private agencies to indigent families and individuals who need money for food, shelter, and other necessities.* A number of specific health organizations are equipped to deal with specific health problems, e.g. blindness, deafness, drug addiction, epilepsy, heart disease, multiple sclerosis, muscular dystrophy, polio, tuberculosis; to provide maternity care and help for retarded or otherwise handicapped children and adults.

* Most welfare monies dispersed by public and private agencies to needy families are given in the form of a *grant* rather than a gift or a loan—a grant meaning that a person in some way has a right to the needed money. In many states, agencies would be working illegally to make loans since they would have to be certified under state banking laws. Many people in real need have such an unrealistic conception of a loan, and approach the parish priest or an agency for something they can never pay back and actually should never be held to pay back. In general, the priest should dissuade the needy family from contemplating any loan that a bank would not grant them. (A bank usually makes a sound investigation of financial realities and potentialities before granting a loan.)

A number of these organizations also provide rehabilitation instruction which enables the afflicted to lead useful and productive lives.

In most cases the parish priest will probably want to make his initial referral to some Catholic agency in the diocese. Most chancery offices include subdepartments which deal in charity and welfare, vocations, St. Vincent de Paul Society activities, hospitals, orphanages, and so on. The priest should come to know the priest-directors of these various organizations, as well as some of the lay officials who staff them.

Catholic welfare and charitable organizations are limited in the kinds of service they can give, and therefore the priest should not hesitate to call upon secular agencies in the vicinity. In the vast majority of cases, priests need have no fear that the faith or morals of the parishioner will be in any way affected or attacked by service personnel in such public or private organizations. Invariably the non-Catholic therapist or social worker will make every effort to respect and facilitate the religious practices and needs of the Catholic client.

More often than not, the priest will find it valuable to himself and to his people if he is as active as he can be in the local community council. This informal interaction of important business, social, political, recreational, and religious leaders within a neighborhood can contribute vitally to the smoother management of referral needs the priest might have.

Finally, we cannot stress enough the importance of knowing key individuals within the parish who can help the priest with his guidance problems, and ease some of the external pressures and difficulties which often complicate the personal difficulties of parishioners. Here are some professional people with whom the priest should be on speaking terms, and who can be "on call" whenever the priest needs advice or even temporary help: The local judge, lawyer, nurses, doctors (psychiatrists in particular), the police, local politicians, newspaper editor, teachers in both public and private schools, guidance and attendance personnel, youth workers, social workers, the undertaker, park department attendants, key merchants in the neighborhood, officers of fraternities and clubs (e.g. Veterans, Elks, Rotarians, Kiwanis) baby-sitters, readers for old people and invalids, rabbis and ministers of local churches and synagogues, and fellow priests in the locality. Interaction between these and other key community personages in matters quite apart from religious affiliation of any kind can make unprecedented and unbelievably productive contributions to so many facets of parish life. They are all too frequently neglected or ignored.

TECHNIQUES OF REFERRAL

Let us attempt to outline what might be called a "philosophy of referral." To begin with, the priest must see the social service agencies, both Catholic and secular, as helpful, and not interfering, organizations. He must not regard them as divisive, or in competition with himself. In some cases a priest feels that these agencies have usurped some important prerogatives of his own vocation. Some priests are reluctant to refer a guidance problem or a psychological difficulty to a professional agency because they think that they should be able to solve everything themselves. Others feel that if they refer certain parish problems to professional organizations they are in some way manifesting their inadequacy and failure as competent shepherds of souls. Nothing is further from the truth. Even a cursory examination of our list of special agencies will reveal to the perceptive priest the impossibility of his being a universal expert on any number of these highly complex subjects. The modern priest must expect to find many problems which he will prudently (and gratefully) refer to the agencies set up to handle them.

It is a real tragedy to find subtle hostilities perpetuated between the professional social worker and the priest. There is plenty of work for both to do, and it can be done so much better by working together. On the other hand, it is also important for the priest to understand that the agencies themselves are often limited in what they can do. Long waiting lists are to be expected; often clients must receive attention on the basis of their financial status or the severity of their problem. Mutual respect for, and understanding of, what each—priest and agency—can and cannot do is the best basis for pleasant and productive co-operation.

Perhaps the single most important suggestion in this chapter is the following: *priests should make every effort to know personally the key people in important service agencies.* His relationship to them should be friendly, intimate, and co-operative. If possible, he should meet them socially, have lunch or dinner with them occasionally, and in general, communicate on a basis of confident understanding. When priest and referral agent are familiar enough with each other's talents and temperaments to gauge with accuracy the expectations each can have of the other, incalculable good can result.

If there is to be collaboration of priest and worker, it is important at the outset of a case to decide which areas are clearly the prerogative of each. Collaboration is often desirable; private interference by either in the other's area of professional competence can make for nothing but dissension, irritation, and confusion.

Here are some specific suggestions for the priest who attempts to use the referral agencies within his community to their maximum potential:

The priest should try to refer cases to local agencies or individuals in the neighborhood whenever possible. For example, if a friendly lawyer across the street can give advice on some legal question, there is no need to send the parishioner to the legal aid society downtown. However, if the problem seems from the outset to be a long-term and expensive undertaking, it is usually better to refer directly to the large professional agency equipped to handle the challenge. Financial potentials must always be considered. If the individual is obviously able to pay for psychiatric treatment, for example, it is better to refer immediately to a private psychiatrist, rather than to send him to the local charity clinic.

The priest should make sure that he is referring to the right agency. As we indicated earlier, many organizations perform very precise kinds of services. For example, we do not send a woman who wishes to adopt a baby to a child placement center. If an individual has a counselling difficulty which centers on a job choice, we should refer him to a vocational guidance center rather than a psychiatric clinic. In other words, it is important that the priest know the work of the agency and the problem of the client before he makes a referral. In many cases the patient or petitioner is shuttled from one agency to another. Each time he must describe anew the details of his problem; in cases where his difficulty involves embarrassing details or painful experiences he suffers pain and irritation again and again in the necessary repetition of his story.

The priest, in reviewing the individual's difficulty, can gather certain preliminary facts which will be of tremendous help to the agency that will finally handle the case. He can make an initial check on the agencies which have helped this individual before, or perhaps are now working on his problem. With the permission of the client he can find out from these agencies whether further referral is really necessary. It is wise to ask if other priests in the parish house (or in neighboring parishes) have been consulted on the problem. There are certain types of people who seem to involve as many professionals as they can, often in a confusing and even deceptive manner. If another priest is already involved, it is best to insist that he be allowed to follow it through. The priest can also interview family members, employers, or other individuals who know the client, to make sure that his needs are as he states them.

In cases where the problem is charged with considerable emotion, it is better not to delve too deeply into details, especially when the patient must go over the subject matter quite soon again with an intake worker or therapist. The priest may be told some details which are highly confidential in nature; in such cases he should first obtain the permission of the client before he transmits them to the referral source. If some kind of collaboration between therapist and priest seems helpful, it is important that there be a free exchange of significant material between the two. It is often desirable that a client give permission for both therapist and priest to interchange freely material which they feel is important to his solution of the problem.

At the initial referral contact, the priest should try to be as co-operative as possible with the service personnel with whom he is in touch. He should communicate carefully, either by phone or by letter, pertinent information which he has collected from the client. The priest should remember that the service agent is a professional person restricted by limited time and often rather rigid schedules. The priest is often in a better position to adjust his communications to the available time of the professional person. Too often the therapist is told, "Father X just called and he wants you to call him back between nine and nine-twenty this morning." (Parish housekeepers often need special instructions to facilitate the communication process.)

Whenever possible, the priest should write a clear and brief account of the pertinent information relating to the case. Either by letter or by phone, he should at the outset indicate the name, address, phone number, and family constellation of the client. He may then include his impression of the core of the difficulty, and the goal which he believes the client is seeking. He may describe key family members or associates who seem particularly involved in the problem. The priest should be most ready to answer pertinent questions the intake worker might ask. He should, if possible, get the name of the referral person to whom the client will be sent. In case of difficulty, friction, or misunderstanding of any kind, the priest should be free to discuss the matter with the director or supervisor of the agency.

In almost all cases, the priest can feel confident in accepting the appraisal or diagnosis of the referral person. The special training of these professional people in the areas of their competence makes it unwise for the priest to arrive at private evaluations on his own unless he has additional and confidential material not available to the worker. A client who is advised by two separate authorities—the priest and the worker—often in contradictory ways, is at best confused, and at worst alienated. Priest and referral person must decide together if a collaboration is desirable, and if so, they must agree (as we have indicated earlier) upon the specific areas to which each will limit himself. This is the kind of team work which eliminates unnecessary repetition and duplication and will best serve the interests of the client himself.

RURAL AREAS

It is undoubtedly obvious to the reader that much of the foregoing material has been written with the urban rather than the rural pastor in mind. Many of the above-mentioned community organizations are at the easy beck and call of the busy city pastor but are not available to the rural clergyman. The following suggestions may be of interest to the pastor or curate of a country parish.

It is as important, and in some cases even more so, for the rural clergyman to have first-class relationships with those important people in his community who can help him with his counselling problems. Prominent medical figures, guidance personnel, and public school officials, for example, can prove invaluable in times of need. It is often the personal relationship of the priest with these personages which assures active aid and fruitful co-operation.

The country pastor should do his best to be a part of any community organization or council which co-ordinates social services for rural areas. He may even be interested in inaugurating such a program. This often means a pooling of professional resources by organizing teams of area experts who are members of different faiths. Again, the priest should be reluctant to presume that non-Catholics will be hostile or unco-operative when he pleads for help. The opposite is more often the case.

More and more rural areas are able to call upon social agencies in near-by cities for help. Extension services will often send out field workers who will set up part-time service centers, or even make house visits. A letter or visit to the nearest big city welfare board or the diocesan Catholic Charities will provide the priest with the proper referral addresses and phone numbers.

A number of governmental and educational institutions provide regular extension services in suburban and rural districts. A letter to the state capital, county headquarters, or city hall, as well as to local university offices, can often pinpoint valuable information and aid. (The rural pastor far from metropolitan centers should be cautious about the way in which he communicates confidential information, particularly in his use of the telephone.)

It is in the uncovered and rural areas that the pastor can perform an especially vital function. Rural public departments seem too parsimonious in allotments to needy families and too tight in budgeting for needful services. The rural pastor can familiarize himself with the policies of such departments and dedicate himself to work for wholesome Christian attitudes of charity among the budget planners and welfare personnel. In areas that are beginning to feel the effects of population explosion, the pastor might, to great advantage, give attention on an advisory level to the promotion of Catholic charitable organization and lend his assistance to the foundation of adequate community services for his parishioners.

The rural priest must learn, as must clergymen everywhere, to be content at times with imperfect results. One man, using even the finest of referral resources, can often do only so much. Where expert care and professional advice are lacking, he must often be content with even less. In any case, he will do what he can, much as a nurse does when no doctor is available. The conscientious shepherd of souls will always do his best to provide the necessities and even some of the "extras" important to many facets of his parishioners' lives. Where he fails, or only partially succeeds, he can comfort himself with the conviction that he has done his best. In any event, the priest must constantly remind himself that he is first and foremost a priest, and that regardless of the unavoidable shortcomings of his social and philanthropical contributions, he is always fully qualified to give to the poor, the suffering, and the frustrated those blessed consolations which only he can give: namely, the grace and holy ministrations of Christ's Church.

PART TWO

MORAL PERSPECTIVES
ON COUNSELLING

10

MORAL ASPECTS OF
MASTURBATION

Theologians are in unanimous agreement that masturbation is always objectively a grave sin, for whatever purpose it is committed. The teaching of the Church is clear upon this matter and all theologians are naturally in agreement with that teaching. The problem of the confessor concerns not so much the objective sinfulness of masturbation as the subjective guilt of the masturbator. The concepts of the "sufficient knowledge" and the "sufficient freedom" required for grave subjective sin require exploration.[1]

Theologians and moralists are far more willing today than in the past to admit that subjective imputability can be greatly diminished in cases of habitual masturbation. Nevertheless, they insist that each individual and each case must be judged upon its own merits and that we cannot lay down blanket rules to cover all situations.[2] Theologians have always admitted that habits and compulsions diminish subjective guilt. Today they are also aware that unconscious motivations may strongly influence the individual who has the habit of masturbation and may, consequently, diminish his responsibility.

One must not assume without proof that the psychologically mature man, even if influenced by unconscious motivations, is so determined by them that his actions are not free or do not have that degree of freedom required for grave sin. The mature man, in his apparently free acts, is probably not so strongly influenced by unconscious motivation that his freedom to act and his responsibility for his choices are substantially vitiated. On the other hand, the evidence for the existence of a dynamic unconscious has raised serious problems for the moralist. We believe that the dynamic unconscious exists and that unconscious motivation does play an important role in the moral life of mature people. This does not mean, however, that the classic principles of moral theology, though more sensitively applied in the light of recent psychological insights, are outmoded.

Unconscious energies or dynamisms undoubtedly exercise pressure on man's activity, but this does not imply that they inevitably compel it or deprive it of all freedom, or of the degree of freedom required for grave sin.[3] Unconscious motivation does pervade human conduct, but one may question whether it destroys or even substantially impairs human freedom in the emotionally adult individual, upon whose existence theology insists (but whom psychology must help define). Normal men and women ordinarily have sufficient freedom in the circumstances of their human existence to merit condemnation for sin and praise for virtue. God does not judge a man on his unconscious motivations but upon his freely chosen acts.

Moral theology is prepared to admit that subjective difficulties and impediments to freedom do excuse the average man and woman from the guilt of grave sin more frequently than one might have supposed in the past, but it insists upon the fact that man is capable of some free choices and that the more normal the man is the more complete his freedom is. We cannot act upon a blanket presumption against mortal guilt in masturbation. Certain authors are too quick to declare, without psychological or theological evidence, that in this or that case of masturbation freedom is diminished below the point required for mortal sin. With this uncritical viewpoint we are not in agreement.

There is, certainly, evidence that leads us to believe that in many cases freedom and knowledge are insufficient for grave sin. Let us discuss first the question of knowledge. It was in the past (and still is) the custom to ask the sinner in the confessional whether or not he knew that the sin was grave at the time he committed it. In other words, the confessor asked if the penitent had free deliberation or sufficient knowledge; that is to say, if his intellect remained sufficiently clear and unclouded to judge about the grave guilt involved in the act he was about to commit. If the penitent answered this question in the affirmative, it was presumed that he had sufficient liberty also to commit grave sin.

Moralists in the past seemed to feel that the major impediment to free choice came from the lack of sufficient advertence or sufficient knowledge. If the mental perception of and attention to the sinfulness of the act was intact, the act was regarded as free. With regard to this we might say that modern moralists are willing to admit that *even granted* correct and sufficient conceptual knowledge of the evil of the act about to be committed, man still may not have the required "sufficient reflection" for grave sin.[4] With the use of reason unimpeded, man can still fail to be free in his choice. The reason for this is that today moralists admit that there is such a thing as "evaluative cognition" required for grave sin. Moreover, *even granted* that man has *habitual evaluative* cognition, it is still possible that his liberty is disturbed by other factors such as passion, fear or unconscious dynamisms, so that he does not, despite his habitual evaluative knowledge, have sufficient freedom to commit grave sin.

Conceptual cognition tells us what the object in question is, whereas evaluative cognition appraises the good or worth or the value present in the object. These are two different aspects of a moral object. The normal adult usually joins these two types of cognition in his everyday judgments concerning practical matters. But it is quite evident that there can be cases in which the notional knowledge or the conceptual knowledge is present without sufficient *evaluative* knowledge, for evaluative knowledge is more complex and more difficult to attain than conceptual. Evaluation can be impeded by so many emotional factors that even though abstract knowledge of the act is present, the emotional factors or habitual factors affecting the evaluative knowledge may drive this knowledge to the background of consciousness. In that case the knowledge sufficient for grave sin is lacking. In other words, if the evaluative knowledge seems to lose all its reality at the moment, man is probably not free. There are times and situations in which man understands with perfect clarity that the act which he is about to commit is a sin and yet the sinfulness of the act seems to make no impression upon him at all, or to make an impression far less strong than that which it would make during the normal course of his daily life. He may then be unable to weigh sufficiently the act he is about to commit.

It is possible that some emotionally disturbed people could be placed in this category of persons who lack evaluative cognition. The psychopathic personality most likely should be placed here also. These people, while recognizing right and wrong in the objective order, find that right makes no appeal to them and wrong causes in them no twinges of conscience. They seem to be completely indifferent to the value embodied in the law at stake. Thus their abstract cognitive faculties work normally, but one could not say that they have sufficient axiological knowledge and advertence for grave imputability. Freedom and imputability, in other words, cannot be measured by the conceptual knowledge alone but require a certain proportion of evaluative knowledge. It is acknowledged that a habit of impurity may seriously disturb evaluative knowledge. Thus a man may know clearly the sinfulness of the act and not be free because his evaluative knowledge is disturbed or inculpably inoperative.

Even if a man, because of his adulthood, is presumed to be endowed with the power of evaluating something, it is still possible that he cannot choose freely or that he is unable to evaluate his actions sufficiently. This inability to evaluate the moral quality of one's proposed action is at times obstructed by an impediment, such as drunkenness, delirium, fever or by a functional defect such as habit, and also by certain mental diseases.[5] Freedom depends on the control which man exercises by his will over his action. But this in turn depends upon man's power to deliberate, to weigh and assess alternative courses of action. But the assessment of a course of action requires a certain amount of cognitive valuation of the act proposed to the will. We do not doubt that certain habits such as those of impurity may disturb evaluative cognition.

It is possible also that the evaluative knowledge necessary for freedom may even be completely effaced momentarily under the influence of habit, passion or other strong emotions. This would explain why certain penitents readily admit that they had clear knowledge of the sinfulness of the action—that is to say, cognitive knowledge—yet sincerely protest that they could not have acted otherwise. They may well be telling the truth, because it is possible that emotion, passion, habit so disturbed or obliterated their evaluative cognition that their freedom was diminished below the level of grave imputability or even diminished below the level of a human act. Obviously the non-existence or the disturbance of evaluative cognition in those who suffer from psychological difficulties is more common. The more serious the psychological imbalance, the more ready moralists are to admit that evaluative cognition may be disturbed.

It is important also to realize that *even granted habitual evaluative cognition,* there are still obstacles to man's freedom which may operate to reduce the level of imputability below that of grave fault. One must distinguish here between philosophical freedom and psychological freedom.[6] Philosophical freedom is that freedom required in order to have a human act. This type of freedom simply means that a man had sufficient cognitive and evaluative knowledge, sufficient rational deliberation and freedom, to have made the opposite choice to the one which he made, or to have refrained from any choice at all. This power of freedom means that, given certain requisites of knowledge and motivation, a man is responsible for his choice since he could, absolutely speaking, have said no instead of yes to the action in question. This type of freedom makes the act a human act. If this much freedom is not had, the act is simply not a human act at all and can in no sense be a moral act, since it is non-free.

But even granted that man had, in an individual situation, this metaphysical freedom to choose the opposite, it does *not* automatically follow that he has sufficient freedom for grave sin. The naked possibility to choose otherwise or not to act at all does not mean that the sinful choice is automatically a grave subjective sin, when the act is objectively, gravely sinful. For mortal sin, besides metaphysical freedom, requires a certain degree of freedom from psychological pressures, obstacles, difficulties, and emotions. What degree is required we cannot state with mathematical accuracy. What we must underscore is that, even if metaphysical freedom is present so that the person chose freely in a metaphysical sense, it is still possible that this person was not sufficiently free to commit mortal sin. We admit, in other words, that emotional stress, habit, obsessions, compulsions limit man's psychological freedom and limit it in some cases below the level required for grave sin.

However, here too the theologian must be careful not to make blanket statements excusing normal men from grave subjective sin. The practice of the Church indicates that she believes that normal men are capable of and actually commit grave sin. This is implicit in the way she administers the sacrament of Penance and also in the requirements she lays down for canonical delicts. We cannot insist too strongly that the judgment in each case must be an individual judgment and is the result of many complex factors. We have explained that mere cognitive knowledge of the rightness or wrongness of an act does not always mean that the subsequent choice of the will is free, or sufficiently free to merit grave sin. In the normal individual the joining of conceptual cognition and evaluative cognition will take place so easily that he will ordinarily have sufficient knowledge for freedom and for sin, but the more pathological the penitent is, the more influenced by unconscious dynamisms, the less probable it is that evaluative cognition will function as it should. Since this evaluation may be disturbed by emotional factors, we believe that emotion may diminish evaluative cognition below the level required for grave sin. In those who have developed the habit of masturbation, it seems that evaluative cognition of the sinfulness of the act may often recede to the background of consciousness because of the pressure of passion and habit.[7]

The influence of a long-sustained habit may be such that the penitent actually does not have sufficient freedom for grave sin. When a habit is of long duration, it often happens that there is good reason for asserting that grave guilt is absent. There are habits also which seem to be engraved not only in the psychology of the individual but in his bodily structure. Inveterate habits of impurity lead us to suspect that grave subjective guilt may possibly be absent.

Further, we should not believe either that even if *all* the conditions required for sufficient knowledge are present, it automatically follows that the act is free. The spiritual will, even granting both types of knowledge, may still be seriously disturbed by the emotions and passions of the body. Moreover, even the external execution of the act commanded by the will may be hampered by bodily passions and instinctive reactions. Man may carry out certain actions, partially at least, in opposition to his free decisions, so that the external execution is not a human act. Pathology can block the normal execution of the will's choice and reduce execution to the level of a non-free action. This is possible *even when the spiritual choice* and intellectual deliberation were free.[8]

We are inclined to believe also that at least in some cases an intolerable situation arises in which the impulse to masturbate may be irresistible because it is no longer physically possible to resist. In this case, we have no question of freedom because there is no human act. The impulse is genuinely irresistible in this situation. In compulsive actions of this sort, there is simply no choice of the will remaining at all. We are in the realm of acts which are not human acts.

No one then would maintain that every external action of man that takes place with clear attention to the sinful nature of the act is a free action under the control of the will. Irresistible impulses and impulsive actions exist. It is possible also that the irresistible impulse in the sensitive appetite of man is so strong that, despite even *evaluative* cognition of the sinful nature of the act to which he is impelled, man's executive powers carry out the act completely or partially as a non-human, non-free act. In this case the "will act" is not positive enough to command external action. The action then is a completely compulsive action and in no sense is moral or immoral action. Moralists today admit that the force of an impulse such as violent anger, fear or passion may in some cases produce these irresistible, compulsive actions.

It is possible also that the threat of an intolerably painful situation continuing, as may happen in the case of the habitual masturbator, causes a genuinely compulsive action.

These situations naturally do not exist as the usual pattern for the normal man. We cannot accept the thesis that original sin took away from man the possibility and the obligation of directing his moral activity through his freedom. Nor can we accept the principle that psychological incapacity represents the normal situation of man. Unconscious motivation is a reality, but we cannot grant that it is the unique or determining factor in a normal man. We grant that there can be a continuing fascination or attraction with an object which obsesses the mind so that the urge towards the object is in fact irresistible. It is also possible that the urge, while absolutely speaking not irresistible to the extent that philosophical or metaphysical freedom vanishes, may be so strong that the degree of freedom required for a gravely imputable act is no longer had. It is very difficult to judge in practice whether or not an act is compulsive.

The compelling fascination with which the habitual masturbator dwells upon the thought of masturbation suggests that in some cases his action is indeed compulsive. However, each case must be judged individually, for what appears to be a compulsive urge will, in the same individual, vary in strength from period to period. Nor can we say that because an urge manifests compulsive symptoms, therefore all of the actions which follow from this urge will be compulsive. On the contrary, in the same individual the urge may be compulsive at one moment of the day and not at another moment of the day.

What one must recall to pass judgment on compulsive urges is this: there must be some kind of proportion between the attraction exerted by the value and the disvalue in question if moral freedom is to operate in such a fashion as to permit serious praise or blame. If consciousness is so narrowed down by the fascination of the immoral object that the moral value in question exerts almost no attractive power, it seems clear that the freedom necessary for sin is excluded. If the object of desire so absorbs one's consciousness that any kind of genuine, realistic, evaluational appraisal of the alternative good is impossible or is greatly reduced, then we believe that freedom is reduced beyond the point where mortal sin is possible.

There are other indications in the practical order which may be helpful to the confessor in judging whether responsibility is limited or eliminated entirely.[9] For example, when the struggle between the desire to masturbate and the desire to obey the objective law is so long continued that considerable mental fatigue results, it is possible that the act finally performed is more an act of passion and weakness than of sin. We also may assume that if the act occurs suddenly, following upon a lengthy period of struggle when the subject was pulled to and fro by temptation, that there was not adequate free will. We may also be lenient in our judgments of those situations where the subject commits acts in a partially conscious state, when half-asleep or under the impulse of very strong emotional excitement or profound depression. So too with the penitent whose falls become rarer and rarer as he tries to collaborate with his confessor. There are indications here that the sin is rather a sin of weakness than of malice and that his will is abnormally weak.

When the confessor is confronted with a case of the individual who uses all the natural and the supernatural means suggested to him by his confessor and yet makes no improvement, he may well suspect here also that the level of freedom is diminished beneath that required for grave guilt. If the individual has rejected his habit voluntarily and wishes to improve his moral status and takes serious means to do so, and if the whole tenor of his religious or spiritual life is otherwise satisfactory, we may legitimately wonder if there is not operative here some psychological deformation which renders him incapable of freedom, or sufficient freedom for grave sin in this sphere. At least, serious doubts may well arise in the confessor's mind about the grave subjective guilt of such a penitent.

It is also noteworthy that we should take into account the psychological age of the individual masturbating. We cannot expect the same adult scale of values from a youth or an adolescent that we would expect to find in an unpressured adult. It is possible therefore that the immature individual, and masturbators of any age are relatively immature individuals, is in some cases prevented by his immaturity from sufficient appraisal of the alternatives offered to his freedom.

We are also prepared to admit that sexual passion, when thoroughly aroused, can overpower human freedom, so that if the individual has resisted until the moment when passion is most intense we can presume that he is not seriously responsible for what then takes place. We should be lenient too in our judgment when there are in the family, or in the history of the individual, indices of mental illness, emotional disturbances, "nerves," breakdowns, etc. In these cases we may have reason for doubting grave guilt. Then too, sudden onslaughts of passion—for example, a sudden fit of rage—may not actually allow for sufficient deliberation.

Some such judgments may perhaps also be made in the case of those whose masturbatory activities far exceed quantitatively the normal man's desires for sexual satisfaction. When a man or woman confesses to abnormally frequent masturbatory activity over a fair period of time, we may suspect that we are in the presence of a psychic abnormality.

When the masturbatory activity of the individual is accompanied by an extraordinary and peculiar fantasy life, deviate in character and weird and unreal in content, one may suspect that the habit of masturbation reflects some inner conflicts or compulsions.

It is not infrequent that the confessor will meet with married men who, while admitting that their marital life is sexually satisfactory, continue the habit of masturbation. In such a situation one may suspect that the sexual side of marital life is actually not so satisfactory as the individual claims. At any rate, it is a situation which puzzles the ordinary confessor; there is probably some deep-rooted conflict which must be brought to light and cured before the habit of masturbation itself can be cured. It is possible that in this case we have one of those psychological anomalies which indicate more or less compulsive activity.

Another type of individual who not infrequently presents himself to the confessor is the masturbator who experiences a highly intense feeling of guilt and anguish over his habit and yet in the same breath protests that he is morally guiltless. Here we must be aware of all the mental and emotional disturbances that may be expressed in the act of masturbation. Frequently this habit is an expression of conflicts of a non-sexual order which one must discover before the individual will be capable of breaking with his habit. In this case, we must do what we can to relieve the torment of the individual without seeming to be permissive towards an act always objectively sinful. When the penitent, however, claims that he is irresistibly impelled to place this act, is not free, hence morally guiltless, we may strongly suspect that he is expressing a complex truth. Whatever may be the objective situation of the penitent in this case (always very difficult for the confessor to discover), at least the confessor should try to alleviate his feelings of anguish, depression, and frustration. Possibly here a personality disturbance is at work that limits or eliminates the freedom of the individual in this particular situation.

As regards the typical adolescent masturbator, we must be careful not to demand of the adolescent a maturity of judgment and evaluative knowledge which is normally not had until adulthood. The period of adolescence is often one of intense confusion and conflict to the normal individual, and it is not surprising if he is not able to integrate his sexual activity into a well-balanced heterosexual life. In this case we should in no sense give acquiescence to his activity but should encourage him to develop himself as a human being and to put aside the disequilibrium and tensions which accompany adolescence and to grow to adulthood. We must judge the adolescent's guilt according to his present structure of personality and psychological maturity. The Church does not judge children as men, and the adolescent is still half-child. This does not mean that the adolescent is not capable of free acts, but it is possible that his evaluative cognition does not keep pace with his cognitive cognition when biological growth and the demands of sexual life break in upon his conscience at adolescence. At least the confessor here may be lenient in judging the guilt of the masturbator who shows good will in attempting to co-operate with the advice of the confessor, and whose general moral life is praiseworthy.

The principles here expressed may be of help to the confessor in forming a judgment concerning the guilt of his penitent. However, we must remember that Pius XII pointed out rather insistently in his addresses that we must not automatically transfer conclusions drawn from the clinical study of abnormal man to the normal man.

Each individual case must be weighed as such. We must not accept the thesis that original sin deprives man of the obligation or power to structure his moral life through his free choices. The normal man will have a moral struggle to keep on the path of virtue, but it does not authorize his drawing back or laying claim to psychic impotence.

Unconscious motivation may well explain much of what takes place in abnormal personalities and to some degree in the normal personality also, but we cannot predicate it too readily in the sexual sphere, of a person who is otherwise psychologically normal. It is certainly not the determining factor in the normal man's moral life.

In his radio message of March 23rd, 1952, Pope Pius XII condemned those who in practice seemed to presume that the sins of impurity in today's youth could not possibly be subjectively grave because of an inevitable influence of antecedent blameless passion. He, on the contrary, declared to educators and youth itself that the demand for divine purity of body and mind retains its full force for the youth of today. Modern youth has the obligation and, with the help of grace, the possibility of persevering in the cultivation of purity. Pius XII rejected as erroneous the assertion of those who regard the attainment of purity in adolescence as an impossibility.

Perhaps we should recall the case of the condemnation of the book of the Abbé Marc Oraison. The fundamental principle condemned in this book seems to be a distorted notion of original sin with the corollary that no one is normal in matters of sex. Hence all human beings, as the victims of sexual pathology, would be presumed to be guilty of material sins only, and this presumption would only yield to contrary proof. It appears to some reviewers at least that the author of this book claims that all sexual sins are, in practice, committed by individuals whose wills have been so interfered with by unconscious dynamisms that they are incapable of serious sin. Hence in the confessional penitents are to be treated on the presumption that they have not been subjectively guilty of mortal sin. The condemnation of this book leads us to restate the necessity for prudence and circumspection in judging individual consciences.

The Holy See encourages us to continue our researches in depth-psychology and psychiatry, but it warns us that the objective principles of morality are inviolable and that we must not overstress the influence of original sin, as if this obliterated human freedom in normal individuals.

NOTES

1. André Snoeck, S.J., "Masturbation and Grave Sin" in *New Problems in Medical Ethics,* ed. Peter Flood (Westminster: Newman Press, 1953), pp. 35–38.

2. John C. Ford, S.J., and Gerald Kelly, S.J., *Contemporary Moral Theology* (Westminster: Newman Press, 1958), Vol. I, pp. 233–234.

3. J. Duhamel, "Theological Aspects of Habitual Sin," *Proceedings of the Eleventh Annual Convention of the Catholic Theological Association of America,,* pp. 148–149.

4. Duhamel, art. cit., pp. 135–138; cf. also J. Lynch, "Notes on Moral Theology," *Theological Studies,* 17 (1956), p. 169.

5. J. Ford, "Criminal Responsibility and Catholic Thought," *Bulletin of the Guild of Catholic Psychiatrists,* 3 (1953), pp. 3–22.

6. Ford and Kelly discuss this at length in their work cited above, pp. 211–214.

7. Dunhamel, art. cit., p. 138.

8. Ford and Kelly, op. cit., p. 228.

9. Duhamel, art. cit., pp. 144–147; cf. also R. Angermair, "Moral and Theological Notes on the Problem of Self-Abuse," printed as an appendix to von Gagern's *The Problem of Onanism* (Westminster: Newman Press, 1955).

11

MORAL ASPECTS OF THE
PROBLEM OF HOMOSEXUALITY

The objective disconformity of homosexuality to the moral law consists in the fact that the sexual appetite and affections are directed to persons of the same sex. The true homosexual personality, while normal from a physical point of view, is entirely disoriented from attraction to the opposite sex. Those persons who do not manifest this fundamental orientation to their own sex, but practice homosexual acts as a substitute or variation, should rather be called pseudo-homosexuals.

The moralist's problem with homosexuality is with the subjective rather than the objective responsibility. As always, subjective responsibility is more difficult to evaluate than objective, because of the many concrete situational, individual, and cultural factors that enter into any judgment concerning subjective morality. All that we can do here is simply point out a few general principles by which the moralist tries to come to a judgment of responsibility.

It must be noted first that the *condition* of homosexuality cannot itself be imputed to the sincere penitent. Even though this state may have arisen as a result of repeated culpable acts on the part of the penitent (a fact which will be disputed by most psychologists), if the penitent has sincerely repented of these lapses his present state may be declared involuntary. It will sometimes be of help to a penitent of this type if it is explained to him that his present condition cannot be imputed to him as sinful.

Secondly, one can note that those spontaneous affections and desires which arise from the sincere penitent's habitual dispositions are not more free or more sinful than are the spontaneous desires of his normal companion. Nor will it always be possible for him to suppress them positively. The best that he can do is to avoid their causes and divert his attention to other objects when these affections become conscious. In doing so he will follow most of the classic rules for those whose sexual desires have a normal object. He may contemn those which arise spontaneously and involuntarily. He should be inspired with the desire to free himself from this abnormality and taught to avoid what are, for him, the occasions of sin.

SPECIAL PROBLEMS OF THE HOMOSEXUAL

Because of the unusual situation in which the homosexual finds himself, attracted to that sex with which social organization forces him to have most contact, one should be careful to avoid giving him the impression that he must isolate himself from his own sex on the grounds that some of its members may be an occasion of sin for him. It is well to remember also that this type of penitent may more often be in necessary occasions of sin than his normal counterpart, simply because he cannot reorganize society to permit him to live with the cultural and social protections that ordinary mores set up between the sexes. This fact may make one more lenient in judging the homosexual in certain situations.

The fact that the homosexual's sex life is *abnormal* does not necessarily mean that his attractions and desires are *insuperable.* The qualitative abnormality does not of itself, by the very fact of its existence, destroy responsibility. On the contrary, the homosexual is to be judged according to the usual principles that determine moral guilt. Because an act is qualitatively abnormal does not automatically mean that its agent is deprived of that use of reason and liberty required for responsibility.

However, the principles that determine responsibility should be applied to the homosexual *as principles,* and should not be imposed upon him as though in the concrete his sexual problem were an exact parallel to that of his normal counterpart. The statement, for example, that the homosexual has no more difficulty controlling his impulses than does the normal man must be accepted with definite reserves, or it will lead to a most unrealistic appraisal of the penitent's situation.

The homosexual also is under many nonsexual pressures which aggravate his sexual tensions and push him in the direction of the false securities of his pathetic love affairs. He lives in constant fear of blackmail, as the normal man does not, even if he indulges in sexual activity outside marriage. He is economically vulnerable in that few employers care to retain homosexual employees if their secret is discovered. He has constantly to suspect his own friendships and normal social dealings with men. This secrecy, loneliness, and insecurity often aggravate the temptation to have at least one chosen companion with whom he can be wholly open.

Lastly, since society approves of attitudes, occupations, and social conduct which are foreign to him, the homosexual's life is rather more egocentric than the normal man's. He has the difficult task of structuring his own ideals for himself according to patterns which he must in many cases determine for himself, since society has not elaborated a rule of conduct governing the details of his confusing situation. In what measure should he apply materially to himself the rules of morality governing those acts which incite *per se* to venereal pleasure? Shall he, for example, avoid all such occasions as nude swimming with men? The moralist would answer this question rapidly for the normal man in our present culture with regard to women. It is perhaps less easy to decide in the case of homosexuals. One must beware of advice which will further complicate their social situation, bringing on new tensions which will seek release in sexual activity.

It must be recognized, however, that the homosexual personality is invariably a psychologically disturbed and frequently a neurotic personality and that his judgments of value will often be distorted by his disturbed condition.

THE SUBJECTIVE GUILT OF THE HOMOSEXUAL

It is admitted by everyone today that sexuality is by no means confined to genital impulses. Sexuality irradiates the entire personality and promotes a general orientation of the entire emotional life so that the whole of life and personality is marked by its influences. Since the elements of sexuality are subject to a psychosexual evolution the normal personality will be one whose development has passed through the various stages of psychosexual evolution. The child's affective and sexual interests must be guided beyond the stage of concentration upon himself to an heterosexual and altruistic stage. Only the man whose evolution is accomplished in a fortunate manner will have that general attitude and moral conduct towards others which is really adult.

The homosexual personality lacks this adulthood of the sexual instinct, taken in its widest sense. His entire affective orientation is disturbed. Because it is disturbed his judgments of value will reflect this disturbance in greater or lesser degree. To think that one can reorientate the genital activities of such a person without affecting first a general re-education of his entire personality structure is an illusion. His sexuality must be re-educated, but as we have seen, sexuality is by no means confined to the genital sphere. Without this general re-education (see chapter 1), it is very doubtful if such a disturbed personality will ever have the psychical equilibrium and energy needed to bring his moral life into accord with the objective laws which foster his genuine development as spirit. To bring one's activity into accord with objective morality, one needs knowledge and one needs freedom. A defect in either will ordinarily imply some lessening of responsibility. The reaction of the neurotic character to his moral problem will not infrequently be: "I know that what I am doing is objectively wrong; I am aware of this and troubled by it, but it is stronger than I, and I am unable to do otherwise."

Such a penitent as this registers both *feelings* of guilt and a tendency to exculpate himself on the grounds of lack of freedom. In approaching this case the confessor must avoid two extremes. One extreme is immediately to absolve the penitent from all responsibility as though freedom were automatically and totally obliterated in every case by the neurotic condition of the penitent. Such an attitude doubtless would end in moral nihilism. Objective moral laws exist which are universally binding, founded upon immutable natures and essences.

At times the invert will experience a relatively high degree of freedom from those psychological conflicts which limit his power to choose. There are periods of his life, periods even of the same day, which vary considerably with regard to freedom. It would be doing the penitent a great disservice to suppose that the mechanisms which inhibit his freedom work always at equal intensity. Hence general statements about the degree of his moral guilt are completely out of place and should never be given to him.

On the other hand, the moralist must avoid an objectivist frame of mind which tends automatically to equate objective disconformity to the moral law with subjective guilt. In cases of overt homosexuality, factors of the subjective, existential, concrete, situational order and psychological mechanisms must be taken into consideration, and usually these factors cannot be established by the confessor unless he is working in collaboration with the psychiatrist.

A matter of particular interest to moralists today is the case of those penitents who claim to lead a rather vigorous interior life on most points, who express a rather determined aspiration to obey God's law in its entirety, but who encounter within themselves a difficulty which they express as an impossibility, in the matter, e.g., of their homosexual desires. It appears to them that the imbalance they experience within themselves is due, at least in part, to causes outside their control. They claim an inability to execute in the real order the fundamental aspirations of their spirit to God. Doubtless in such cases we must recall that our characters and our moral worth are to be judged by our deepest *attitudes* as well as by our external acts.

We are called by God not only to act well but to *be good*. We must take into the consideration of the invert's guilt the whole fundamental orientation of his life. Is it to God or to self? In the strata of motivation which are not directly translatable in act does he manifest a desire to serve God, practice virtue and lead a good life? Is his moral life in other matters conformed to the laws of God and the Church? Does he try to make use of the religious help offered to him in the sacraments, prayer, and the advice given him by his confessor? If so, one may judge that he is sincerely trying to help himself, and this fact should make the confessor more lenient in judging the occasional fall which may occur.

NEED OF VALUATIONAL APPRECIATION OF WRONGDOING

In order to establish adequate responsibility for grave sin our knowledge should proceed, not only from an abstract, juridical understanding of the moral disvalue in question, but also from some type of *interior comprehension* of the law and the value it embodies. It is recognized today by moralists that the clear knowledge required for mortal sin is not always satisfied by a purely *conceptual* knowledge even when this is explicit. The fact that the law of God and the Church forbids this particular action may be quite clear to the invert at the moment of his temptation without giving him the requisite *valuational appreciation* of the good involved in this law. If this value-aspect of the law, its inner goodness, its inner sweetness and beauty, is separated from the majesty of law, the moral knowledge that results may be schematic, theoretical, notional, but, in the sense of Newman, unreal. In that case, not only does the good-for-me aspect of the value recede to the periphery of consciousness, but the inner goodness in itself, the importance of the value-in-itself, tends to be obscured in the mind of the subject, and the remaining conceptual knowledge may be insufficient to found grave responsibility.

This affective valuation will be found lacking in many homosexuals with respect to their particular situation. And of course liberty is dependent upon knowledge. But even when theoretical knowledge is adequate for responsibility it can happen that the individual describes himself as blinded and chained when called upon to resist temptation. This indeed seems to be the case with many inverts. Here we must recognize that traditional moral theology admits that an individual, because of conditioning and habit, may indeed be emotionally incapable, at a precise moment, of observing objectively this or that commandment.

Thus even when valuational knowledge is actually had, the individual may experience such neurotic pressures that his liberty does not retain that degree of energy required for grave sin. The emotional drives upsetting his spiritual equilibrium may be such as to exert an almost hypnotic effect upon his will, giving an air of unreality to the good embodied in the moral law. Even with valuational knowledge present, the tangle of neurotic pressures and emotions to which he is subject may, as it were, *anesthetize* the appeal of the good for the moment. Realizing this may help the confessor to understand that the penitent is not entirely insincere when he describes himself as irresistibly drawn by the object of his sin.

It should also be noted that the will, even if its decision is free, does not have despotic control over the external faculties. Thus it is possible that there will exist, even in the sincere penitent, a considerable gap between objective and subjective morality. He has, however, always the obligation of striving to close this gap in his life between objective and subjective morality. The gap which may exist in a particular case between the order of intention and the order of execution does not dispense the subject from effort.

HOMOSEXUALITY ONLY SECONDARILY A MORAL PROBLEM

If one group of extremists seem to feel that any responsibility is out of the question in the case of inverts, it is another extreme to think that the action of grace will cure all psychical defects. Grace is not given for that purpose in the usual scheme of things. Its function is not to cure the malfunctioning of nature in the order of psychology. In the degree that a particular nature is subject to a natural psychological imbalance, grace meets with obstacles in restoring that nature to objective conformity to the moral law. In the ordinary course of events we should not expect grace to perform miracles in the natural order or to ensure clinical cures. Grace is given for interior, subjective spiritual success in our dialogue-life with God, and will not ordinarily remove all the clinical obstacles to objective success in the moral life.

It is undeniable that there exist unfortunate psychisms which ill dispose their owners for objective conformity to the moral law. There are types who probably never will know the lucidity in judgments of value that the normal man knows. But if we avoid confusing *sanctity* with objective *moral perfection* we will not despair of these types, among which seems to be the invert.

In forming any moral judgment of the subjective guilt of this class of neurotic personalities, it is obvious that the confessor and the psychiatrist must work in common. The problem of homosexuality is primarily a problem for the psychiatrist and only secondarily a moral problem. Insofar as it is a moral problem it lies particularly in the domain of those principles which seek to establish subjective responsibility. The confessor who approaches this problem should then be aware of the researches of modern psychology and the assistance that this science offers to him in determining the presence or absence of moral knowledge and moral freedom.

The real is always complex, and it is quite impossible, in dealing with this class of penitents, to lay down simple rules of thumb for determining the extent and degree of subjective responsibility. Nor may the penitent always be believed completely when he testifies against himself. Many of them are unaware of the conditions required for freedom and confuse freedom from external forces with psychical freedom. Moreover, they do not usually evaluate justly the *non*sexual neurotic pressures to which they are subject, living as they do in a society which considers them as outcasts and thus aggravates their sexual tensions.

The universal moral law governing these cases is intransigent, as binding as in any other cases. But the Christian conception of morality has never been one of mechanical conformism, of objectified legalism. The experience of generations of spiritual directors and confessors and an increasing body of psychological information are rich sources for understanding the complexity and limits of human freedom. They should not be neglected in favor of some neatly codified rule of thumb capable of an automatic application to all individuals.

THE PRIEST AND THE HOMOSEXUAL

In his pastoral work the confessor and the counsellor has an excellent opportunity to encourage the homosexual to seek that medical treatment which may restore to him the freedom needed for accomplishing objectively the demands of a Christian moral life. The counsellor should avoid, however, holding up too glowing a promise for future recovery since prognosis, especially in the case of older and habitual inverts of overt activity, is quite poor. Since the homosexual is already in a difficult social position the counsellor must do what he can to encourage him to make some positive contribution to the community in which he lives and should avoid a censorious, accusatory, rejecting attitude.

Above all he must stimulate the penitent to seek the requisite help and must do what he can to see to it that human needs in the nonsexual area are satisfied, so that further tensions are not built up in the penitent by frustrations of a purely social order. Anything that contributes to the human equilibrium of the penitent will have its effects on the moral order. The entire personality needs reorganization, and usually the treatment will be long, since areas of the personality have to be explored that are not immediately accessible to the therapist. Moreover, many homosexuals will feel that no real change is either possible or especially desirable. Their attitude is usually pessimistic, fatalistic. Here the priest-counsellor may play an important role in stimulating a desire for recovery and treatment, or in helping the patient resign himself to the inevitability of his temptation, while still determined to fight against it.

If the counsellor or confessor can take the time to explain the differing roles of the natural and the supernatural in effecting a cure, and if the priest does not lead the penitent to a *magical* conception of the sacrament's efficacy, much good can be done by the sacraments. The quantitative aspect of the case may be helped and the number of overt acts diminished by reception of the sacraments. The attitude of the confessor or counsellor should remain encouraging and should stress that the penitent must extend the area of his self-control gradually, with the combined strength of natural and supernatural helps.

The penitent must also be helped to gain insight into his own situation, and for this he needs as complete a picture as possible of the factors that may contribute to that situation. Besides an understanding of the role of sex and love in human life he should be brought to realize, in a very general fashion, the mechanisms that effect his freedom and the principles that determine his responsibility. This will usually be done by the collaboration of priest and therapist. The priest must stress that whatever may be the appearance to the contrary, interior, spiritual peace lies ahead for the penitent who co-operates with God's grace. The dogmatic truths concerning both the distribution and the efficacy of grace may be stressed with advantage, providing always that the penitent is not led to some magical idea of grace as a substitute for human effort or for therapy.

To present grace in such a fashion may only cause rebellion and loss of faith, for the invert will reply to these magical promises with a cold denial based upon experience. A counsellor should not ordinarily undertake the direction of a homosexual personality without collaboration with a therapist. Nor should he take it upon himself to promise cures or to determine the limits of recovery possible. In some cases the best that will be achieved is a relatively successful adjustment to a nonsexual social life with no overt acts. If the priest-counsellor realizes this ahead of time he will save all concerned much distress. The necessity of regular and consistent encouragement for this type of penitent should not need to be stressed. It is obvious.

NOTES

The following readings will be found particularly helpful:
1. J. Duhamel, S.J., and J. Hayden, O.S.B., "Theological and Psy-

chiatric Aspects of Habitual Sin," *Preceedings of the Eleventh Annual Convention of the Catholic Theological Society of America,* pp. 130–167.

2. P. Flood (ed.), *New Problems in Medical Ethics,* Vol. I (Westminster: Newman Press, 1953).

3. J. C. Ford, S.J., and G. Kelly, S.J., "Psychiatry and Moral Responsibility," *Theological Studies,* 15 (1954), pp. 59–67.

4. J. F. Harvey, O.S.F.S., "Homosexuality as a Pastoral Problem," *Theological Studies,* 16 (1955), pp. 86–108.

5. N. Mailloux, O.P., "Psychic Determinism, Freedom and Personality Development" in *The Human Person,* ed. J. A. Gasson, S.J., and M. B. Arnold (New York: Ronald, 1954), pp. 264–280.

6. T. V. Moore, O.S.B., "The Pathogenesis and the Treatment of Homosexual Disorders," *The Journal of Personality,* 14 (1945), pp. 46–83.

7. *The Proceedings of the Institute for the Clergy on Problems in Pastoral Psychology* (New York: Fordham University Press, 1956), pp. 140–191.

12

ALCOHOLISM AND
MORAL GUILT

The ordinary moral textbook gives us the requisite information to judge the guilt of an individual case of *drunkenness*. We are chiefly concerned in this chapter with the case of *alcoholism* itself. By alcoholism we mean the condition of those whose excessive drinking causes problems in life adjustment and is rooted in compulsion. The genuine alcoholic is a compulsive drinker.[1] He can never learn to drink moderately and he cannot stop drinking permanently unless he receives assistance from without.[2] The alcoholic is compulsive in the sense that he is fascinated by the thought of alcohol. In genuine alcoholism this fascination reaches abnormal proportions so that the alternative—not to drink—really cannot be realistically appraised. The compulsion in the alcoholic operates at different times with different degrees of force. On certain occasions his thinking about alcohol becomes a positive fascination which takes possession of his imagination and seems to force him to drink even against his genuine determination to avoid alcohol.[3] In this situation there is really no realistic appraisal of the alternative not to drink. The craving for alcohol becomes, from a moral and psychological point of view, as strong as the craving of an addict for dope. When the individual suffers this type of interference with his power of freedom, it is clear that his responsibility and culpability are diminished or eliminated.

Is the alcoholic responsible for his condition? With some alco-

239

holics it seems possible that from their first drink they were already compulsive alcoholics and therefore have no responsibility for their present condition. In others, compulsive drinking seems to have some physiological basis over which they have no control, and for which, consequently, they have no responsibility. Certain personalities seem to be addictive personalities. They seem unable to resist the appeal of pleasure. If he ceased to be an alcoholic, this addictive personality would become addicted to some other type of pleasure.[4]

Of course, if it were possible that self-indulgence could lead to compulsive drinking, the drinker would be responsible for his alcoholism to the extent that he freely chose to drink despite the probable addiction he foresaw would result. Alcoholics, however, are in a sense born and not made. Whether they realize it or not, most of them are alcoholics from almost the first drink on. Only the stress of circumstances brings out the potential that is there from the beginning. Most alcoholics do not believe, in the early stages of their drinking, that they are compulsive drinkers or that they will become such. Many approach their compulsive drinking and the realization that they are alcoholics very gradually, over a long period of years. Apparently they have been drinking socially for years with temporary excesses, not realizing that they are caught in addiction. Occasional sprees may have warned them of the possibility of addiction, but frequently the alcoholic dismisses this possibility as nonoperative for him. They are experts in self-deception.

Normally speaking, one can say that the ordinary alcoholic rarely believes he is a compulsive drinker. The moral law does not oblige us to forego legitimate pleasures simply because of a *remote* possibility of a future danger or a future evil.[5] The dangers involved in drinking are hardly ever apparent to the beginner who will discover in time that his drinking is compulsive. If we understand this, we will realize that there are not too many addictive drinkers who are actually responsible *in causa* for their condition of alcoholism. Most of them deceive themselves about the seriousness of the danger in their own particular case. Although others warn them, they do not accept these warnings. Frequently, too, they take certain steps towards periodic abstinence, which they believe protects them from the dangers of future addiction. It seems unlikely, therefore, that the alcoholic analyzes his situation with sufficient clarity to be guilty of mortal sin in causing the condition itself.

What is the responsibility of the alcoholic with regard to his particular sprees? To begin with, we must remember that since alcoholism is a compulsion, the alcoholic is an ill man, whether he recognizes the fact or not. All authorities insist that alcoholism is an illness, at least in part. The alcoholic's condition is not normal; he suffers from an addiction which seriously diminishes his liberty. There is no doubt that the narrowing of awareness about the idea of alcohol exercises, at times, an almost obliterating influence on his freedom. This does not mean, of course, that each drinking spree shows the same degree of diminished culpability. There are times when an alcoholic experiences more freedom and other times less freedom with regard to his compulsion. Compulsions do not always operate in an absolute fashion.[6]

It appears to be clear that after one or two drinks the alcoholic is usually controlled by his active urge to drink. In such cases, it is probable that after the first, second, or third drink, he is no longer sufficiently free to incur grave guilt.

We repeat here what we have said about other moral problems. We cannot lay down any blanket rules which excuse this or that individual drinker from serious guilt. Each situation, each day, each hour, must be concretely judged. There are so many kinds of alcoholics, so many varieties and stages of compulsive attraction, that it is impossible to lay down any mathematical norms to judge responsibility. Certainly there are many cases where alcoholics are not mortally guilty of their sins of drunkenness.

We must realize also that alcoholics frequently do not have a sufficient evaluation and grasp of the sinfulness of drunkenness itself. At times they seem to be misled by certain false ideas. Some think that since their drunkenness does not affect others it cannot possibly be a serious sin. Still other alcoholics will maintain that they were not seriously drunk since some use of reason remained to them in the sense that some consciousness remained. This inculpable ignorance or confusion as to the immorality of drunkenness may excuse them in certain cases. The alcoholic ordinarily shows a certain degree of mental confusion which may help him to escape grave guilt. It is possible also that his mental confusion is brought about by neurotic conflict within himself. Whatever be the cause, the genuine alcoholic does not ordinarily have that clarity and sobriety of judgment which is required for grave sin.

Then too, the desire to relieve intolerable tensions enters in to such an extent that the taking of a drink may actually be an irresistible impulse. Often the alcoholic cannot bear the psychological tensions within himself which arise from the deprivation of alcohol. This craving certainly diminishes his liberty. In certain cases it would seem almost like the physiological craving of a drug addict for his dope. But even though purely psychological, it can arise so strongly in many types of alcoholics that the act of drinking seems compulsive and not free.

In the case of individuals who have formed a *habit* of heavy drinking we would have to apply the ordinary theology of habit and examine its principles with regard to the diminution of responsibility. There are many excessive drinkers who are *not* compulsive drinkers yet who bring hardship and distress to themselves, their families, and their work because of *habitual* drinking bouts. They are to be judged and exhorted by the priest as he would deal with others enmeshed in habits of sin. With proper motivation and effort the heavy drinker who is not an alcoholic can curtail his problem by self-control.

The alcoholic is an addictive personality and suffers from all the psychological imbalances and the hindrances to freedom which addicts suffer from. Hence, even in the individual drinking bouts of the alcoholic, it is probable that his responsibility is frequently diminished below the level required for grave sins, if it is not eliminated entirely. After the alcoholic has begun to take his second or third drink, his imputability is substantially diminished. Even before taking the first drink, it is considerably diminished by the psychological factors which we have mentioned.[7]

Occasionally it will help to ask the alcoholic himself to form a judgment concerning his responsibility. It is possible that in some cases he may be able to explain his conduct and make a moral judgment thereon. But usually he will either excuse himself wholly or condemn himself point-blank, and his testimony will be of little use to the confessor. Since the condition of the alcoholic is definitely abnormal and since his desire for alcohol is decidedly pathological, one certainly should be lenient in judging his subjective responsibility. It is difficult to give more definite or exact norms than this, but we can trust him to the mercy of God and do what we can for him.

The alcoholic has the responsibility to help himself insofar as is in his power. It will not be in his power to stop drinking immediately. It may not be in his power to stop drinking at all, but it may be in his power to take the steps suggested by his confessor and to collaborate with a physician or a psychiatrist. Most alcoholics need psychiatric, medical, and spiritual help. The confessor can be of great assistance in suggesting these aids, and in helping to clear up the confusion which generally reigns in the alcoholic's mind concerning subjective responsibility. He can also encourage the alcoholic and relieve him of that *neurotic* anguish which often accompanies his drinking.

An expert on the subject of alcoholism, Mark Keller, has written, "The alcoholic's lack of coöperation—and he is a notorious noncoöperator—is really a part of his disease. It is a symptom like everything else in his behavior. . . . A patient sometimes needs to drink; he also needs not to coöperate. He just can't help himself. The doctor [and priest] should understand this lack of coöperation as a symptom which he must treat."[8] The priest, therefore, should spend his time thinking about how he might convert the alcoholic's unwillingness to co-operate into willingness, rather than trying to puzzle out how responsible the penitent might be here and now for his lack of good will.

Ordinarily it will not be helpful to tell the alcoholic that he is obliged under pain of mortal sin to refuse even one drink. It may well be true that objectively one drink is a free proximate occasion of serious sin and hence should be avoided as seriously sinful in itself. However, telling the alcoholic this will usually not help him to avoid that first drink. Secondly, it may increase his frustration and anguish.

It is better pastoral practice, therefore, to adopt other methods of direction. Usually the alcoholic will be incapable of recognizing that for him personally one drink will inevitably entail more. Even if he recognizes it, he will be incapable of obeying such advice. The priest should rather help the alcoholic to admit to himself that he is an alcoholic and requires medical, moral, and psychological assistance.[9] The priest can also put the alcoholic in touch with agencies capable of giving him this help.

The alcoholic can be responsible for acts performed while drunk. If the drunkenness was sought precisely in order to commit the crime, then obviously the man is guilty both of the drunkenness and the crime. More often, however, sins such as murder, fighting, impurity, etc., committed by an alcoholic during his drunken sprees were not foreseen by the alcoholic as likely to happen. If he does see that these are likely to happen and deliberately continues to drink, he is guilty of these acts *in causa*. He is not guilty of acts committed while he was completely drunk unless he foresaw the probability that such acts would occur and was willing to accept responsibility for this probability. If he does foresee such a probability and accepts such a responsibility, he is guilty of the acts whether they follow or not in the objective order. But normally speaking, this will not be the case. The alcoholic usually believes that he is exempt from the general rules that govern the likelihood of such occurrences.

When a person is not completely drunk and does not foresee the evil consequences of drunkenness, then we have to judge his guilt by how much rational control he maintained at the time when he committed the individual act. Here we must determine the degree to which alcohol has deprived the individual of the use of reason. Certain alcoholics are able to drink consistently and heavily for long periods of time without losing the use of reason except for rare intervals. In such cases they are normally responsible for their activities with the exception of those committed during these rare intervals.[10]

Occasionally, too, the alcoholic experiences the phenomenon of a loss of memory with regard to a period of time, a type of amnesia. It is possible for very heavy drinkers to black out at times so that memory of the blackout period is completely lost, and yet to conduct themselves during the blackout in a fashion that seems quite rational. These blackouts, as described by alcoholics, may come and go over a period of days or weeks. One should remember here that the mere fact that the alcoholic does not *remember* much of what he did during the blackout does not free him from all responsibility. It is possible that he was acting rationally although he is no longer able to *recall* the actions of that period. In such condition, alcoholics have been known to perform actions with all the appearances of sobriety. They have entered marriage, for example, or conducted professional or business affairs. However, it is difficult for us to believe that an alcoholic in such an abnormal condition should be held *fully* responsible for the acts performed in this state. The fact that continued excess has had such a violently disturbing effect upon the personality as to render him incapable of all memory of what occurred during this period suggests to us that he is at least not fully responsible and that his apparently rational conduct proceeded from a genuinely disturbed personality.[11]

NOTES

1. M. Lomash, "Alcoholism—Vice or Disease?" *The Sign*, 32 (1953), pp. 22–24.

2. F. A. Rea, *Alcoholism, Its Psychology and Cure* (New York: Philosophical Library, 1956).

3. R. G. McCarthy and E. M. Douglass, *Alcohol and Social Responsibility* (New York: Crowell, 1949).

4. Ford and Kelly, *Contemporary Moral Theology*, Vol. I, pp. 289–290.

5. J. Ford, S.J., *Man Takes a Drink* (New York: Kenedy, 1955). This volume discusses this and allied questions.

6. Ford and Kelly, op. cit., 291–293.

7. Ibid., pp. 294–295.

8. "The Alcoholic as a Patient," *State of Mind*, May 1957, pp. 4–5.

9. R. Murphy, "A Plea for the Alcoholic," *Australasian Catholic Record*, 28 (1951), pp. 28–30.

10. R. E. Britt, "Alcoholism and Some Moral Issues," *Linacre Quarterly*, 13 (1945), pp. 15–24.

11. Ford and Kelly, op. cit., pp. 299–300.

13

CATHOLICISM AND PSYCHIATRY

It seems that Catholics frequently feel a bit uneasy about psychiatry and psychiatrists. Such a feeling has its own history and its own partial justification.[1] To many Catholics, psychiatry is identifiable with the name of Freud. This is, of course, not an accurate conception, since there are many schools of psychiatry and perhaps hardly any absolutely "orthodox" Freudians practicing today. Nevertheless, Catholic thought tends to identify psychoanalysis (which is only one branch of psychiatry) and psychiatry in general, with Freud. Psychoanalysis is a theory which grants to man's unconscious an unusually ample and dynamic role in human behavior. It is especially this, perhaps, that renders the Catholic ill at ease. He is afraid free will may evaporate under the "unconscious dynamisms" of the psychiatrist. He wonders where will power and character training come into play and he is aware that free will is a tenet of his Faith.[2]

FREUD AND RELIGION

If the initial position of religion towards psychiatry was one of opposition and hostility, the fault lies historically with Freud. He himself was dominated by an attitude of hostility towards religion, and he repeatedly took up the subject of religion only to attack it. In 1907 he published a paper entitled "Obsessive Acts and Religious Practices." He observed in this paper the resemblances which he had noted in clinical practice between religion and the obsessive, neurotic characteristics of certain of his patients. Unfortunately, he did not stop at noting the similarities between neurotic obsession and religious practices but ended by postulating the identity of neurosis and personal piety. He developed further the idea that religion itself is a universal obsession of man. *Totem and Taboo, The Future of An Illusion, Civilization and Its Discontents, Moses and Monotheism* all develop the same distortions of religious belief and practice. From his early period until right before his death Freud never relinquished this belief that most religious phenomena are to be understood on the model of an obsessional neurosis.[3]

In such an atmosphere, where psychiatry cast the first stone, religion reacted vigorously. It is undeniable that many religious people do manifest neurotic symptoms; but this correlation of religion and neurosis was pushed too far by some of the early psychiatrists. It is possible for man to develop neurotic behavior concerning almost anything that touches him deeply, whether it be fraternal, paternal, or maternal love, sex, aggression, or religion. Unfortunately, many of the early psychiatrists did not seem to realize that the neurotic manifestations of religion in many cases simply indicated that religion is a deep source of values and therefore, possibly, of conflict also.[4]

Some of the earlier disciples of Freud believed also that there is an inevitable conflict between religion and mental health. At first Catholicism showed an almost united front in opposing psychiatry, doubtless because of these prejudices among psychiatrists against religion. From the beginning theologians rejected Freud's pseudo-theology and especially Freud's philosophical materialism. Gradually they began to examine certain of the theoretical bases of psychoanalysis itself. Freud's theories of sex were received with distaste by religious groups, since they seemed to leave no room for freedom or God or morality and appeared to put undue emphasis upon sexual material. Even the practice of psychiatry raised certain doubts in the minds of some Catholics, since the Freudian method seemed to put so much emphasis on sex. Moreover, there was always the fear that the psychiatrist would not distinguish between neurotic guilt and real guilt. They feared that in attempting to relieve neurotic guilt he might remove all sense of genuine guilt and all sense of morality along with it. Because of this background, Catholicism, until the second quarter of this century, seemed dubious and suspicious of psychiatry, and of psychoanalysis in particular.[5]

A prime factor which caused Catholic concern about psychiatry was the materialism of Freud himself. Freud professed to be irreligious* and completely materialistic in his speculative philosophy. This does not, of course, imply that his personal, ethical life was gross, but it does mean that Freud's philosophical theory of human existence placed matter at the summit of reality. Consequently, for Freud, man is simply a highly developed animal. He did not concern himself with a spiritual soul in man distinct from matter. Hence in Freudian *philosophy,* which must be distinguished, as we shall see, from Freudian *psychology* and Freudian *therapeutic* techniques, man is really a highly sensitive animal. Perhaps no one has so brilliantly analyzed the animal and the infrahuman drives in man as has Freud. Nevertheless, the Catholic who realizes that Freud is a materialist realizes also that there is a conflict between Catholic *philosophy* and Freudian *philosophy.*[6]

Moreover, Freud did not take into account a personal God whose wise providence extends over man and man's universe. Rather, God is simply a product of man's unconscious, an enlarged Father-Image, and nothing more. Freud was also a mechanist. He did not profess a belief in human free will, and Catholic philosophy could not accept any theory of human behavior which seemed to deny freedom. It is only normal that a man who apparently disregards free will will come into conflict with Catholic doctrine on many levels. Pope Pius XII has stated that "our knowledge of God and

* Freud's view of religion, and its power to influence much of man's functioning, was by no means unremittingly hostile. His explanations of religious phenomena are different from ours, but he is far from disdainful when he describes their effects. There is a section in *Moses and Monotheism* beginning "How we who have little belief envy those who are convinced of the existence of a Supreme Being. . . ." which the reader will find a powerful defense of religion as a valuable psychological force in mental health.

our worship of Him do not proceed from the unconscious or the subconscious, but from the positive revelation of God and His natural revelation in creation."[7] What we would call free choices are for some Freudians really products of unconscious factors which not only *influence* but absolutely *determine* us when we imagine that we are free. Pope Pius XII, on the contrary, has said that "these psychic dynamisms may indeed exist in the soul and may indeed exert pressure upon our activity, but they do not compel it, and to place them at the helm as the controlling factor of man's psychology would be to deny his humanity."[8] With his philosophical background, it is obvious that Freud the materialist would have difficulty winning acceptance among Catholics since many would fail to distinguish his metaphysics from his psychology.

PSYCHIATRY AND THEOLOGY

There are other reasons which historically have militated against the easy acceptance of Freud in Catholic thought. The psychiatrist is concerned with psychological problems which sometimes have moral overtones. The theologian is concerned with sin and the free moral activity of man. When the theologian encounters a psychiatrist whose philosophy runs distinctly contrary to revealed truth, it is natural that he takes a somewhat cautious point of view, particularly since both of them are concerned with man's behavior, personal conduct and system of values. Since many psychiatrists have a view of human nature directly contrary to revealed truth, and deny certain facts such as freedom, the theologian becomes suspicious of the psychiatrist.[9] Moreover, some psychiatrists disagree with theologians on what is concretely good for man and what is permissible for him in the moral field. Such a disagreement flows naturally out of the disagreement concerning the very nature of man himself. The conflict is sharpened by the fact that both psychiatrist and theologian are often dealing with the same object, man's human behavior, but from different motivational points of view.[10]

Moreover, psychoanalysis especially was born in an atmosphere hostile to traditional sexual morality. Theoretically, a psychiatrist does not recommend to his patients anything which goes contrary to the client's moral or religious beliefs. This is true, at least, in theory. And yet the Catholic feels—often erroneously—that it is difficult for a client to be associated with someone over a long period of time without being influenced by the moral attitudes and viewpoints of the one who is treating him.

Then, too, the sexual sphere is frequently touched upon by psychiatry. The Catholic Church has very definite ideas on sexual morality and rejects such notions as "pansexualism," the theory that all human behavior is motivated by and controlled by unconscious sexual drives. Today, psychiatry has been freed of much that was interpreted as objectionable in the original Freudian theory with regard to sex. And yet the popular mind still associates Freud and psychiatry in general with over-insistence upon sex. This has also given rise in the popular mind to much prejudice against psychology.

It is true that some Freudian views of religion, morality, human nature and human behavior are in opposition to revealed religion. Yet we should distinguish, and this is not always done, between the Freudian materialistic *philosophy* and his *psychology,* that is, his understanding of the structure of personality, the id, ego, and superego (see chapter 1), instincts, etc., and his medical *techniques* and theories. It is quite impossible to reconcile Freud's philosophy, atheistic and materialistic, with Catholicism. It is useless to attempt to do so; God is a myth to Freud, the ultimate reality is matter. There is no point in denying this about Freud, nor can any Catholic subscribe to his pseudo-theological views.[11]

But beyond this, Freud has given us an empirical psychology of human nature which is not necessarily identified with his philosophy. He has given us methods of exploring the unconscious. These therapeutic techniques are not necessarily in conflict with Catholic teaching.[12] We can admit Freud's analysis of the unconscious and its dynamisms, we can admire his discussions and explorations of the nature of instinct and emotional drives and of the sex instinct itself. We need not necessarily subscribe to his theoretical ideas concerning freedom or lack of freedom in this sphere. While it is true that Freud explores with particular success those elements in human nature which are really less human since they are infrarational, still the Catholic psychiatrist or the Catholic philosopher can accept and profit from much of this. The theologians may consider that Freud perhaps overemphasizes the irrational elements in human nature. But this does not imply that he need deny the value of many of Freud's clinical discoveries.

DYNAMIC PSYCHOLOGY: AN EXPOSITION

There are scholars who feel that the answers which modern psychology has given in the last fifty years to the question "What is man?" are second in importance only to that great and more basic answer which has been enunciated by the Christian tradition itself. The distinguished convert Karl Stern has dubbed this new knowledge and its influence upon the present and the future of humanity "The Third Revolution." He believes that these new insights into man's psychological nature will have far greater influence upon the future of mankind than have the two preceding modern ideologies which purported to change the world, namely Marxism and Racism.

The new dynamic psychology is as different from traditional scholastic or rational psychology as physiology is from anatomy: not superior, but different. Rational psychology tends to stress the control and influence which the intellect and the will should have over the lower faculties and passions. Dynamic psychology studies ways in which the emotions influence, cripple, and sometimes even cancel out the effective functioning of man's higher faculties, his intellect and will. Dynamic psychology is interested in the degree to which the early years of childhood influence the likes and dislikes, the temptations and talent, the strengths and weakness of the adult. Dynamic psychology is interested in determining the degrees to which human motivation and behavior are influenced by the unconscious, that vast storehouse of buried yet active forces and energies which have been built up in those years before the use of reason during which the young human being is living almost wholly on his emotions.

Thus dynamic psychology helps the moralist, the confessor, and the penitent himself to make clearer judgments as to whether this or that behavior belongs more to the category of compulsive and unconsciously motivated *acts of man* or to the rationally chosen *human acts* for which he is responsible.

Finally, even those human failings which are to a large degree deliberately chosen and for which the individual is culpable are to some extent bound up with emotional and temperamental influences which environment and upbringing have set in motion. Thus, new ways of achieving self-knowledge by gaining deeper insight into the emotional roots of human behavior not only make it possible for the psychiatrist to heal sick minds, but help the confessor and spiritual director to deal more effectively with the particular faults of their floundering penitents.

As a philosopher and theologian one need not pass judgment upon the psychological discoveries of Freud until these come in conflict with Catholic philosophy or revealed doctrine. We need not therefore reject Freudianism whole and entire. We cannot accept the system as it stands as a unit, unified by its philosophy. But it appears that today very few psychiatrists or analysts accept Freudianism in this form either. If we take Freud's insights into human nature, lift them out of the materialistic philosophy in which they are embodied, and supplement them by what Catholic philosophy and theology teach of human nature, we can frequently find a great deal that is of help in understanding man, even of help to the Christian philosopher and theologian.[13]

There are certain aspects of Freudian therapeutic technique which have given rise to some uneasy feelings in Catholic circles. The process of *transference*—the emotional identification of client with the therapist—stirs some misgivings.

While it is an indisputable fact that some unethical psychiatrists have at times advised clients to follow procedures contrary to the religious and moral convictions of the patient, we should not therefore suspect that this happens regularly. Evidence suggests that it does not. The competent psychiatrist accepts the proposition that he is not to dictate to his clients procedures contrary to their moral tenets. And the more competent the psychiatrist, the closer he adheres to this norm, not only from ethical reasons but from medical ones. Yet, as there are competent doctors and less competent doctors, so doubtless there are competent psychiatrists and less competent psychiatrists. Psychiatrists, of course, are not the only people in the world to give bad advice. But since they are very closely associated with man's moral life and particularly with that phase of it which touches sexuality, it is natural that the Christian should be cautious when placing someone he loves in the hands of one who must deal directly with this sphere.[14]

At times too, Christians distrust anyone who enters into the sphere of morality, which is most personal to man, and reveals the unconscious sources of man's conduct. A patient may be greatly distressed upon learning that his motives might not always have been those which appeared in clear consciousness. In "self-defense" he may impute religious or moral theories and attitudes to the psychiatrist which the doctor may not hold at all.

Some Catholics are also apprehensive about the dangers inherent in the phenomena known as *abreaction* (the emotional release which accompanies the emergence and integration into consciousness of traumatic experiences of the past) and *free association* of ideas (the spontaneous process of connective thought by which the significant past is brought to consciousness). Some Catholics are further disturbed by the assertion that the analyst must remain neutral and nondirective, no matter what sort of moral material the patient brings up. These critics cite the words of Pius XII forbidding the psychiatrist to counsel or encourage material sin, and further remind us that a Catholic cannot remain neutral where conscious acts of sin are concerned. Such misgivings in the minds of non-medical laymen are quite understandable. Most of these concepts do not involve either philosophical or psychological precepts, but rather the therapeutic process itself. In a very real sense it can be said of psychoanalysis that to define and evaluate the process adequately, one must undergo the experience. Consequently some questioners will have to be content with the unimpeachable testimony of Catholic doctors (priests among them) and patients who have themselves conducted or undergone analytic treatment. They have told us that the various techniques under consideration do not, if properly employed, violate in any way the tenets of traditional Catholic morality.[15]

DYNAMIC PSYCHOLOGY: DEFENSE

In defense of sound psychoanalytic theory, the following points should be noted:

If the analysis encourages the *actual execution* of a sinful desire or a sinful experience of the past, this would be quite unjustifiable. Classic psychoanalytic treatment aims simply at a *conscious recognition* of a hitherto unconscious desire or experience in order that such past emotional landmarks may be interpreted rationally, integrated into one's consciousness, and in this way lose their motive force. This need not involve the risk of either formal or material sin. It does not imply approval of past sin, desire to commit sin in the future, or morose delectation of a sinful emotional experience or action in the present.

It is a misconception to think that psychoanalysis interprets every man as so strongly influenced by unconscious motivations that the greater part of his conscious activity is removed from free choice. Catholicism strongly insists upon the fact that the normal man's life is under the influence of his free will and that at least some of his choices are free. Catholicism has a view of human nature and of human destiny which does not accept the theory that the normal man is actually not free in all or most of what he considers his free actions. The fear is present among some Catholics that psychiatrists who constantly deal with sick people in their clinics and medical treatment too often transfer their convictions concerning the sick man to the normal and healthy man. Catholic theology considers the normal man a responsible individual capable of choosing between good and evil. Moreover, it presumes that unless there is some form of mental sickness present, to a greater or lesser degree the ordinary man is normal.[16]

There are no doubt a large group of borderline cases which it would be difficult to classify as either normal or abnormal. But there are certain people who *freely* choose to conduct themselves in an asocial fashion, in what Christianity would call an immoral fashion. There are no doubt compulsive thieves, kleptomaniacs, but there can be thieves who freely and deliberately choose theft as their way of life, without the domination of compelling traumatic experiences or unconscious motivation. There are compulsive liars and there are those who lie freely because it is to their advantage. Some are clearly mentally ill, some are clearly not mentally ill. Some Catholics fear that psychiatry tends to interpret us all as mentally ill and to grant too large a measure of influence to unconscious dynamisms. Catholicism will not relinquish its position that the normal man is an individual responsible for many free choices.

Difficult to determine in these days of fear, crisis, and confusion is, Who is, emotionally speaking, "normal"? Father James Royce's mental health figures (see chapter 8, p. 180) seem to indicate that the majority of today's young people are emotionally damaged in one way or another. He does not imply that most of these will suffer a grave impairment of freedom as adults. Because of these personality shortcomings, however, many people are liable to be blocked in their efforts to meet effectively *some* of the emotional and moral challenges of their daily lives. Psychotherapy or counselling will not absolve the sinner from his responsibilities; but treatment can help bring even greater insight and conscious control over those emotional flaws which respond to clinical attention.

The single most important fact for the Catholic to remember is that psychoanalytic therapy deals almost exclusively with *unconscious* influences on man's feelings, thoughts, and behavior. The reader will remember that the *unconscious* content of man's mind is here and now beyond his control and divorced from responsible choice; it cannot fall under the direct domain of the moralist. So long as the psychoanalyst concerns himself with these enslaving, unconscious forces in his patient, he cannot violate Catholic morality.

Indeed Catholic psychoanalysts have taken pains to point out that the analytic process, far from absolving man from guilt, can make him more responsible. Psychoanalysis brings to the surface those unconscious pressures which propel man to compulsive activity and limit his freedom. As the patient comes to understand himself better, he is less and less influenced by the dictates of unknown and unconscious drives and motivations. With self-knowledge comes more and more freedom, and, of course, more and more responsibility. It is for this reason that Catholic scholars value psychoanalysis not only as a therapeutic process but as a device leading to personal insight, growth, and even increased virtue. (Once the unconscious blocks to more responsible behavior have been removed, some "ego-psychologists" feel that they can also contribute to the moral and even spiritual development of the individual. In collaboration with a clergyman, they feel they can help to integrate man's instinctive life with the totality of his emotional, intellectual, and spiritual aspirations.) *

Another of the difficulties raised about psychiatry is that the psychiatrist frequently does not understand the notion of original sin as it is presented by Catholic theology. For the Catholic, original sin deprives the individual of those supernatural and preternatural gifts of integrity, grace, and immortality which were given to Adam, but it does not intrinsically *corrupt* his nature. Consequently, although man in the present order has *difficulty* bringing unity and order into his emotional life, he has the means granted to him by the Redemption to bring this unity into his moral life; he has the freely offered grace of Christ. He is not intrinsically corrupt or condemned to evil.

The idea that everyone is "abnormal" can mean that everyone has imperfect and not despotic control over the instinctual life. If this is seen as what psychiatry is insisting upon, Catholicism goes along with it. Man's instincts constantly belabor him, attempt to control his entire life and to escape from the control of the higher faculties of intellect and will. But this struggle between instinct and reason, while it may be increased by unconscious conflicts, is not in

* For the sense in which the word *instinct* is used here, and throughout the book, please see our note in chapter 1 (p. 29).

the normal man (upon whose existence theology insists) a struggle destined to failure. While man does not have that gift of integrity granted to Adam which would give him perfect freedom from concupiscence, he has freedom of choice and he can structure his life according to self-chosen ideals, if he is normal. Neither theology nor psychiatry should imagine that it can restore the normal man to the perfect freedom from instinctive rebellion which was characteristic of Adam and Eve before the Fall.[17]

CATHOLICISM AND PSYCHIATRY

We have described some of the historical and speculative reasons why some Catholics maintain a certain reserve when dealing with psychiatry. However, this caution should not be exaggerated. Frequently, intelligent caution has been replaced by crude prejudices which are completely unfounded. Such statements as "what this disturbed person needs is a good confession rather than a psychiatrist's couch" indicate a rather naive approach to the problem. People do suffer from mental illnesses. It is only part of Catholic tradition to use every legitimate means at its disposal to help the sick person. It would be absurd and unchristian to discard psychiatry as an effective means of helping sick persons simply because one or another psychiatrist disagrees with Catholic principles or gives unwise advice to his patients. Others besides psychiatrists have been known to give bad advice. We do not therefore cease to summon doctors because one or another doctor makes a wrong diagnosis or offers unwise or immoral advice to his patient, any more than we cease to recommend confession because one or another priest gives wrong direction or counsel to his penitent.

It is obviously a problem for the Catholic to know exactly where to choose his professional help in this delicate sphere. Frequently it is a help if the priest, to whom the case is often first presented, has referral sources at his disposition. The prudent choice of a psychiatrist may be helped by appealing to a Catholic hospital. Too, a good non-Catholic psychiatrist may be better than a poorly trained Catholic one.

We must remember also that the official attitude of Catholicism to psychiatry is one of encouragement. In 1953 Pope Pius XII addressed the Fifth International Congress of Psychotherapy and Clinical Psychology. He assured the members of his audience that the Catholic Church followed their research and their practice with warm interest. He admitted that the subject matter with which they deal presents many difficulties, and yet he pointed out that psychotherapy is not only capable of achieving very genuine results for medicine and for the knowledge of the soul's operation in general but can be a great help for the development of religious life in man. (See chapter 8, paragraph 1.)

The ethical and religious directives for Catholic hospitals published by the Catholic Hospital Association at St. Louis, which is an official ethical handbook used in all Catholic hospitals in Canada and in many dioceses of the United States, comments that there is no objection on principle to using psychoanalysis or any other form of therapy for the treatment of Catholics. By avoiding disproportionate risk of moral dangers and observing the cautions dictated by sound morality, the conscientious therapist need not weaken his therapy to remain in agreement with Catholic thought. What is desirable in this sphere is obviously a genuine co-operation between the priest and the psychiatrist, for frequently both are dealing with different aspects of the same problem.

There can, however, exist no genuine co-operation unless both priest and psychiatrist understand the limits of their competence in their respective fields. The priest should not substitute the confessional for therapy, nor should he attempt to play the role of an amateur psychologist. It is certainly a great deal of help if the priest has at least an elementary understanding of psychiatry's aims and of the various types of therapy that can be used for helping penitents. It is also a great deal of help if he understands the common symptoms which will enable him to make such an elementary diagnosis of the illness as to decide if the penitent needs referral. (See Appendix I.) For frequently it is the priest who is first called upon to determine whether or not the patient requires professional psychiatric treatment. It is one of the purposes of this book to give to the priest certain practical norms for judging the existence of the deeper personality disturbances which require psychiatric help and also provide him with certain practical referral resources. The priest must frequently make a very practical judgment concerning his penitents. In some cases it will be inadvisable to send them on for further help because of foreseen difficulties involved.

Recently there has been introduced by Rome an extra year of priestly study devoted to Pastoral Theology, and it is suggested that this include certain lectures in pastoral psychology. This again makes it evident that the Church officially admits the necessity for some knowledge of psychology on the part of the priest and also points up the fact that co-operation is expected between the priest and the psychologist. The priest needs to put aside certain prejudices in dealing with psychology and to approach the psychologist with respect. Obviously there can be no genuine respect unless he understands what the psychologist is attempting to do. It is so common today to refer disturbed personalities to the psychiatrist that the priest should understand the limits of his own competence in this sphere and not believe he can cure mental illness by exclusively supernatural means.

The psychologist, on the other hand, must be aware of the fact that sin is the province rather of the priest and the theologian than of the psychiatrist. In the case of essentially moral problems and moral difficulties he should collaborate with the spiritual director or religious director of the patient. The priest has at his disposal supernatural means to assist the penitent to a better-balanced religious and spiritual life. Nevertheless, the priest knows from experience that there are stubborn cases which simply do not yield to the supernatural means which he applies to them. Frequently the situation is such that the penitent is at once a sinner and a neurotic or a psychotic personality and has need of both priest and psychiatrist.[18]

The priest may find it extremely difficult to collaborate unless he puts aside his misconceptions and respects the medical capacities of the psychiatrist. Prejudices should be discarded. The priest should not presume without proof that the psychiatrist is a person who will suggest to his penitent immoral practices, or treat him in a fashion which is not consonant with his religion. It is uncharitable and unreasonable to judge an entire profession on the exaggerations of one or another of its members. Priests might remember also that the isolated cases of unethical conduct on the part of psychiatrists of which they have heard do not usually refer to the most competent members of that profession.

It would be unwise also to dismiss all the help psychiatry can give to the individual by simply deciding that the patient has need of strong "will power." It is not possible for the disturbed individual to utilize his God-given freedom of will until he acquires more psychical balance. There are a great number of mentally ill persons today, and they are clearly not all found in mental hospitals. Many more outside need professional help.

Nowadays, the prejudices against psychiatry are losing strength. Those occupied with religious guidance began to realize in the second quarter of this century that, although Freud is one of the leading figures of modern psychiatry, neo-Freudian psychiatrists and non-Freudian theories of psychiatry have also had their influence. Alfred Adler's emphasis upon individual psychology, and his popularization by the Catholic Rudolph Allers, contributed much to a better understanding on the part of Catholics of what psychiatry can contribute to religious mental health. Carl Jung also emphasized, more than Freud had done, the values which religion can supply in mental health as a synthesizing factor. Every life to be healthy must have some philosophy or basic unity to give it meaning, and psychiatrists were not slow to recognize that religion in many cases offers this unifying principle. Such psychiatrists as Karen Horney, the Menningers, Erich Fromm and Harry Stack Sullivan also helped to mitigate the attitude of hostility which had been predominant among religious people.

The fundamental principles of psychoanalysis and psychiatry, Catholic writers began to realize, may be accepted by any Catholic and may be of considerable help to the religious life of the individual. It is now accepted as self-evident that Freud's concern with religion was a personal concern and perhaps an obsessional neurosis on his part. Freud generalized his personal problems with religion and introduced them illegitimately into his schematic theories.

Today it is generally accepted that his method may be used to advantage if one discards Freud's pseudo-theology and pseudo-philosophy. A number of recent Catholic books such as those of Vander-Veldt and Odenwald, Nuttin, Stern, and Braceland point out that Freud's philosophy and theology may be rejected while one accepts the principles of his therapy. After all, Freud had long clinical experience with therapy before he began to philosophize about the principles which he thought lay at the basis of this therapy. His materialistic philosophy was popular at the time of the late nineteenth century, and he incorporated his insights regarding human personality into this philosophy. The Catholic may drop the philosophy and retain the insights. The Catholic philosopher, theologian, or psychiatrist who uses Freud's techniques simply incorporates these into basic Catholic philosophy and theology.

It is also accepted today that there is such a thing as neurotic guilt, and there is such a thing as genuine moral guilt, and that they are different. No Catholic objects to a psychiatrist's effort to remove neurotic guilt from his patient, on the contrary he urges him to do it. And the psychiatrist today is more aware of the fact that genuine sins and genuine moral guilt exist and that this guilt is not matter for therapy but for the confessional.

Pope Pius XII, in his discourses on psychiatry, found no general objection to its method on moral grounds, but he pointed out the dangers which may be involved in it. Freudian psychoanalysis, as it is practiced by many Catholics today, is not condemned by the Holy Father's discourses—at least, in the opinion of Gemelli, the rector of the Catholic University of Milan. In *Psychoanalysis Today*,[19] Father Gemelli observes that many present-day analysts no longer make the sexual instinct the be-all and and-all of their theoretical philosophy or of their clinical procedures. It is no longer an accepted belief even among Freudians that sexual disorders are the *exclusive* source of *psychological* disorders. Freudian analysts today admit, for example, the great importance that must be given to aggressivity and to the individual's striving for power. In April 1953, in speaking to the Fifth Congress of Psychotherapy and Clinical Psychology, the Pope indicated that there are limits imposed by religious and moral convictions on the psychologist; yet the general attitude of this document is very encouraging.

COLLABORATORS: PRIESTS AND PSYCHIATRISTS

There are, moreover, many signs that Catholics are beginning positively to appreciate the value of psychiatry more and more. The conflict has notably subsided, and co-operation is taking its place. Catholic, Jewish, and Protestant ministers of religion co-operate in seminars with psychiatrists, philosophers, psychologists and psychoanalysts. Also, recently organized institutions help the clergy get a better understanding of psychology and psychiatry for their pastoral work. Protestant seminaries throughout the country have invited psychiatrists to lecture to their theological students. Catholic seminaries are following closely behind. There are several workshops under the auspices of various religious groups. There is the pioneer summer workshop at St. John's University, Collegeville, Minnesota, on Pastoral Care and Psychotherapy. Fordham University also conducts an Institute for the Clergy on Problems in Pastoral Psychology every other year. Gonzaga University, Detroit University, Spokane University, and Loras College, Dubuque, have all co-operated in workshops of this type.

There are also a number of clinics operating under religious auspices. There is the Marble Collegiate Church Clinic under Protestant auspices in New York. There is also the Academy of Religion and Mental Health in the New York Academy of Medicine Building, based upon Jewish, Catholic, and Protestant co-operation. Recently there have been organized many groups of priests and psychiatrists working in unity on some of these difficult problems. The very existence of such associations as the Gallahue Seminar at the Menninger Foundation, Topeka, Kansas, and the Workshop on Pastoral Care and Psychiatry at Collegeville, Minnesota, and the Summer

Institutes on Pastoral Psychology at Fordham University, Detroit University, and in other places makes it obvious that today, intelligent priests and intelligent psychiatrists recognize the need of collaboration. A sympathetic atmosphere is replacing the atmosphere of prejudice and conflict which at one time seemed to reign in the non-official attitude of the Church towards psychiatry.

The serene atmosphere in which these discussions have been carried on, as anyone can bear witness who has been present at them, makes it evident too that closer collaboration is becoming possible between psychiatrist and priest. Moreover, today, all the Catholic hospitals in the United States normally have on their staffs psychiatrists whose services they make use of in dealing with disturbed personalities. Many Catholic schools throughout the country also have clinical psychologists and psychiatrists engaged in counselling services for the disturbed youth of the school. It is also noteworthy that many of the Roman ecclesiastical courts use the testimony of psychiatric experts. The diocesan Catholic Charities in many dioceses in the United States also employ regular staff psychologists and psychiatrists, psychiatric case workers, and so forth.

This is the official attitude of the Church towards psychiatry. It is unfortunate that this attitude is not always that of the ordinary Catholic, for charity demands of us that we use every means at our disposal to help the individual Christian lead a well-balanced Christian life.

Through these co-operative interchanges, the psychiatrist often comes to learn and respect the profession of the priest. If the psychiatrist believes that the priest normally does harm to his patients by his insistence on unchanging moral principles, or by dealing with mental illness as if it were moral illness, his attitude of scarcely veiled hostility will inevitably militate against peaceful collaboration. The psychiatrist doubtless can mention cases of priests who have done genuine harm to disturbed young persons by their advice. But he, too, sometimes has to see that he need not judge an entire profession by the less enlightened members of that profession. He can learn to presume that the priest is competent in his own field until the opposite is proved. If the uninformed psychiatrist believes that Christian morality is simply an illusion or that religion itself is a myth, he cannot approach the priest or the religious guide of the penitent with that objectivity which fosters co-operation.

The psychiatrist must learn that he need not accept any particular teaching of any religious body in order to be of help to his patient. He can come to respect these beliefs in the patient and not attack or undermine them. As a philosopher he can recognize that there is a religious side to human nature, and in dealing with this aspect of man he should respect the beliefs of his patient. The psychiatrist obviously should not undertake to give theological or moral advice to his client but should send the penitent to one who is trained to give this advice. No more, of course, should a priest attempt to give psychiatric direction to his penitent. Each should remain within the field of his own competence. It is obviously difficult at times to draw the line between that place where psychological help ends and the priest's help begins, but with mutual co-operation, understanding, and respect there can certainly be much more fruitful co-operation between psychologist and priest.[20]

At times, theologians object that the psychologists are trying to restore a balance in human nature which will never be restored as long as man is a fallen and redeemed human nature. Here again it would be very helpful for the professional psychiatrist to have an understanding of Catholic theology and of what dangers Catholicism sees in psychiatry. It is not necessary that he be a trained theologian; mutual discussion will often help to solve apparent difficulties.

The psychiatrist should also be aware that religion accepts the possibility of genuine freedom in man and consequently of genuine guilt. This does not mean that religion accepts the idea that all *feelings* of guilt represent genuine moral faults. Nevertheless, psychology cannot explain away all guilt feelings if there is genuine guilt in the patient. Psychiatry would deceive itself and the patient if, in order to do away with a neurotic sense of guilt, it pretended that the possibility of real guilt does not exist. Pius XII has pointed out that it is not the task of psychiatric treatment to eliminate *genuine* guilt. This is the role of contrition and sacramental absolution by the priest.[21]

In pathological cases there may indeed exist the common phenomenon of neurotic guilt. But, as Karl Stern has pointed out, neurotic guilt has several characteristics which distinguish it from real guilt. Real guilt is proportionate to the fault committed. Neurotic guilt is without any proportion to the fault committed. Real guilt can be lifted when the guilt is removed in confession. The neurotic guilt remains, however, and can never be assuaged. Thirdly, objective guilt does not depend upon emotion, whereas neurotic guilt does. Neurotic guilt is so bound up with anxiety that even when there is no *conscious* feeling of guilt, *anxiety* remains. Neurotic guilt obviously refers to repressed drives even more than to objective acts committed by the patient, whereas real guilt refers to objective, fully conscious and responsible acts, even though these acts be internal. Both priest and psychiatrist should be aware of the difference between these guilts. The psychiatrist can be of invaluable assistance to the priest in evaluating real and neurotic guilt. He must not attempt to eliminate from the working concepts of the penitent the idea of genuine moral guilt, should it be present. Neither, on the other hand, should the priest constantly act as though it was the aim of the psychiatrist to eliminate all sense of moral guilt.[22]

Another frequent occasion of confusion between theology and psychiatry is the question of guilt feelings. Certain theologians seem to feel that some psychiatrists believe that all guilt feelings are undesirable. This is obviously in conflict with revelation (as well as with most psychiatric theory). Sin itself is always undesirable, but the feeling of guilt which results from objective sin may be put to constructive use. Obviously we cannot say that whenever there is a feeling of guilt there is sin. Sin is a violation of the moral law set by the Supreme Lawgiver; it presupposes that the sinner has full awareness at the time of committing the sin, that he deliberately offends God. There is obviously no such thing as unconscious sin; and a purely material breach of the law is not a sin in the formal sense. But he who actually commits formally objective and subjective sin is guilty, and the feeling of guilt is a perfectly normal accompaniment to his reasoned assent.

We should not believe that the guilty feelings caused by an objective formal sin are an undesirable phenomenon which must be eliminated from man's psychic life. Rather, they are a normal accompaniment to human failing and they motivate man to see his dependency upon God and to alter his way of life. It is humiliating to realize that one has committed formal sin and to understand that one has imperfections and limitations, but this feeling may be put to constructive uses. On the other hand, psychologists and moralists are in agreement that guilt feelings not based upon objective guilt are undesirable and should be eliminated from the patient's moral life. Religion in no sense opposes psychiatry on this point.

The theologian does not always understand what attitude psychiatry takes towards objective, formal sin. The physician does not moralize concerning sin. But it is obvious that the psychiatrist *can* take a viewpoint towards sin which helps the neurotic patient to eliminate it from his life. Because the psychiatrist helps appraise the conflicts and motives underlying man's action, he is often able to bring to clarity certain motivations which in their unclear and confused state have hampered the religious development of the individual. Psychiatry thus can help the individual to strive towards self-perfection by removing emotional blocks to self-understanding and free choice, thereby integrating his life and enabling him to come to a fuller grasp of his own goals, aspirations, and motives.

The situation then is thus at the present moment: The official attitude of the Catholic Church invites closer and closer collaboration between psychiatrist and priest, with each remaining within his respective sphere. Mutual understanding and mutual respect based upon an intellectual grasp of the principles of each other's disciplines can be greatly improved by study on the part of both priest and psychiatrist. Those conventions and congresses and institutes which endeavor to bring together priest and psychiatrist can be of great assistance to both. Both priest and psychiatrist can collaborate for the great spiritual benefit of the Christian, and they will collaborate most effectively if they will put aside prejudices and try to understand the limits and possibilities of each other's science.

For while some Freudians may consider religion to be the universal obsessional neurosis, a pure fiction, an illusion of no value, from which psychoanalysis will liberate mankind, their whole argument rests upon all sorts of unproved assumptions. For some who deny the existence of God psychoanalysis has possibly become a substitute for religious conviction. But the fact that they make it a substitute does not prove the nonexistence of God. Long before Freud, innumerable people professed religions of one sort or another and on the whole were no more neurotic than Freud and some of his followers. It may well be true that religious problems are the basis of a patient's difficulty, but the psychiatrist can often help to solve these problems on the psychological level if he will not treat his patient's religion as an illusion.

The Catholic concept of religion is quite clear in its meaning. Religion is not born solely out of a need of security but out of an obligation to adore. Religion therefore, to the Catholic, is neither the mere projection of a father image nor a common denominator of all sorts of vague religious teaching. Religion *can* help the individual to overcome that egocentricity and selfishness which often underlies certain psychological difficulties. People who can sublimate certain of their selfish tendencies into religious, altruistic channels often create more satisfactory interpersonal relationships with other men and generally have less neurotic difficulties than the completely self-centered individual.[23]

It is also true that a healthy dependence upon God can be of great assistance to the mental health of man, for it can prevent him from becoming unduly dependent upon other people and things. Religion helps man's balance when it teaches him that he is not absolute in himself but is supported by God. This conviction often gives a patient the courage and the self-respect to continue his efforts at self-fulfillment. Moreover, religion can help a person to accept, with some degree of serenity, suffering and frustration, and therefore it gives to man a basic happiness within his suffering. When man has a theology of life he endures more easily life's disappointments, routine or serious, and can more easily weather the emotional difficulties and crises which arise in almost every life.

Moreover, psychiatrists can at times bring the patient to a point where divine grace can more easily operate in the personality. Psychiatry is not an ordinary means of divine grace. The psychiatrist does not aim at giving grace but may reduce the tensions and conflicts of the individual and bring about a better natural equilibrium, thus enabling the patient to conform to the dictates of his conscience with more facility. Grace then operates to achieve the visible and tangible results of a good moral life. If the psychiatrist believes that it is to the benefit of his patient to revise his religious ideals, he should not attempt to substitute himself for the clergyman. It will not ordinarily help the patient if his doctor stimulates him in a religious direction without the collaboration of the priest, minister, or rabbi.

Hence it is clear that sincere religious convictions can be a powerful aid to the psychiatric method and have genuine value for the individual's mental health. On the other hand, religion is not a substitute for psychiatry. When a person's mental health has been seriously disturbed, it will not do to appeal to divine grace to work miracles. In setting a stable moral standard for the individual, and in assuring him of the protection of a loving God, religion frequently co-operates with the means used in analytical psychology. But the two actually work on a different level. Psychology works to a great extent on the subconscious and unconscious level, and religion is essentially an affair of man's conscious mind.

The two disciplines are different, but collaboration and mutual insight on the part of doctor and priest can be enormously beneficial to the patient. Since such great strides have been made in the last quarter of a century we can hope that progress will continue to be made.

NOTES

1. William C. Bier, S.J., "Sigmund Freud and the Faith," *America*, November 17, 1956, pp. 192–195.

2. Joseph Donceel, S.J., "Second Thoughts on Freud," *Thought*, 24 (September 1959), pp. 466–467; cf. R. Allers, *The Successful Error* (New York: Sheed and Ward, 1940), p. 259.

3. Bier, art. cit., p. 192.

4. Gregory Zilboorg, "Some Denials and Assertions of Religious Faith" in *Faith, Reason and Modern Psychiatry,* ed. Francis Braceland (New York: Kenedy, 1955), pp. 110–113. See also ch. 9 of Zilboorg's *Mind, Medicine and Man* (New York: Harcourt, 1943).

5. Donceel, art. cit., p. 466.

6. Ford and Kelly, *Contemporary Modern Theology,* Vol. I, p. 321.

7. *A. A. S.,* 45 (1953), p. 284.

8. Ibid., p. 279.

9. Joseph Donceel, S.J., "La psychologie profonde et le Service social," *Progrès scientifique et Service social* (Rome, 1950).

10. Bier, art. cit., p. 193.

11. Ford and Kelly, op. cit., pp. 320–323.

12. For a sympathetic view of Freudian techniques and their relationship to religion, see Joseph Nuttin, *Psychoanalysis and Personality: A Dynamic Theory of Normal Personality* (New York: Sheed and Ward, 1953), and R. Dalbiez, *Psychoanalytical Method and the Doctrine of Freud* (New York: Longmans, 1941).

13. Donceel, "Second Thoughts on Freud," p. 484.

14. Ford and Kelly, op. cit., p. 327.

15. André Snoeck, S.J., "Moral Reflections on Psychiatric Abreactions," *Theological Studies,* 13 (1952), pp. 173–189.

16. Ford and Kelly, op. cit., p. 182.

17. W. Bier, "Psychological Aspects of Pastoral Works," *Proceedings of the Archdiocesan Institute of Ecclesiastical Studies* (New York, 1957), pp. 57–61.

18. Ford and Kelly, op. cit., pp. 338–343.

19. New York: Kenedy, 1955.

20. J. VanderVeldt and R. Odenwald, *Psychiatry and Catholicism* (New York: McGraw-Hill, 1952), ch. 11.

21. Ibid., p. 205.

22. K. Stern, *The Third Revolution* (New York: Harcourt, 1954), pp. 202–203.

23. VanderVeldt and Odenwald, op. cit., pp. 197–198.

APPENDIX I: THE CHIEF
MENTAL ILLNESSES

An ever increasing number of priests find that they must give part of their time to chaplaincy work in hospitals and sanitaria within the local parish, and to consultation with psychiatrists who are treating Catholic parishioners. Such priests will be reading and hearing about various psychiatric disorders, often described in rather technical terminology. If such priests are to work well with patient and psychiatrist, they should endeavor to understand each emotionally disturbed patient in terms of the particular mental components involved in the illness. In order to bring about a more understanding relationship between priest and psychiatrist so that both may better serve their purposes in restoring the emotionally disturbed patient to better mental health, we shall here try to give a brief and simple description of each group of the chief mental illnesses. We shall also try to outline the main dynamics, or interplay, of the mental processes at work.*

Excepting certain physical or chemical causes, most mental illnesses are caused by a faulty interrelationship of the chief psychic components of the mind. These components are primarily (1) urges from within, e.g., love and hate; (2) an opposing conscience, which consists of a "moral" *conscious* conscience and *unconscious* conscience; and (3) the ego or conscious rational part of the mind which must deal with both the surging urges and the authority of the conscience. (See chapter 1, pp. 18 ff.) Besides the urges and the conscience, the ego part of the mind must also handle demands

---

* The authors are indebted to Dr. M. John Schumacher of the Hacker Clinic, Beverly Hills, California, for his major contributions to this glossary.

from the world or external reality. Emotionally disturbed patients are those in whom one or another psychic component of the mind has overwhelmed the ego or rational part of the mind.

PSYCHIATRIC DISORDERS* AND REACTIONS

Psychoneurotic Disorders

Psychoneurotic disorders are the result of the automatic pushing back of powerful feelings of love or hate from the conscious and rational part of the mind. These powerful charges of love and hate are usually attached to the developmental experiences in infancy and early childhood. Patients who suffer an acute or sudden illness of this kind are usually temporarily overwhelmed by strong feelings of love and hate reactivated from powerfully significant events and attitudes of the past. They do not experience these strong feelings consciously, but rather as symptoms of tension and nervousness, with or without depression, unwarranted fears, or memory disturbance. The life histories of psychoneurotic persons reveal periodic outbursts of their present symptoms alternating with periods of normal, tensionless adjustment.

The chief feature of psychoneurotic disorders is anxiety, also called tension or general nervousness. Nervousness may be "free floating," which means that the tension of the person is diffuse; he is liable to worry about everything. If nervousness is bound up or attached to specific objects or symbols, such as fear of heights, crossing bridges, or braving traffic, the disorders are also psychoneurotic, but special names are usually given to them. They are broadly classified as phobias.

In contrast to psychotic (insane) patients, persons with psychoneurotic disorders do not distort facts or the realities of the world; they do not experience illusions, hallucinations, or delusions. Psychoneurotic patients usually do not falsify. They are in touch with reality, but often are unable to cope with it; they are quite

* The word "disorder" is used to designate a specific psychological reaction in terms of its causes. Subclassified titles are descriptive of one specific aspect of a general emotional problem.

aware of the conflict between themselves and their environment. The psychoneurotic patient realizes that the difficulty is largely within himself, and much of his suffering stems from his inability to relate to disturbing life situations which he knows are quite inconsequential for the more normal people around him.

The various ways in which psychoneurotic patients tend to handle their anxieties result in a variety of *reactions*.

A. *Simple anxiety reactions*. In these cases nervousness is diffuse and not restricted to meeting definite situations or objects. Such persons are nervous about everything. Often certain body functions are sufficiently upset, so that sweaty palms, dilated pupils, night sweats, and a rapid pulse are common symptoms. Simple anxiety reactions should be distinguished from normal apprehensiveness or fear. Fear is experienced by every human being when there is a rational reason for it. For example, almost everyone who faces an examination shows some kind of fear and apprehension. In contrast to this normal fear, neurotic fear or simple anxiety reactions is "free floating"—it occurs without any apparent rational basis. However, depth exploration of the personality will uncover reasons for the tension. These reasons are not conscious in the patient. By making them conscious in treatment the neurotic fear and anxiety are dissipated.

B. *Dissociative reactions*. These reactions may be described as acute instances of "freezing up" or aimless running about. In such cases the personality make-up is suddenly overwhelmed by deep urges which the patient attempts to discharge by immobility or hyperactivity. Such persons do not know what urges are attempting to overwhelm them. They may also suffer memory losses for the period of the disturbance; this is called amnesia. (Dissociative reactions must not be confused with certain forms of epilepsy or acute psychotic breakdowns.)

C. *Phobic reactions*. Phobic reactions involve one or more fears which seem unwarranted. Fear of germs, high places, open places, crossing the street, dirt, spiders, noise, the dark are examples. There are many more. People who suffer from phobias are aware that they fear certain specific objects or situations. The cause of their fear, however, is tension about some problem or attitude which they have pushed back deep into their mind. This conflict presses forward towards conscious expression but cannot be faced. As a result, the tension and the conflict are released obliquely through a symbolic object. For example, a woman's fear of men, or of relating closely to men, may be released through a fear of spiders, mice, or other animals. Fear of the dark frequently represents fear of physical pain or injury; darkness is symbolic of the person or persons who the patient fears might harm him.

D. *Psychosomatic reactions.* Nervous tension is sometimes relieved by channeling the tension and conflict through the autonomic nervous system into body organ symptoms and complaints. These psychosomatic reactions represent the body's way of complaining of such unbearable inner discord and strain. It is socially, culturally, and even morally more acceptable to complain of nausea and vomiting, for example, than to state openly that one "cannot stomach" a conflict with husband, wife, son or daughter. The stomach attempts to relieve the conflict by contracting, causing nausea and vomiting. Symbolically it is an attempt to "throw up" the conflict and discharge the tension. Incidentally, other psychosomatic symptoms are not so simply described and explained.

Psychosomatic reactions are generally classified according to the organ or bodily systems through which the anxiety or tensions discharge themselves as symptoms. Therefore, these diagnoses are usually written as:

1. PSYCHOSOMATIC GASTRO-INTESTINAL REACTION, which includes chronic gastritis, mucus, colitis, constipation, heartburn, irritated colon, hyperacidity, pyloric spasm, etc.

2. PSYCHOSOMATIC CARDIOVASCULAR REACTIONS include such common types as rapid heart and pulse rate, missing heart beats and double heart beats, episodes of chest pain, some cases of high blood pressure and hypertension. Headaches and migraines may be at least partially caused by such nervous tension.

3. PSYCHOSOMATIC GENITO-URINARY REACTIONS include premenstrual depressions and menstrual cramping, erection difficulties in men, sexual coldness in women, frequent urination at night.

4. PSYCHOSOMATIC ALLERGIC REACTIONS include cases of hives, rashes, unusual swellings, especially when they are bilateral, and cases of so-called "skin writing." In the latter, brushing the skin with a finger nail produces a red mark.

5. PSYCHOGENIC-ASTHENIC REACTION is a condition where fatigue is the dominant characteristic and is usually mixed with symptoms relating to various organs in the body. Sometimes the word "weakness" is used by the patient to describe his condition.

6. Certain BRONCHIAL DISTURBANCES, in particular asthmatic and allergy afflictions, can often be complicated by emotional as well as organic involvements.

Psychosomatic symptoms can be treated by organic medicine, but the only permanent solution lies in unearthing the conflicts being channeled into the organ and helping the patient to resolve them. It is important to remember that when psychosomatic reactions become chronic and prolonged an actual alteration of the tissue of the involved organ occurs. Once tissue changes have taken place it is usually very difficult to relieve the medical symptoms of the patient permanently by psychological treatment alone. If, on the other hand, psychosomatic problems are detected early, chronic tissue changes in heart, lung, stomach, etc., can be avoided or reversed and psychological treatment can alleviate symptoms permanently.

The foregoing is an important note for priests in that many persons with psychosomatic complaints come to see them for reassurance. As aspirin relieves a headache, comfort and reassurance temporarily alleviate these people's symptoms. But like aspirin, consolation alone is no cure. In fact misplaced comfort and reassurance may only prolong the period of time these people avoid skilled psychiatric help. Meantime irreversible organic changes can occur so that complete asymptomatic recovery will be almost impossible, even with the most intensive psychiatric help.

E. *Hysteria reaction.* The unconsciously caused symptomatic simulation of almost any known disease. Symptoms can include paralysis of various sorts, twitching, pseudo-pregnancy, dramatic faintings, fits and convulsions, amnesia. Severe, unbearable anxiety causes the automatic suspension or complete closing off of organic activity or feeling. This is seen as an unconscious way of escaping kinds of activity which are too painful or threatening to manage at the moment (e.g., a concert pianist in a panic may develop paralysis in his hands).

F. *Obsessive-compulsive reactions.* People with this reaction reflect or discharge their nervousness through nagging and persistent anxiety impulses which they feel are uncontrollable. For example, a mother may be obsessed with the idea that she may hurt or even kill her child, or that if she lets her child play in the street he may get run over by an automobile. Obsessional reactions are purely mental processes—scrupulosity, constant preoccupation with death, guilt, and punishment, an inordinate fear of hell are often characteristic of the Catholic patient. Sometimes patients have monotonously recurring (obsessive) thoughts, usually of a sexual nature. Sometimes compulsions are the symptom of nervousness. A compulsive person temporarily controls his anxiousness by isolating the conflict from the rational mind and displacing it by engaging in excessive or useless and repetitive activity. Such repetitive actions are deeply symbolic and, for the moment, temporarily protect the patient against his inner conflicts and urges. Even though the patient knows his compulsive ritual is unreasonable and calls it foolish, he still feels a compelling force within himself to carry it out.

Compulsive mechanisms are seen at work in excessive handwashers, persons who must touch each crack in the sidewalk with their feet, or must count each telephone pole as they drive along in the car. Sometimes compulsions are expressed as ceremonials: e.g., a person must always get up at a certain time, must shave or dress in a particular way, then eat breakfast at a certain hour with specific foods demanded or avoided, each act being performed in a specified and over-precise manner.

G. *Hypochondriacal conditions.* These people are concerned in an obsessive and brooding way about their health. They have a multitude of complaints about many organs or body systems. If the doctor treats the liver, they develop a complaint in the stomach; if he treats the stomach, they then develop a complaint elsewhere. Reassurance, and the treatment of the organ complained about, result in the symptom leaving that organ and hopping to another. What *really* is hopping is the anxiety and tension around a buried conflict.

The prime irritators of the average doctor, and of many priests, these people by their constant complaints and harassment frequently invite rejection, which only furthers their need to complain. The more the hypochondriac is belittled and urged to recognize the absurdity of his worries, the more he feels compelled to defend his sickness, and new symptoms usually develop.

H. *Reactive depressions.* In these cases the nervous tension within the patient is reduced or alleviated through self-depreciation and self-blame. The depressed reaction may be related to extreme feelings of guilt for past misdeeds and failures. Sometimes it is related to a personal and emotional loss of the patient, such as the death of a loved one. Dynamically this depression is usually caused by pushed-back "anger." For example, upon the death of a loved one a person is beset by real grief over the loss of love and protection which the departed had offered. Another feeling, however, is strong anger over the loss of one upon whom he had depended. Conscience forbids such a person the right to be angry at someone who dies and leaves him alone. This anger therefore is pushed deep into the mind and may be experienced consciously as depression. The degree of depression is related to the strength of the initial love *and* hate which was present for the loved one. If the intensity of the patient's mixed feelings toward the loss of his loved one is strong, the depression will be more profound. Thus, a spinster, who, swallowing her resentment, sacrifices a good part of her life to care for an ailing parent may be plunged into a severe depression at the death of the parent. The ambivalent feelings of dependency and resentment which are so often involved in such situations will suggest that the death is a result of "wishful thinking" which often goes on in the unconscious. The guilt associated with such thoughts may overwhelm the survivor with remorse.

It is not only the loss of a loved one which can precipitate severe neurotic depressions. The loss of possessions, money, important convictions or beliefs, etc., can also bring on depressive reactions.

Character and Behavior Disorders

These disorders are largely problems involving defective early conscience development which result in antisocial or asocial tendencies. People so affected have little tension. They sense no distress when they do wrong. Literally they are persons who have developed conscience in one area but have little or no conscience in another area. For example, such people do not feel out of harmony with themselves when they are promiscuous or uncouth; but they may be excessively clean in their personal habits. They feel little or no guilt about violations of the moral law, but they can have strong feelings over a dirty shirt, or dress, or an unpressed blouse.

Persons afflicted with character and behavior disorders cannot stand tension but seek immediate pleasure in life. They cannot wait for long-term goals. They cannot plan effectively because they seek immediate gratification, whether sexual, social, or vocational. They have not learned to postpone immediate gratification for future gain even when that future gain promises more reward or enjoyment than the immediate, self-satisfying pleasure.

Character and behavior disorders may be divided into the following groups.

A. *Pathological personality types.* Pathological personalities are individuals who show some general but serious flaws in character formation. They have little or no tension or anxiety. Their main personality is described by others as "seclusive, eccentric, envious, stubborn, jealous, moody, with alternating periods of depression and excitement." At times pathological personality types show antisocial or asocial behavior. Despite a normal moral upbringing they are always in trouble; experience or punishment does not teach them. They usually defy cultural, social, and moral codes. They cannot remain loyal to causes, groups, or persons. They are sometimes on the verge of criminal conduct. In this group fall gangsters, prostitutes, and certain types of juvenile delinquents. A special type of pathological personality is the sexual deviate, including the homosexual, transvestite (wears clothes of other sex), pedophiliac (molests children), rapist and sexual mutilator. (Most sexual deviations are extreme symptoms of more serious underlying illnesses such as schizophrenia and severe obsessional neurosis.)

B. *Drug addicts.* Addicts are persons who utilize alcohol, drugs, or both to release very deep-seated inner tensions. This character disturbance has been fixated in earliest infancy by painful psychological blows. The use of alcohol or drugs is unconsciously intended by the addict to reduce the inner tension and insecurity which he cannot endure any other way. Under the influence of alcohol or drugs antisocial and asocial behavior may also occur.

C. *Immaturity reactions.* These adult individuals fail to maintain an emotional balance under minor stresses because of gaps in their emotional development. In some life situations behavior is mature and appropriate, but when faced with a major stress and under severe duress behavior becomes immature. Tensions and nervousness are not involved. The basic way in which the early personality develops is the important factor. (Physical immaturity may or may not accompany emotional immaturity.)

Emotionally immature people, reacting with excitement to minor stress, are ineffective in emergency situations. At sudden crises, such as a fire, they show poor judgment; their feelings disclose a mixture of strong guilt, poorly controlled anger. They usually react explosively and inappropriately to hide their sense of inadequacy or to ward off sudden, overwhelming anger and intense guilt.

Dependency is another characteristic of immature people. Persons with strong "dependency needs" cling to others for help, are indecisive, and feel helpless in any situation which requires assertion or leadership. Inappropriate aggressiveness is also an expression of immaturity. This aggressiveness is usually seen in passive forms such as pouting, obstructionism, stubbornness, and whining. Or such immature persons will react to frustrating situations with marked irritation, temper tantrums and destructive acts. As a rule this kind of infantile aggressiveness is used to ward off a deeper, underlying dependency. Immaturity may also be associated with uncontrollable habits such as bed-wetting, speech disorders, finger-sucking, and nail-biting.

Disorders of Intelligence

Disorders of intelligence can be primary or secondary mental deficiencies. *Primary mental deficiency* is usually a case of mental retardation which has been present since birth or infancy without known brain disease. It includes hereditary cases. *Secondary mental deficiency* is applied to cases of mental retardation which have resulted from some organic disease or lesion of the brain. Feeble-mindedness, with its classification of idiot, imbecile and moron, falls under the general heading of intelligence disorders. It is the moron (with a mental age of from seven to ten) who occasionally has a difficult time in school because the deficiency is not detected soon enough. He is often pushed to efforts beyond his capacities, and the resulting emotional strain and stress can produce mental difficulties over and above his retarded intellectual acumen.

Psychotic Disorders

The psychotic disorder is a personality disintegration; it is a failure on the part of the rational mind to test and evaluate reality correctly in various spheres. Further, psychotic persons are unable to become sufficiently involved with people to be happy or to work effectively. It is to these patients that the term "insanity" is most commonly applied.

A. *Schizophrenic disorders.* The schizophrenic patient suffers from a psychosis which is characterized by a fundamental confusion of reality relationships. His ideational formations are awry, and there is a consequent disturbance of feelings and intelligence in varying degrees and mixtures. These people retreat from reality, and in doing so are unaware of the split between their feelings and their thoughts (hence "split personality"). Their stream of thinking is unpredictable, compulsive, and sometimes verbally long-winded. They tend to speak of things in a flat, unfeeling voice. They may describe a terrifying incident or experience without showing the expected and proper emotions.

The disordered conceptual thinking of schizophrenics (sometimes called categorical thinking) can be tested by asking such a patient the meaning of proverbs. For example: ask a schizophrenic patient, "What does it mean to you when I say 'A rolling stone gathers no moss'?" He will respond, "Just what it says—a stone can roll down a hill and will not pick up moss on it." The schizophrenic is unable to abstract from the literal meaning of the proverb the general principle "If you keep busy you will not age."

Schizophrenic reactions show themselves in four prominent types. These are by no means distinct and untouched by symptoms more pronounced in other classifications.

1. SIMPLE SCHIZOPHRENIA is a reaction seen frequently in tramps or "bums." Such people are unable to make any kind of attachment to other people, cultures, society, groups or codes. They suffer from an impoverishment of human relationships. They lack interest in everything. They are apathetic, indifferent, find life perplexing, and neglect their own appearance. They usually have bodily complaints of one kind or another. They are devoid of feeling regardless of stimulations from the world outside. Although they rarely suffer conspicuous delusions or hallucinations, they seem to undergo a progressive deterioration which seems unresponsive to current treatments.

2. PARANOID SCHIZOPHRENIA is characterized chiefly by suspicion, delusions, guilt feelings, feelings of persecution and/or grandeur. Such persons feel they are being followed by the police, abused by employers or certain racial groups; are convinced that people are talking about them.

3. THE HEBEPHRENIC SCHIZOPHRENIC is characterized by shallow, inappropriate emotions, unpredictable, childish behavior, and mannerisms often involving silliness, grins, incoherent babbling, giggling and bizarre gestures.

4. CATATONIC SCHIZOPHRENIA involves general immobility, with muscular rigidity or inflexibility. Alternating periods of physical hyperactivity or excitability may occur. Usually the patient is markedly inaccessible and impervious to ordinary methods of communication. Such patients will remain for hours at a time in the precise position in which they have been placed; automatic obedience and explosive violence may often be a part of their symptom pattern.

B. *Manic-depressive psychosis* is a major emotional illness marked by severe mood swings (elation-depression). In most cases, the patient suffers more obviously from one emotional extreme. The depressed type is characterized by a despondent mood, retardation and inhibition of both thinking and physical activity. Feelings of unworthiness and often of sinfulness and utter desolation, with delusions of persecution and a tendency to suicide, are often present. The manic type is characterized by elation, overtalkativeness, extremely rapid skipping from one idea to another, and increased motor activity. He often seems to be mildly intoxicated, exhibiting at first social, aggressive and brilliant characteristics, but eventually becoming domineering, erratic, and lacking in moral restraint.

C. *Involutional melancholia* is a psychotic reaction of a prolonged course which begins during the male or female climacteric. This is perhaps one of the most common mental disorders which the priest will encounter in women in their menopause. It is usually marked by depression and occasional paranoid thinking; it almost always includes feelings of guilt, anxiety, agitation, delusional ideas, insomnia and preoccupation with self. This is one of the diseases which shock treatment often effectively arrests.

In addition to these psychoses, which are essentially functional (no physical cause) in origin, there are the organic psychoses, which result from defects, damage, infection, drug or alcohol impairment, tumor or other organic pathology of the brain.

D. *Senile psychosis* is a mental illness of old age characterized by personality deterioration, progressive loss of memory, eccentricity and irritability. Still other forms which do not seem to fit into these somewhat arbitrary categories are cerebral arteriosclerosis and epilepsy.

APPENDIX II: REFERRAL FACILITIES

The busy priest who does not know of appropriate local agencies to advise him on his many counselling and referral problems may find the following selection of professional and charitable organizations helpful. Listed are the titles of *national* agencies which are prepared to inform the inquirer of state, local, and neighborhood specialized facilities. These main offices will also send pertinent literature upon request, and many of them are prepared to offer practical and individual suggestions by mail. A simple statement of the problem in a written plea for information is usually sufficient to bring a helpful response.

AGED

American Association of Retired Persons, New York City
American Society for the Aged, New York City
Federal Council on the Aging (U.S. Department of Health, Education and Welfare, Washington, D.C.)
National Committee on the Aging, New York City
Senior Citizens of America, Washington, D.C.

ALCOHOL

Alcoholics Anonymous, General Service Board, New York City
Catholic Total Abstinence Union of America, Philadelphia, Pennsylvania
National Clergy Conference on Alcoholism, Indianapolis, Indiana
National Council on Alcoholism, New York City
National States' Conference on Alcoholism, Richmond, Virginia
Yale Center of Alcohol Studies, New Haven, Connecticut

ARMED FORCES AND VETERANS
  American Legion, Indianapolis, Indiana
  American Veterans Committee, Washington, D.C.
  Army Relief Society, New York City
  Catholic War Veterans, Washington, D.C.
  Chaplains Aid Association, Inc., New York City
  Disabled American Veterans, Cincinnati, Ohio
  Federal Civil Defense Board, Battle Creek, Michigan
  National Catholic Community Service, Washington, D.C.
  Navy Relief Society (Department of the Navy), Washington,
    D.C.
  Selective Service System, Washington, D.C.
  Veterans Administration, Washington, D.C.
  Veterans of Foreign Wars of the U.S., Kansas City, Kansas

CHILDREN
  (cf. also MARRIAGE AND THE FAMILY)
  American Camping Association, Bradford Woods, Martinsville,
    Indiana
  American Youth Hostels, New York City
  Association of Junior Leagues of America, New York City
  Big Brothers of America, Philadelphia, Pennsylvania
  Boy Scouts of America (National Council), New Brunswick, New
    Jersey
  Boys Clubs of America, New York City
  Camp Fire Girls, New York City
  Catholic Central Union of America Youth Movements, St. Louis,
    Missouri
  Child Study Association of America, New York City
  Child Welfare League of America, New York City
  Girl Scouts of the U.S. of America, New York City
  Girls Clubs of America, Springfield, Massachusetts
  Interdepartmental Committee on Children and Youth (U.S.
    Department of Health, Education, and Welfare, Washington,
    D.C.)
  Junior Achievement (Teen-age work groups), New York City

National Association of the Prevention of Juvenile Delinquency, Inc., New York City

National Catholic Camping Association, Washington, D.C.

National Committee on Boys and Girls Club Work, Chicago, Illinois

National Council of Catholic Youth, Washington, D.C.

Pathfinders of America (Guidance for Children), Cleveland, Ohio

United Nations Children's Fund, United Nations Building, New York City

United Nations Educational, Scientific, and Cultural Organization (UNESCO), United Nations Building, New York City

CRIME

American Catholic Correctional Chaplains Association, Iowa State Penitentiary, Fort Madison, Iowa

American Correctional Association, New York City

Board of Parole, U.S. Department of Justice, Washington, D.C.

Guild of Our Lady of Ransom, Charlestown, Massachusetts

National Jail Association, New York City

National Probation and Parole Association, New York City

EDUCATION

Adult Education Association of the U.S.A., Chicago, Illinois

American Association for Gifted Children, New York City

American Council on Education, Washington, D.C.

American Library Association, Chicago, Illinois

American Schools and Colleges Association, New York City

Catechetical Guild Education Society, St. Paul, Minnesota

Catholic Library Association, Villanova, Pennsylvania

Confraternity of Christian Doctrine, Washington, D.C.

Institute of Adult Education, New York City

National Association of Foreign Student Advisors, New York City

National Association for Nursery Education, University of Rhode Island, Kingston, Rhode Island

National Catholic Educational Association, Washington, D.C.

National Congress of Parents and Teachers, Chicago 11, Illinois

National Educational Association of the U.S.A., Washington, D.C.

The National Federation of Catholic College Students, National Catholic Welfare Conference, Washington, D.C.

National Newman Club Federation, National Catholic Welfare Conference, Washington, D.C.

Office of Education, U.S. Department of Health, Education and Welfare, Washington, D.C.

Play Schools Association, New York City

Serra International (Education of Seminarians), Chicago, Illinois

Sodality for Deferred Vocations, New York City

The Young Christian Students, Chicago, Illinois

HEALTH AND REHABILITATION

(cf. also SICK AND HANDICAPPED)

A. G. Bell Association for the Deaf, Washington, D.C.

American Association for Health, Physical Education, and Recreation, Washington, D.C.

American Association for Workers for the Blind, New York City

American Cancer Society, New York City

American Dental Association, New York City

American Federation for the Blind, New York City

American Federation of Catholic Workers for the Blind, Philadelphia, Pennsylvania

American Hearing Society, Washington, D.C.

American Heart Association, New York City

American Medical Association, Chicago, Illinois

American Nurses Association, New York City

American Occupational Therapy Association, New York City

American Printing House for the Blind, Louisville, Kentucky

American Public Health Association, New York City

American Rehabilitation Committee, New York City

American Speech and Hearing Association, Wayne University, Detroit 1, Michigan

Arthritis and Rheumatism Foundation, New York City

Association for Aid of Crippled Children, New York City

Braille Institute of America, Los Angeles, California

Catholic Hospital Association of the U.S. and Canada, St. Louis, Missouri

Federation of Catholic Physicians Guilds, St. Louis, Missouri

Guild of St. Apollonia (Dental Aid), Boston, Massachusetts

Ladies Catholic Benevolent Association (Aid for the Deaf), Erie, Pennsylvania

League of St. Dymphna (Mental Health), New York City

Muscular Dystrophy Association of America, New York City

National Association for Crippled Children and Adults, Chicago, Illinois

National Association for Retarded Children, New York City

National Association of the Deaf, Berkeley, California

National Blood Bank, Inc., New York City

National Cancer Foundation, New York City

National Committee on Social Aspects of Epilepsy, Butlerville, Indiana

National Council of Catholic Nurses, Washington, D.C.

National Foundation for Infantile Paralysis, New York City

National Foundation for Muscular Dystrophy, Inc., New York City

National Foundation Industries for the Blind, New York City

National Multiple Sclerosis Society, New York City

National Tuberculosis Association, New York City

Office of Vocational Rehabilitation, U.S. Department of Health, Education, and Welfare, Washington, D.C.

President's Committee on Employment of the Physically Handicapped, Washington, D.C.

Public Health Service, U.S. Department of Health, Welfare, and Education, Washington, D.C.

United Cerebral Palsy Association, New York City

U.S. Department of Health, Welfare, and Education, Washington, D.C.

HOUSING AND IMMIGRATION

(cf. also WELFARE; NATIONAL GROUPS)

American Association for Better Housing, Inc., New York City

Bishops' Committee for Migrant Workers, Washington, D.C.

Catholic Committee for Refugees, National Catholic Welfare Council, New York City

Housing and Home Finance Agency, Washington, D.C.

Immigration and Naturalization Service, U.S. Department of Justice, Washington, D.C.

National Catholic Resettlement Council, New York City

National Catholic Welfare Conference, Immigration Department, Washington, D.C.

National Federation of Settlements and Neighborhood Centers, New York City

National Housing Conference, Washington, D.C.

LABOR

American Federation of Labor, Congress of Industrial Relations, AFL-CIO Building, Washington, D.C.

Religion and Labor Foundation, Columbus, Ohio

U.S. Civil Service Commission, Washington, D.C.

U.S. Department of Labor, Washington, D.C.

Women's Bureau, U.S. Department of Labor, Washington, D.C.

Young Christian Workers, Chicago, Illinois

LEGAL AID

American Bar Association, Chicago, Illinois

American Civil Liberties Union, New York City

Guild of Catholic Lawyers, New York City

National Legal Aid Association, American Bar Center, Chicago, Illinois

MARRIAGE AND THE FAMILY

American Association of Marriage Counselors, Inc., New York City

American Institute of Family Relations, Los Angeles, California

American Parents Committee, New York City

Archconfraternity of Christian Mothers, Pittsburgh, Pennsylvania

Cana Conference, Chicago, Illinois

Catholic Guardian Society, New York City

Catholic Maternity Guild Apostolate, St. Mary's College, Ilchester, Maryland

Christian Family Movement, Chicago, Illinois

Family Location Service (Desertion), New York City

Family Service Association of America, New York City

Federation of Catholic Family Action, St. Paul, Minnesota

Foster Parents Plan, New York City

Maternity Center Association, New York City

National Association on Service to Unmarried Parents, New York City

National Catholic Conference on Family Life, Washington, D.C.

National Committee for Education in Family Finance, New York City

National Council on Family Relations, Minneapolis, Minnesota

National Family Council on Drug Addiction, New York City

MENTAL HEALTH AND ILLNESS

Academy of Religion and Mental Health, New York City

American Academy of Psychotherapists, New York City

American Association of Psychiatric Clinics for Children, New York City

American Association on Mental Deficiency, Mansfield Depot, Connecticut

American Catholic Psychological Association, Fordham University, New York City

American Foundation of Religion and Psychiatry, New York City

American Group Psychotherapy Association, Inc., New York City

American Institute for Psychoanalysis, New York City

American Mental Health Foundation, Inc., New York City

American Personnel and Guidance Association, Washington, D.C.

American Psychiatric Association, New York City
American Psychoanalytic Association, New York City
American Psychological Association, Washington, D.C.
Guild of Catholic Psychiatrists, Stamford, Connecticut
Mental Health Materials Center, New York City
National Association for Mental Health, New York City
National Committee against Mental Illness, New York City
National Organization for Mentally Ill Children, Inc., New York City
National Psychological Association for Psychoanalysis, Inc., New York City

MISCELLANY

Apostleship of the Sea, New Orleans, Lousiana
Catholic Daughters of America, New York City
The Catholic Film Library Service, Newark, New Jersey
Convert Makers of America, Pontiac, Michigan
General Federation of Women's Clubs, Washington, D.C.
Knights of Columbus Supreme Council, Columbian Squires, New Haven, Connecticut
National Catholic Cemetery Conference, Washington, D.C.
National Catholic Laymen's Retreat Conference, Covington, Kentucky
National Conference of Christians and Jews, New York City
National Council of Catholic Men Film Center, New York City
National Council of Catholic Men, Washington, D.C.
National Council of Catholic Women, Washington, D.C.
National Legion of Decency, New York City
National Travelers Aid Association, New York City
Rashob Foundation for Catholic Activities, Wilmington, Delaware
Sodalities of Our Lady, St. Louis, Missouri

NATIONAL GROUPS

American Committee on Italian Migration, New York City
Ancient Order of Hibernians in America, Brooklyn, New York

Bishops' Committee for the Spanish-Speaking, Austin, Texas
Catholic Central Union (Czech), Chicago, Illinois
Catholic Kolping Society (German Workers Club), Chicago, Illinois
Edith Stein Guild (Jewish Converts), East Elmhurst, New York
First Catholic Slovak Union, Cleveland, Ohio
Hungarian Catholic League of America, Inc., New York City
Lithuanian Roman Catholic Alliance of America, Wilkes-Barre, Pennsylvania
National Alliance of Czech Catholics, Chicago, Illinois
St. Ansgar's Scandinavian Catholic League, New York City
Slovak Catholic Federation of America, Lansford, Pennsylvania

NEGRO

Catholic Committee of the South, Rock Hill, South Carolina
Catholic Scholarships for Negroes, Springfield, Massachusetts
Friendship Houses, Chicago, Illinois
Knights of Peter Claver, New Orleans, Louisiana
National Association for the Advancement of Colored People, New York City
National Association of Intergroup Relations Officials, Detroit, Michigan
National Congress of Colored Parents and Teachers, Dover, Delaware
National Council of Negro Women, Washington, D.C.
National Scholarship Service and Fund for Negro Students, New York City
National Urban League, New York City
Southern Education Foundation, Atlanta, Georgia
United Negro College Fund, New York City

PSYCHIATRY
(cf. MENTAL HEALTH AND ILLNESS)

PSYCHOLOGY
(cf. MENTAL HEALTH AND ILLNESS)

RECREATION

American Recreation Society, Washington, D.C.

Cooperative Recreation Service, Delaware, Ohio

Federal Inter-Agency Committee on Recreation, Washington, D.C.

National Industrial Recreation Association, Chicago, Illinois

National Recreation Association, New York City

RURAL LIFE

Alliance for Guidance of Rural Youth, Inc., Washington, D.C.

American County Life Association, Washington, D.C.

Extension Service, U.S. Department of Agriculture, Washington, D.C.

Farm Foundation, Chicago, Illinois

National Catholic Rural Life Conference, Des Moines, Iowa

National Council on Agricultural Life and Labor, Washington, D.C.

Rural Youth of the United States of America, Marietta, Ohio

SICK AND HANDICAPPED

(cf. also HEALTH AND REHABILITATION)

Apostolate of Suffering, Milwaukee, Wisconsin

Apostolate to Aid the Dying, Sisters of the Poor of St. Francis, Hartwell, Cincinnati, Ohio

Catholic Union of the Sick in America, Inc., New York City

League of Shut-In Sodalists, Marcus, Iowa

National Association of Sheltered Workshops and Homebound Programs, New York City

The Shut-In Society, New York City

SOCIAL SERVICE

(cf. WELFARE)

SOCIOLOGY

American Catholic Sociological Society, Loyola University, Chicago, Illinois

American Sociological Association, New York University, New York City

American Sociological Society, New York City

Community Research Association, New York City

VETERANS

(cf. ARMED FORCES)

WELFARE

Alumni Association of the National Catholic School of Social Service, Catholic University of America, Washington 17, D.C.

American Foundations Information Service, New York City

American National Red Cross, Washington, D.C.

American Public Welfare Association, Chicago, Illinois

American Women's Voluntary Services, New York City

Bureau of Employment Security, U.S. Department of Labor, Washington, D.C.

Catholic Relief Services, Washington, D.C.

Federal Home Loan Bank Board, Washington, D.C.

National Association of Social Workers, New York City

Guild of St. Paul (Aid to Converts), Lexington, Kentucky

National Catholic Community Service, Washington, D.C.

National Catholic Social Action Conference, Washington, D.C.

National Catholic Welfare Conference, Washington, D.C.

National Conference on Catholic Charities, Washington, D.C.

National Conference on Social Welfare, New York City

National Information Bureau, New York City

National Social Welfare Assembly, New York City

St. Paul's Guild, Inc. (Aid to Convert Ministers), New York City

Social Security Administration, U.S. Department of Health, Education, and Welfare, Washington, D.C.

Society of St. Vincent de Paul, Superior Council of the United States, New York City

United Community Funds and Councils of America, New York City

United Service Organizations, New York City

YOUNG ADULTS

American Youth Hostels, New York City
Carroll Club, Inc., New York City
The Grail Movement, Loveland, Ohio
Young Ladies Institute, San Francisco, California
Young Men's Institute, San Francisco, California

BIBLIOGRAPHY

The following books constitute only a sampling of the vast body of current literature in the fields treated in this book. Several of the volumes listed do not agree in every respect with Catholic teaching, but all of them have much to offer the judicious and perceptive reader.

Allport, G., *The Individual and His Religion*. New York: Macmillan, 1950.

Anon., *Alcoholics Anonymous Comes of Age*. New York: Harper, 1957.

Anon., *The Invert and His Social Adjustment*. London: Baillière, Tindall & Cox, 1948.

Bergler, E., *Homosexuality: Disease, or Way of Life?* New York: Hill & Wang, 1956.

Biddle, W. E., *Integration of Religion and Psychiatry*. New York: Macmillan, 1955.

Blum, G. S., *Psychoanalytic Theories of Personality*. New York: McGraw-Hill, 1953.

Blum, M. L., and Balinsky, B., *Counseling and Psychology*. Englewood Cliffs: Prentice-Hall, 1951.

Braceland, F. J., ed., *Faith, Reason, and Modern Psychiatry*. New York: Kenedy, 1955.

Brady, L., and Kurtz, E., *Essentials of Gynecology*. New York: Macmillan, 1945.

Bruno de Jésus-Marie (O.C.D.), ed., *Conflict and Light*. New York: Sheed and Ward, 1953.

Carroll, H. A., *Mental Hygiene* (3d ed.). Englewood Cliffs: Prentice-Hall, 1956.

Clemens, A. H., *Marriage and the Family: An Integrated Approach for Catholics*. Englewood Cliffs: Prentice-Hall, 1957.

Clinebell, H. J., *Understanding and Counseling the Alcoholic*. New York: Abingdon, 1956.

Curran, C., *Counseling in Catholic Life and Education*. New York: Macmillan, 1952.

———— *Personality Factors in Counseling*. New York: Grune & Stratton, 1945.

Demal, W. (O.S.B.), *Pastoral Psychology in Practice*. New York: Kenedy, 1955.

Dempsey, P. J. R. (O.F.M. Cap.), *Freud, Psychoanalysis, Catholicism*. Chicago: Regnery, 1956.

D'Evelyn, Katherine, *Meeting Children's Emotional Needs*. Englewood Cliffs: Prentice-Hall, 1957.

Dobbelstein, H., *Psychiatry for Priests*. New York: Kenedy, 1953.

Duvall, Evelyn, *Facts of Life and Love for Teenagers*. New York: Popular Library, 1958.

Eisenstein, V., *Neurotic Interaction in Marriage*. New York: Basic Books, 1956.

English, O. S., and Pearson, G. H. J., *Common Neuroses of Children and Adults*. New York: Norton, 1937.

Erickson, E. H., *Childhood and Society*. New York: Norton, 1950.

Ferm, V., *A Dictionary of Pastoral Psychology*. New York: Philosophical Library, 1955.

Finn, J. P., *A Study of the Problems of Certain Catholic High School Boys*. Washington, D.C.: Catholic University Press, 1950.

Fleege, U., *Self-Revelation of the Adolescent Boy*. Milwaukee: Bruce, 1945.

Flood, Peter (O.S.B.), ed., *New Problems in Medical Ethics*. 3 vols. Westminster, Md.: Newman, 1955.

Ford, J. C. (S.J.), *Depth Psychology, Morality, and Alcoholism*. Weston, Mass.: Weston College Press, 1951.

———— *Man Takes a Drink*. New York: Kenedy, 1954.

———— and Kelly, G. (S.J.), *Contemporary Moral Theology*. Westminster, Md.: Newman, 1958.

Fox, Ruth, and Lyon, P., *Alcoholism, Its Scope, Cause and Treatment*. New York: Random House, 1955.

Frankl, V., *The Doctor and the Soul*. New York: Knopf, 1955.

Freud, S., *A General Introduction to Psychoanalysis*. New York: Doubleday, 1956.

Fromm, E., *Psychoanalysis and Religion*. New Haven: Yale University Press, 1950.

Gemelli, A. (O.F.M.), *Psychoanalysis Today*. New York: Kenedy, 1955.

Goldbrunner, J., *Cure of Mind and Cure of Soul*. New York: Pantheon, 1958.

———— *Holiness Is Wholeness*. New York: Pantheon, 1955.

Goodenough, Florence L., *Developmental Psychology* (2d. ed.). New York: Appleton-Century-Crofts, 1945.

Gross, L., *God and Freud*. New York: David McKay, 1959.

Gruenberg, Sidonie, ed. (in cooperation with the Child Study Association of America), *Our Children Today*. New York: Viking, 1955.

Hall, C. S., and Lindzey, G., *Theories of Personality*. New York: Wiley, 1957.

Harsh, C. M., and Schrickel, H. G., *Personality: Development and Assessment* (2d. ed.). New York: Ronald, 1959.

Henry, G. W., *All the Sexes*. New York: Rinehart, 1955.

Hiltner, S., *Pastoral Counseling*. New York: Abingdon, 1949.

Horney, Karen, *Neurosis and Human Growth*. New York: Norton, 1950.

Hostie, R. (S.J.), *Religion and the Psychology of Jung*. New York: Sheed and Ward, 1957.

Hunter, Edith, *The Questioning Child and Religion*. Boston: The Starr King Press, 1956.

Jersild, A., *Child Psychology*. Englewood Cliffs: Prentice-Hall, 1954.

———— *In Search of Self*. New York: Teachers College, 1952.

———— *The Psychology of Adolescence*. New York: Macmillan, 1957.

———— *When Teachers Face Themselves*. New York: Teachers College, 1955.

Joseph, H., and Zern, G., *The Emotional Problems of Children: A Guide for Parents*. New York: Crown, 1954.

Josselyn, Irene, *The Happy Child*. New York: Random House, 1955.

Kelly, G. A., *The Catholic Marriage Manual*. New York: Random House, 1958.

Kuhlen, R. G., and Thompson, G. G., *Studies in the Psychology of Human Development*. New York: Appleton-Century-Crofts, 1952.

Linn, L., and Schwarz, L. W., *Psychiatry and Religious Experience*. New York: Random House, 1958.

Mailloux, N. (O.P.), "The Problem of Scrupulosity in Pastoral Work" in A. A. Schneiders, *Proceedings of the Institute for the Clergy on Problems in Pastoral Psychology*. New York: Fordham University Press, 1956.

——— "Psychic Determinism, Freedom and Personality Development" in J. A. Gasson (S.J.) and Magda Arnold, eds., *The Human Person*. New York: Ronald, 1954.

Mann, Marty, *New Primer on Alcoholism*. New York: Rinehart, 1958.

McCarthy, R., *Drinking and Intoxication*. Glencoe, Ill.: Free Press, 1959.

——— and Douglass, E. M., *Alcohol and Social Responsibility*. New York: Crowell, 1949.

Menninger, K., *The Human Mind*. New York: Knopf, 1957.

Mihanovich, C. S., Schnepp, G. J. (S.M.), and Thomas, J. L. (S.J.), *A Guide to Catholic Marriage*. Milwaukee: Bruce, 1955.

——— *Marriage and the Family*. Milwaukee: Bruce, 1952.

Misiak, H., and Staudt, Virginia, *Catholics in Psychology*. New York: McGraw-Hill, 1954.

Moore, T. V. (O.S.B.), *Personal Mental Hygiene*. New York: Grune & Stratton, 1944.

Mullen, J. J., "Psychological Factors in the Pastoral Treatment of Scruples," *Studies in Psychology and Psychiatry,* Vol. 1, No. 3. Washington, D.C.: Catholic University Press.

Nuttin, J., *Psychoanalysis and Personality*. New York: Sheed and Ward, 1953.

Osborne, E., *Understanding Your Parents*. New York: Association Press, 1956.

Patterson, C. H., *Counseling the Emotionally Disturbed*. New York: Harper, 1958.

Philp, H. L., "Alcohol, Science, and Society." New Haven: *Quarterly Journal of Studies on Alcohol*, 1954.

———— *Freud and Religious Belief*. New York: Pitman Publishing Co., 1956.

Rea, F. B., *Alcoholism, Its Psychology and Cure*. New York: Philosophical Library, 1956.

Redlich, F., and Bingham, Ruth, *The Inside Story: Psychiatry and Everyday Life*. New York: Knopf, 1953.

Riesman, D., *The Lonely Crowd*. New York: Doubleday, 1956.

Ringel, E., and Van Lun, W., *The Priest and the Unconscious*. Westminster, Md.: Newman, 1954.

Schneiders, A. A., *Personal Adjustment and Mental Health*. New York: Rinehart, 1955.

Seidman, J., *The Child: A Book of Readings*. New York: Rinehart, 1958.

Snoeck, A. (S.J.), "Masturbation and Grave Sin" in Peter Flood (O.S.B.), ed., *New Problems in Medical Ethics*. Westminster, Md.: Newman, 1953.

Social Work Year Book. National Association of Social Workers, 1957.

Stern, K., *The Third Revolution*. New York: Harcourt, 1954.

Strang, Ruth, *Counseling Techniques in College and Secondary School*. New York: Harper, 1949.

Sullivan, H. S., *The Interpersonal Theory of Psychiatry*. New York: Norton, 1953.

Terruwe, A. A., *Psychopathic Personality and Neurosis,* trans. by Conrad W. Baars, ed. by Jordan Aumann, O.P. New York: Kenedy, 1958.

Thomas, J. L., (S.J.), *Marriage and the Family*. See Mihanovich, C. S.

Thorne, F. C., "Principles of Personality Counseling." Brandon, Vt.: *Journal of Clinical Psychology*.

VanderVeldt, J. (O.F.M.), and Odenwald, R., *Psychiatry and Catholicism* (2d ed.). New York: McGraw-Hill, 1958.

Von Gagern, F., *Difficulties in Sex Education*. Cork, Ireland: Mercier Press, 1958.

—— *The Problem of Onanism*. Westminster, Md.: Newman, 1955.

White, V. (O.P.), *God and the Unconscious*. London: Harvill, 1952.

Winter, G., *Love and Conflict: New Patterns in Family Life*. New York: Doubleday, 1958.

Wise, Carroll, *Pastoral Counseling*. New York: Harper, 1951.

Zilboorg, G., *A History of Medical Psychology*. New York: Norton, 1941.

—— *Freud and Religion*. Westminster, Md.: Newman, 1958.

—— *Mind, Medicine, and Man*. New York: Harcourt, 1943.

Zimmerman, C. C., and Cervantes, L. F. (S.J.), *Marriage and the Family*. Chicago: Regnery, 1956.

We recommend with great enthusiasm the short pamphlets dealing with a great variety of counselling topics published by the two following houses. Catalogs listing hundreds of titles can be obtained by writing for them:

Public Affairs Pamphlets   Science Research Associates
22 East 38th Street   57 West Grand Avenue
New York 16, N.Y.   Chicago 10, Illinois

The following periodicals are also recommended for frequent consultation:

The Academy Reporter (Academy of Religion and Mental Health), New York, N.Y.

The American Catholic Sociological Review, Loyola University, Chicago

The American Ecclesiastical Review, Catholic University, Washington, D.C.

The American Journal of Sociology, University of Chicago, Chicago, Ill.

The American Psychologist, Washington, D.C.
The American Sociological Review, New York, N.Y.
The Catholic Counselor, St. Francis College, Brooklyn, New York
Contemporary Psychology, Washington, D.C.
The Homiletic and Pastoral Review, New York, N.Y.
The Journal of the Guild of Catholic Psychiatrists, Washington, D.C.
The Journal of the National Council on Family Relations, Minneapolis, Minn.
Newsletter of the American Catholic Psychological Association, Fordham University, New York, N.Y.
Pastoral Psychology, Great Neck, New York
The Priest, Huntington, Indiana
Social Order, St. Louis, Mo.